Theory and Management of Collective
Strategies in International Business

Theory and Management of Collective Strategies in International Business

The Impact of Globalization on Japanese–German Business Collaboration in Asia

René Haak

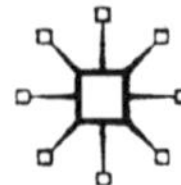

First published 2004 by
PALGRAVE MACMILLAN
Houndmills, Basingstoke, Hampshire RG21 6XS and
175 Fifth Avenue, New York, N.Y. 10010
Companies and representatives throughout the world

PALGRAVE MACMILLAN is the global academic imprint of the Palgrave Macmillan division of St. Martin's Press, LLC and of Palgrave Macmillan Ltd. Macmillan® is a registered trademark in the United States, United Kingdom and other countries. Palgrave is a registered trademark in the European Union and other countries.

ISBN 1–4039–1127–4

This book is printed on paper suitable for recycling and made from fully managed and sustained forest sources.

A catalogue record for this book is available from the British Library.

Library of Congress Cataloging-in-Publication Data
Haak, René.
    Theory and management of collective strategies in international
    business: the impact of globalization on Japanese–German business
    collaboration in Asia/René Haak.
        p. cm.
    Includes bibliographical references and index.
    ISBN 1–4039–1127–4
        1. Strategic alliances (Business) – Japan. 2. Strategic alliances (Business) – Germany. 3. Corporations, Japanese – Asia – Management. 4. Corporations, German – Asia – Management. 5. International business enterprises – Japan – Management. 6. International business enterprises – Germany – Management. 7. Joint ventures – Japan. 8. Joint ventures – Germany. 9. Joint ventures – Asia. 10. Industrial management – Japan. 11. Industrial management – Germany. I. Title.
HD69.S8H33 2004
658'.044—dc22   2003053660

10 9 8 7 6 5 4 3 2 1
13 12 11 10 09 08 07 06 05 04

Printed and bound in Great Britain by
Antony Rowe Ltd, Chippenham and Eastbourne

To Ulrike Maria, with love

Contents

List of Figures

List of Abbreviations

ADB	Asian Development Bank
AFTA	ASEAN Free Trade Area
AG	Aktiengesellschaft (limited company)
APEC	Asia Pacific Economic Cooperation
ARF	ASEAN Regional Forum
ASEAN	Association of Southeast Asian Nations
CEPT	Common effective preferential tariff
CNC	Computer numerical control
CSCAP	Council for Security Cooperation in Asia-Pacific
EFTA	European Free Trade Association
EAEC	East Asian Economic Caucus
EU	European Union
FANUC	Fujitsu Automatic Numerical Control
FDI	Foreign direct investment
GATT	General Agreement on Tariffs and Trade
GDP	Gross domestic product
GNP	Gross national product
HRM	Human resource management
IT	Information technology
JBIC	Japan Bank for International Cooperation
JETRO	Japan External Trade Organization
Jexim	Export and Import Bank of Japan
JV	Joint venture
JPY	Japanese yen
KEDO	Korean Peninsula Energy Development Organization
METI	Ministry of Economic, Trade and Industry (Japan)
MIT	Massachusetts Institute of Technology
MITI	Ministry of International Trade and Industry (Japan)
MNE	Multinational enterprise
MOF	Ministry of Finance (Japan)
NAFTA	North American Free Trade Agreement
NIE(s)	Newly industrializing economy(ies)
NC	Numerical control
OECD	Organisation for Economic Co-operation and Development
OECF	Overseas Economic Cooperation Fund

PECC	Pacific Economic Cooperation Council
PTA	Preferential Trading Arrangement
R&D	Research & Development
SEANWFZ	Southeast Asia Nuclear Weapon-Free Zone
SME	Small and medium-sized enterprise
SOE	State-owned enterprise
TAC	Treaty of Amity and Cooperation
TQC	Total quality control
TQM	Total quality management
USA	United States of America
USD	US Dollar
WTO	World Trade Organization
ZOPFAN	Zone of Peace, Freedom and Neutrality

Preface

From the point of view of politics, economics and also science, Asia is today one of the influential regions of the world. Following the crisis in 1997 and 1998, which had a considerable impact on global economic development, the economic situation in most countries in East and Southeast Asia stabilized and, in some cases, even improved. However, as this book will show, Japan plays a special part in this scenario. Increasing globalization of the world economy and its consequences are creating a different political and economic situation in this region to which German and Japanese companies need to adjust. As the process of globalization accelerates, the companies see themselves forced more and more to optimize at all stages of the value-added chain in order to maintain competitiveness. As markets in East and Southeast Asia, particularly the significant Chinese market, have opened up and developed rapidly, promising opportunities have emerged for German and Japanese companies engaged in international business.

Under these circumstances, international management is faced with the key question of which internationalization strategy will best allow them to assume a successful competitive position in the international arena. Should they choose an export strategy or a global strategy to provide the driving force behind the internationalization of their company? What are the advantages and disadvantages associated with the strategy that they choose? Will a strategy based on cooperation provide them with the success they are seeking in Asian countries?

These are only a few of the questions for which the management in German and Japanese companies have to find answers. This is the starting point, the central issue, of this book: does Japanese–German collaboration in third countries offer a promising, indeed a successful way of engaging in the dynamic and difficult markets in East and Southeast Asia, particularly in China? What reasons do German and Japanese management give for entering into a joint venture? Where are the areas of conflict and what role is played by trust in Japanese–German third-country collaboration? Can Japanese companies learn and do they learn from collective internationalization strategies? For operative German and Japanese management, the question of the key factors for success in a joint strategic venture in East and Southeast Asia continues to be of paramount importance.

I found answers to these questions in the course of my research project *Collective Internationalization Strategies in German and Japanese Manufacturing and Technology Companies in Asia* (Haak, 2002b), which I worked on within the framework of the long-term study carried out by the German Institute for Japanese Studies with its focus on 'Japan in Asia'. Drawing on critical and comparative analysis and interpretation of unpublished sources, primary and secondary literature on economic science and interviews with managers and experts about the different phases in designing and implementing collective strategies in an international environment, the work offers a study of internationalization strategies that goes beyond theory, providing a practical contribution to understanding the complex processes of collective internationalization which could also be developed effectively in structuring an operative business.

My special thanks go to Irmela Hijiya-Kirschnereit, Director of the German Institute for Japanese Studies, whose active support of the research project was instrumental in contributing to the emergence of the book. I would also like to thank Keiko Asano and Matthias Hoop from the German Institute for Japanese Studies for their help in editing and reviewing the bibliographical references and Josefine Moorman for her technical help in implementing the research project and the book.

I also owe thanks to the staff at JETRO, particularly Kazuaki Yuoka, Daizo Miyahara, Takeshi Waragai, Misa Toriumim, Yasuhiko Sumita and Yoshihiro Onizuka, who supported the project by providing important research data quickly and unbureaucratically and by giving numerous interviews.

I am also grateful to the many interviewees from economic science and from industry in Japan, Germany and China. Special thanks to Wolfgang Haas, Freudenberg & Co. Japan, Shi Lei, Freudenberg & Vilene Co. Ltd. Suzhou, China, Thomas Seidel, Freudenberg & Co. Shanghai and Urs Heggli, Freudenberg & Vilene International Ltd., Christian Gebauer, ShinEtsu Quartz Products Co. Ltd, Japan and Christian Brutzer, Heraeus Shanghai Dental Ltd, China, who contributed to the success of the research with intensive interviews and discussions.

Further, I would like to thank Klaus Grimm and Bernd Reitmeier, Delegation of German Chamber of Industry and Commerce Shanghai, Ekkehard Goetting, German Chamber of Industry and Commerce Hong Kong, Manfred Dransfeld, German Chamber of Industry and Commerce Japan, Axel Bartkus, German Trade Office Taipei, Jürgen Maurer, German Federal Office of Foreign Trade Information, Shinji Tahara, Nikkei Business Publication, Inc. Hong Kong and the experienced managers Horst Hornberger, Mannesmann Japan Corporation, Jörn Kunde, Mannesmann China Ltd., Hans-Peter Bauer, Bosch China Investment Ltd, Michael Gotschlich, German Centre for Industry and Trade Shanghai, Norio Gomi, Matsushita Electric Industrial Co. Ltd, Yasuhiro Nishi, Matsushita Electric (China) Co. Ltd, Hiroshi Okayama, Lion Home Products International Ltd., Hartmut Heine, ThyssenKrupp Rep. Office China, Raimund Frese, ThyssenKrupp Group Japan, José E. Martino, Schering Ltd. Hong Kong, Wang Ping, Prettl Shanghai Rep. Office, Erhard Reiber, Merck AG Japan Ltd., Haruhito Takeda, Fujitsu China Co. Ltd, Dirk Westphalen, Siemens Ltd, China, Ian Wood, Bayer China Company, Ltd, Detlef Melzer, Bayer Zhongxi Consumer Care Co. Ltd, Kaname Tomita, Toshiba Corporation, Jörg Wuttke, BASF China Company Ltd, Michael Zipp, Henkel China Investment Co. Ltd, Ralf Bergholz and Joerg Blecker, Shanghai Volkswagen Automotive Co. Ltd, who all willingly breathed life into the research with their interviews which were sometimes very time-consuming.

From the scientific side, I thank Hanns Günther Hilpert, formerly of the German Institute for Japanese Studies, and now at the Stiftung Wissenschaft und Politik in Berlin, with whom I worked as coeditor on two book projects on the relationship between Japan and China (Hilpert and Haak, 2002; Haak and Hilpert, 2003) and who was instrumental in providing impetus in discussions on 'Japanese–German Co-operation'. For their ideas and help I would also like to thank Akira Kudo, University of Tokyo, Jain Min Jin, Fujitsu Research Institute, Dennis Tachiki, Tamagawa University, Tadamasa Imaguchi, Keio University, Dieter Specht, Brandenburg University of Technology, Rolf Caspers, European Business School, Wolfgang Dorow, European University Viadrina, Haruo Horaguchi, Hosei University, Toshiharu Fujisawa, Hosei University, Shigeru Matsushima, Hosei University, Ryoichi Koda, Kumamoto Gakuen University, Hiroshi Itagaki, Musahi University, Sisira Jayasuriya, The University of Melbourne, John Benson, The University of Melbourne, Frank B. Tipton, The University of Sydney, Elise K. Tipton, The University of Sydney, Stephanie Fahey, The University of Sydney, Blair Odo, Japan America Institute of Management Science, Hawaii, and Craig Freedman, Macquarie University, Sydney.

I am especially grateful to my family who supported me unfailingly in all the important stages of the research project. Throughout the years of working on this project, I have benefited from sound advice from my wife, Ulrike Maria, who also provided critical analysis and helpful impetus to continue. Our two sons, Friedrich Antonius Taro and Adrian

Francis Takeo, who were born during the years of research in Tokyo, were more interested in being free to play boisterous games than in the completion of the manuscript. This book is dedicated to my wife, Ulrike Maria.

I would also like to express special thanks to Caitlin Cornish and Jacky Kippenberger at Palgrave Macmillan for their excellent commitment and support.

René Haak

1
Introduction

It's a difficult time for Japan. Obscured by cloud, the rising sun no longer shines so brightly: it's raining in Japan. Less than ten years ago, Western industry was at pains to master Japanese management concepts, hoping to share in the rising sales and profits promised by the Japanese way to success. Lean management and lean production, *kaizen* and *kanban* events, and total quality management seminars were all included in the training schedules for European and American managers. Today, only a few years after the incontrovertible successes enjoyed by Japanese industry with its impressive growth and innovative management concepts, many Japanese companies are in crisis.

The Japanese economy has been suffering for more than a decade: production has been moved to cheaper neighbouring countries, there have been crises in banking, companies have collapsed, unemployment has risen, domestic consumption has stagnated and the state is massively in debt. The most obvious crisis symptoms are:

- hollowing out;
- banking system crises;
- the collapse of numerous businesses;
- stagnation of domestic consumption;
- massive state debt; and
- slowdown in economic development.

These are just the most obvious symptoms exhibited by the exhausted economic giant. Politics, which can by no means be considered innovative, is searching for ways to escape the crisis. Prime Minister Koizumi's current government has taken steps to manage the crisis, but up to now there have been no drastic structural reforms. With some notable exceptions such as Toyota, Honda and NTTdocomo, industrial development has been sluggish in recent years and, faced with the acceleration and globalization of international competition, Japanese management is currently seeking new ways to increase competitive capability. The strategies that served them well in the boom years are no longer of any help.

More than ever there is a need for analyses and conceptions to provide a way out of this vale of tears. At this early stage, I would like to bring to the reader's attention just one book, as a representative of other publications and conceptions which has appeared on the market at exactly the right time. I have in mind *Can Japan Compete?* by Michael E. Porter, Takeuchi Hirotaka and Sakakibara Mariko (2000). I would like to look at the provenance of this book, as it is important for understanding its significance. The starting point, or rather the foundation, was a 1990 study published under the title *The Competitive Advantage of Nations*. The scientific theory is rooted in the 1980s and firmly linked with one name – Michael E. Porter, Professor at Harvard. In those years of raging economic growth, against the background of leading products and production technology, Japan appeared to be 'the world's pre-eminent economic power' (Porter *et al.*, 2000, p. ix). However, even in this study, for which Takeuchi and Sakakibara also undertook research, the point was made that there was a second economic world existing parallel to the competitive Japanese industry which showed no sign of any ability to compete on an international level. This is a discovery that the authors in their most recent work succinctly condense into the statement 'there were two Japans' (*ibid.*).

'Can Japan compete?' Why is the subject of Japanese competitiveness of such great interest at home and abroad? For Japan, the answer is obvious. The meticulous statistics published by the Ministry of Economy, Trade and Industry (METI) and the Ministry of Finance (MoF) convey just one message: without a fundamental change to its structure, the Japanese economy, with its seriously weakened industries and companies racked by crises, cannot exist in the face of the demands made by internationalization and globalization. The avid interest shown by the Western industrial nations could be based in the cynical spite Western managers feel for the failed wonder-boy, once top of the class, who set out to conquer the world at the end of the 1970s and brought American and European companies in many markets to their knees. This surely contributes to the considerable resonance engendered by Japan's economic and structural problems, but an emotional explanation falls short.

A more objective view is helpful and shows that at the core is the issue of the conditions which result from progress in societies, economic organizations or countries, the 'why' of the dynamics of success or failure. Scientists, managers and politicians have thought about this fascinating issue since the beginnings of civilization, borne by more or less organized social, economic or political elements, from city states like the Greek polis or territorial states such as modern Japan. Key disciplines of research have been:

- Sociology
- Economics and management science
- History
- Political science.

Such disciplines have endeavoured, sometimes on an interdisciplinary basis, to acquire an understanding of the driving forces and mechanisms behind the success of some economic organizations and the failure of others.

Politicians and managers look for patterns of explanation, for recipes which will maintain their countries' competitiveness and, if possible, help to increase it. At the centre of these observations are the Japanese companies trying to improve their international competitiveness. It's not the taking part that counts here, but the gold medal to be won in the arena of international competitiveness.

Discussion about the competitiveness of a country has been going on for years and covers a lot of ground in the debates about globalization. Japan and Germany, the second and third largest industrial nations in the world, have been debating for years, and in recent months more intensely than ever. The German government, under the leadership of Chancellor Gerhard Schröder, has been making a final effort to turn economic development round with the 2010 programme agenda. There are to be radical changes to the economic and social framework to give the corporate dynamic a new foundation. Politicians are hoping for results from increased entrepreneurial competitiveness, which for large parts of the population can simply be summed up with the following key words and associations: making companies more competitive means increased economic growth resulting in more employment leading to greater prosperity which will increase revenue from taxes and the state will win back more power to act in a political capacity. Unfortunately, scientific-sounding buzzwords and slogans are often used in heated saloon-bar discussions, whilst the economic reality is complex: indeed in contrast to causal associations there are many interactions which cannot always be anticipated. Porter has the merit of bringing clarity and an analytical structure to the discussion. He has done the theoretical and practical groundwork which has inspired managers and economists in equal measure. Justified criticism of Porter's models focuses on his industrial economy-related concepts which are rooted in his observation of market-oriented strategies which make it difficult 'if not impossible' to 'identify internal resources [of the company] as strategic potential for success' (Staehle, 1999, p. 606). It is therefore not surprising that Porter's market-oriented approach in recent years has been compared to a resource-oriented approach to strategy (Barney, 1991; Barney and Ouchi, 1986; Grant, 1998; Knyphausen-Aufseß, 1995). Nowadays, a combined resource-based and market-oriented approach is called for (Grant, 1998, Knyphausen-Aufseß, 1995), a goal which has already been met in practice in industry.

Without Porter's early work, when he made the nature of competition in individual industries and companies and then in whole national economies the central object of his research and interest, the provenance of his work on the competitive strength of Japan remains incomprehensible. With his first pioneering investigation which was published under the title *Competitive Strategy: Techniques for Analyzing Industries and Competitors* (1980), Porter was looking at the structure of industrial sectors and the positioning of companies within an industry. *Competitive Advantage: Creating and Sustaining Superior Performance* (1985), which appeared five years later then opened up a new analytical framework for understanding the causes and interactions of competitive advantage in a business. In *Competition in Global Industries* which appeared in 1986, he expanded his analytical framework by the demands of international competition. Up until the late 1980s, competition between nations had played a minor role in Porter's research system. When he was appointed to the US government committee for industrial competitiveness, Porter developed the 'firm conviction' (Porter, 1999, p. 12) that the national environment was crucial to corporate competitive success. Against this theoretical background, the publication mentioned previously, *The Competitive Advantage of Nations* (1990a), emerged. In many ways this helped with the work for *Can Japan Compete?* by Porter, Takeuchi and Sakakibara. It was the basic theoretical framework, a welcome insight and not least a catalyst for testing the analyses, conclusions and prognoses about Japan, or more precisely about the central issue of *Can Japan Compete?* And if so, how?

In order to address this complex issue more closely, the authors carried out a massive amount of work: they investigated 20 sectors of industry which they saw as 'representing all the important parts of the Japanese economy', and they used case studies complemented by statistical material to analyse the impact of fundamental political decisions on industrial development. They also made clear that the economic and technological problems that would need solving in the future would need more interpretation in which the historical comparison of successful and failed industrial development would be helpful.

The authors were concerned mainly with the analysis of the 'Japanese government model and its rationale' (Porter *et al.*, 2000, p. 16), and with Japanese management. The result of the first set of investigations surely grabbed the attention of Japanese bureaucracy and political representatives, for it stated bluntly with very plausible and convincing examples that 'The Japanese government model could not have been the driver of Japanese competitiveness' (Porter *et al.*, 2000, p. 44).

Expecting new discoveries, the authors turned their attention to the second set of central investigations: Japanese management. The analysis (*ibid.*, pp. 29–32, 69–76) focused on the known elements of Japanese success, which have been well-documented in economic and management literature:

- high quality and low cost;
- wide array of models and features;
- lean production and lean management;
- employees as assets;
- permanent employment;
- leadership by consensus;
- intercorporate networks;
- long-term goals;
- internal diversification into high-growth industries; and
- close working relationships with government.

At this point I would like to make reference to two central factors of Japanese success: the quality of the products, processes and systems, and corporate management according to the principles of *kaizen*, which sees the Japanese company as a learning organization (see especially Chapter 6).

It is well-known that in the Japanese production system, quality is central to the efforts to improve products and processes and to innovate. Quality is the lynchpin of Japanese competitiveness, and economic success only comes when the customer is convinced of the quality of the product. The high quality of Japanese products and the quality management practised in Japanese companies are still considered exemplary and have defined research into production since the end of the

Second World War and the state of manufacturing science today. Total quality management (TQM) today is no longer limited to production. Created in response to technological problems with products and production particularly in association with American developments and applications, it is used as a management concept throughout companies.

Another central element of competitiveness is often overlooked: the interplay between the manufacturing and the organizational structure of a factory's operation. Today, development and the use of modern means of production are characterized by the integration of information technology which derives primarily from initial development in America and from Japanese and West European product and process-oriented applications. There have been radical changes to traditional methods of organization as the result of this development. The different options for the manufacturing and organizational structure of an operation, the heart of the production process, challenge not only research and industrial practice, but also form the point at which international competitiveness crystallizes.

Developments in this area create economically justifiable leeway in the design of factory operations and perceive both the areas of work organization and technology as strategic variables (Bechtle, 1980; Kern and Schumann, 1986) that will effectively determine the competitiveness of a company. All these well-documented elements of Japanese management still apply more or less today. However, there is justification for asking where the weaknesses in the Japanese economy are – why is it not exhibiting dynamic growth?

The conclusions drawn by Porter, Takeuchi and Sakakibara offer a clear and initially surprising answer. They state succinctly 'Japanese companies remain highly successful when they have strategies'. The Japanese problem with competitiveness is summed up as follows: 'The challenge is that only a handful of large, established Japanese companies have one [a strategy]' (*ibid.*, p. 98). The authors answer the central question 'Can Japan compete?' with a single sentence 'Japan can compete' (*ibid.*, p. 182).

Asking the more important and more interesting 'how' elicits a pointed exhortation: 'Japanese companies will need to develop distinctive strategies that result in true profitability' (*ibid.*, p. 190). The authors are merciless, acknowledging that while Japanese companies have 'the capacity to move rapidly', they state unequivocally that 'incremental improvement in best practice will not be enough'. The only way out of the Japanese vale of tears in their opinion is the development of new and improved strategies.

And this is the starting point for this book, for the competitiveness of a company depends on its level of strategic potential. The question of 'how' which was not answered in detail by Porter, Takeuchi and Sakakibara is central here, and of the numerous possible strategic options the focus is on collective internationalization strategies to take account of how companies are really internationalizing – in the form of collaboration.

One thing is quite clear: at the end of the 1990s and the beginning of the twenty-first century, one of the factors determining the management process of designing collective internationalization strategies has been the increasing speed at which corporate activity has internationalized in the course of globalization. The last two decades of the twentieth century in particular saw some dramatic turning points and far-reaching changes in company environments which have had a lasting effect on the way business is done.

The establishment of new dynamic companies in fast-developing countries such as South Korea, Taiwan, Hong Kong and Singapore, together with the increasing presence of companies operating on a global basis from Japan and Germany and other Western industrialized countries, are examples of the rapid changes the company world has undergone in recent years. The collapse of planned economies in Eastern Europe, the economic transformation of China and the evolution and consolidation of large unified economic entities such as the European Union (EU), the North American Free Trade Agreement (NAFTA) and ASEAN have all drawn new features on the economic map of the world. Features such as internationalization, globalization and interculturality now characterize this development, which is challenging management anew to maintain or gain competitive advantage (Haak, 2003). It poses demands on the strategies and organizational concepts of international companies, but also offers numerous opportunities for entrepreneurial creativity (Fieten *et al.*, 1997).

The increasing speed of globalization will have a lasting effect on the way Japanese and German companies do business. For a long time, their national economies were dominated by companies whose imports and exports were scaled to the size of the business. Along with the globalization of companies and developments in information technology, companies are increasingly forced to optimize all the stages of the value-added chain at a global level. China has also offered promising opportunities for participation to both German and Japanese companies since it opened up at the end of the 1970s (Haak, 2003).

The conditions created by the rapid development of the Chinese economy in the last two decades give rise to questions regarding the most appropriate internationalization strategy in German and Japanese companies. This economic area is new and unfamiliar to many companies and although it offers opportunities it also involves considerable political, economic and social risks. German and Japanese management need to decide whether their targets will be better met by traditional export or import strategies, or by direct investment strategies (for example, establishing a new subsidiary or acquiring a company in China). Furthermore, management also needs to consider the question of whether a collective internationalization strategy based on collaboration might be successful. One of the forms of collective internationalization is 'third-country collaboration', a particular kind of general cooperative venture. The organizational forms of business collaboration are subject to strategic considerations, and in concrete terms are an expression of the collective internationalization strategy of a company (Haak, 2003).

The main question of this book is: Can Japanese–German third-country collaboration as an expression of collective internationalization, as distinct from collaboration in the domestic market of the other partner, be an appropriate way to achieve successful internationalization in the East and Southeast Asian economic region? Or, in other words, can Japanese–German third-country collaboration improve competitiveness in foreign markets?

Organizational learning is the key factor for success in business. Is it possible for Japanese companies to learn to improve their position in international competition through collective internationalization strategies, especially through Japanese–German business collaboration? What specifically motivates German management to enter into a third-country collaboration with a Japanese company, and what motivates Japanese managers to work together with German companies? What are the advantages and disadvantages of Japanese–German business collaboration? What are the criteria that determine the success of a Japanese–German cooperative venture in a third country; and last but not least, what are the areas of conflict that must be overcome when Japanese and German companies enter into third-country collaboration in China, and for this background, what is the role of trust in handling conflict in Japanese–German third-country collaboration?

It is not the intention of this book to give a complete overview of the complex and varied outcome of research into the abundance of internationalization strategies. Its concern is much more to offer an initial approach to the theoretical understanding of the collective internationalization strategy and one of its most significant manifestations, third-country collaboration, which this book presents to international and

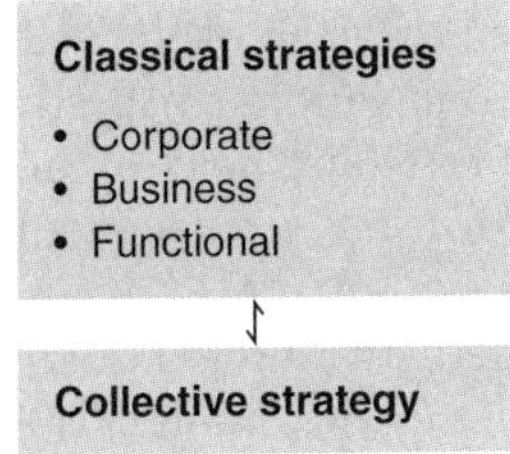

Figure 1.1 Business and internationalization strategies

strategic management for serious consideration. Collective internationalization strategies are developing against a background of discussion on central internationalization strategies from a systematic and theoretical perspective. Furthermore, I argue that in addition to the three classical forms of strategy, corporate strategy, business strategy and functional strategy, which in their internal logic form an interrelated hierarchy, a fourth is needed to represent the current reality of Japanese and German companies' internationalization, which increasingly is taking the form of collaboration (networks, strategic alliances, and so on) (Figure 1.1).

Collective strategy should be understood to mean strategy which references both in its formulation and in its implementation the other layers of strategy and creates a framework for the discovery of other strategies. Collective strategy may be understood as the guiding principle of corporate activity, or, in other words, it represents the view of international management of how the company intends to conduct its internationalization process in the target region in the future.

In order to answer the various questions, the book is structured logically into nine chapters. Following this introduction, Chapter 2 will illustrate the ideal process of internationalization, which in international management practice seems increasingly to lead to forms of collective internationalization. It is the intention of this section to show that formulating strategy today in international companies increasingly takes place in the many different organizational forms of collaboration.

This is followed in Chapter 3 by an examination of the relevant theories from the point of view of their benefits to collective internationalization. Deficiencies in the theories will be highlighted, and following the theoretical discussion targets and motivation for collective internationalization strategies will be considered (Chapter 4). Chapter 5 investigates the factors for success and the potential conflicts in collective internationalization strategies, particularly those of interest in corporate practice. Implementation of the collective strategy is covered in detail and analysed from various perspectives in Chapter 6, especially in relation to the important field of organizational learning through technology and knowledge transfer and through *kaizen* and the various drivers for implementation. In Chapter 7, the characteristics and motives of Japanese–German third-country collaboration in East and Southeast Asia will be discussed; and in Chapter 8 the conflicts and elements of success of Japanese–German third-country collaboration, especially trust, human-resource management, organizational structure and technology transfer, will be analysed in detail. Finally, Chapter 9 presents a conclusion and brief summary of Japanese–German third-country collaboration in East and Southeast Asia.

2
Forms of International Business: Theoretical Foundation and Characteristics

Internationalization of the firm

Seen from a historical perspective, international company activity has its roots in the eighteenth and nineteenth centuries, particularly in colonial areas. Closer examination reveals that this form of international activity was strongly national in nature and carried out within an empire (Perridon and Rössler, 1980, p. 121). At the end of the nineteenth century, activity on the part of still effectively national companies became increasingly internationalized. This development was aided by liberal economic policy and the increasing political independence of nations.

From the point of view of the colonial powers of the eighteenth and nineteenth centuries, this early phase in international company activity was limited mainly to the export of finished products (Sydow, 1993, p. 51). However, securing sources of raw materials also represented a significant factor for the early internationalization of corporate activity. Companies began increasingly to engage in business across national boundaries, and as part of their international business strategy targeted promising markets abroad quite specifically with finished products, without however, and this is very important for the classical definition of international strategy, taking account of or adapting to country-specific features (Kutschker and Schmid, 2002; Perlitz, 1997a; Sydow, 1993; Anderson, 1997). In contrast, the multinational strategy does take account of country-specific features, and, as a rule, in addition to the sales function realized on the foreign market, production, research and development are also undertaken in the foreign country (see also Boddewyn, 1988).

With a simple global strategy, the world market is supplied with largely standardized products and services (Kutschker and Schmid, 2002). A dual strategy is the attempt to manage both the demands of global coordination of activities and country-specific differentiation (Sydow, 1993, p. 52), and the term 'transnational strategy' is increasingly used to describe this dual strategy (Bartlett, 1989, pp. 430–42). The forms of internationalization strategies may be summarized as:

- export strategy;
- internationalization strategy;
- multinational strategy;
- global strategy;
- transnational strategy.

One of the most interesting questions to emerge from consideration of the different strategies is what do they all have in common? First of all, it is certainly the case that each of them, starting from export strategy up to transnational strategy with the exception of direct investment (or export) can be 'realized by collective strategies in the course of international business co-operation' (Sydow, 1993, p. 53). This would be the case when franchises or licences are granted and in the establishment of joint ventures, entering into strategic alliances or implementing international subcontracting (Kumar, 1989; Doz *et al.*, 1990).

Export strategy

Let us start by looking at internationalization and its organizational manifestations in traditional export strategy. Traditionally, export-oriented strategy embodies an early stage of internationalization, but as it has developed it has lost currency in favour of other internationalization strategies. Nevertheless it continues to be pursued by many companies as a promising means of internationalization.

An export strategy is the marketing of finished products or services across borders. It lends itself to exploiting economies of scale when a domestic market has reached saturation point, and if there is a requirement to gather information about a foreign market and at the same time keep risk low, then export strategy is the correct choice. A prerequisite for this strategy, however, is that there are no obstructions or limitations to international trade. As the export-oriented company is not particularly sensitive to the peculiarities of foreign markets – primarily due to domestic restrictions on its structures – and furthermore cannot realize the benefits of a global resource allocation, its potential for growth is limited (Sydow, 1993, p. 54).

How is the export strategy reflected in the organization of the company? There are various organizational solutions. The export company can be incorporated as a function or a division, or even possibly as an export department with a profit centre in its own right. As well as finding a place in the organization, the company also needs to create information and communication routes in order to make available timely and comprehensive information about the opportunities and risks associated with the exchange of goods and services beyond national boundaries. The culture of the organizational units dealing with export should also be of a nature to promote business abroad. Furthermore, exporting very complex goods and systems can make it necessary for engineers and managers to work abroad, and in this case forms of international project management are deployed (Dülfer, 1982; Grün, 1989), resulting in an overlap of pure export strategy and international project management.

Internationalization strategy

Ideally, in a typical case, the internationalization of a company via direct investment, for example in setting up its own branches, sales offices and possibly production and research locations, represents the second stage of internationalization in a company. An 'international undertaking' is created in the course of this process. This undertaking is characterized initially by a head office or home-country-dominated strategy. According to Meffert (1986, p. 690) the limited capacity of these companies to take account of country-specific features (ethnocentric orientation) is typical of this stage of internationalization.

The home-country-dominated international strategy proves successful when 'foreign markets still require development and competitors have not yet adapted strategically or organizationally to specific conditions in the foreign markets' (Sydow, 1993, p. 55). With this strategy, one can assume that most companies have already acquired some experience in foreign markets, possibly as part of an export strategy. One feature of the organizational structure of the international undertaking is the high degree of centralized decision-making (Sydow, 1993, p. 56); the management of the foreign subsidiary often reports directly to a member of the Board of the parent company. Foreign branches often have 'a considerable degree of autonomy' (*ibid.*), which can be ascribed to their development history and their knowledge of the local area. Many resources, responsibilities and decisions are decentralized but are managed from headquarters (Figure 2.1) by strongly formalized planning and control systems (Bartlett and Ghoshal, 1990, p. 76).

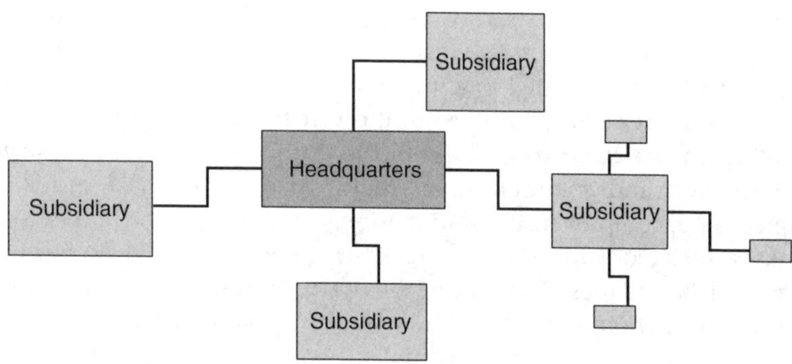

Figure 2.1   Schematic organizational structure of the international company

Source: Based on Bartlett and Ghoshal (1990a) and Sydow (1993).

Note: International strategy: high degree of centralized decision-making, main role of headquarters for the development of business strategies.

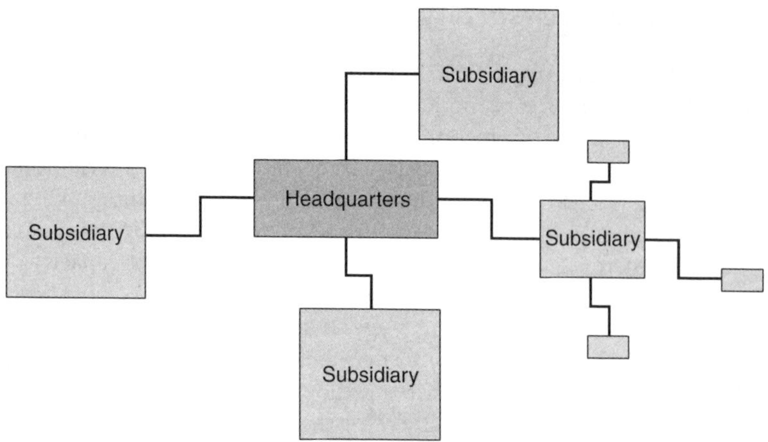

Figure 2.2   Organizational structure of the multinational or multidomestic company

Source: Based on Bartlett and Ghoshal (1990a) and Sydow (1993).

Note: Multinational or multidomestic strategy: decentralized decision-making, main role of the subsidiaries for the development of business strategies.

Multinational or multidomestic strategy

The multinational company pursues a multinational or country-specific strategy rather than an international strategy dominated by a headquarters or the home-country (Porter, 1989, p. 29; see also Buckley and Casson, 1976). The multinational company is frequently the result of continuing internationalization, particularly in US or European companies, but also increasingly in Japanese companies since the 1990s (Figure 2.2).

Where foreign markets are very different from each other and where they deviate from the domestic market of the international company, the multinational strategy is more likely to be successful. Behind the motivation for pursuing this strategy are, for example, cultural differences, differing legal systems, state-imposed conditions and company-specific tradition.

The decentralized federation is the characteristic configuration of organizational structure for a multinational company. The parent company overlays the organizational structure, which is divided into regions, with a confederation. This allows strategic country-specific adaptation of products, advertising, marketing channels and possibly also manufacturing processes (Sydow, 1993, p. 56). At management level, the decentralized structure has a counterpart in polycentric orientation as designated by Perlmutter (1969).

Global strategy

The global company (Figure 2.3) should be distinguished in principle from the multinational company. According to Porter (1989) this type

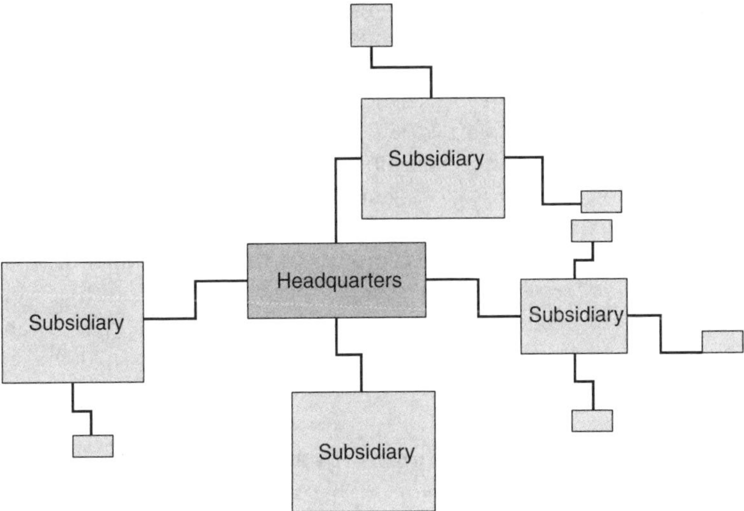

Figure 2.3   Organizational structure of the global company

Source: Based on Bartlett and Ghoshal (1990a) and Sydow (1993).

Note: Global strategy: high degree of centralized decision-making, acceptance of suboptimal business strategies developed by subsidiaries.

of company pursues strategies largely oriented towards the world market, so-called global strategies, and has a global organizational structure. The global company does not differentiate activity on a country-specific basis; at the heart of its strategy is global standardization and configuration of marketing, production and logistics, and so on, 'under conscious acceptance of nationally suboptimal strategies' (Meffert, 1986, p. 692; Sydow, 1993, p. 57). There are two different versions of global strategies – the broad market strategy or the niche strategy which focuses on selected market segments.

A global strategy assumes a continuing homogenization of living standards and styles, of international legal systems and of the technology used in each country. In this context, one should not see a global company strategy merely as an isolated reaction to possibly increasing globalization. It is also the case that global companies will 'tend to contribute towards further homogenization'. The formal identifier for the organizational structure in a global company is the 'centralized node structure' (Sydow, 1993, p. 58), characterized by the fact that the strategic decisions are as a rule made in the parent company which is structured into product divisions, and their realization is strictly monitored with formal plans and, with increasing frequency, staff integration mechanisms via the foreign companies. The result is little autonomy for the foreign companies.

Resources flow freely between the parent and the subsidiary and are not limited to capital, but can also include products, services, technology and much more. Japanese companies have preferred this organizational model, 'which is based on both centralization and the global standardization of products and product strategies' (Sydow, 1993, p. 58), as their form of a comparatively late internationalization strategy (Bartlett, 1989, pp. 432–5).

This structure allows the global company to realize economies of scale and scope or exploit comparative cost benefits. The global company can be more flexible in making decisions about the international distribution of work processes and the resources needed to carry out that work than can other organizations and strategy types (Sydow, 1993, p. 56). Country-specific differences in sales and procurement markets are exploited to the full by global companies (Ghoshal, 1987; Porter, 1989).

Transnational strategy and interfirm networks

The transnational company sees efficiency, flexibility and the ability to learn as equally valid strategic goals. At its core is a network-like organizational model (Bartlett, 1989, p. 438; Bartlett and Ghosal, 1990, p. 79) as indicated in Figure 2.4. The transnational strategy concentrates

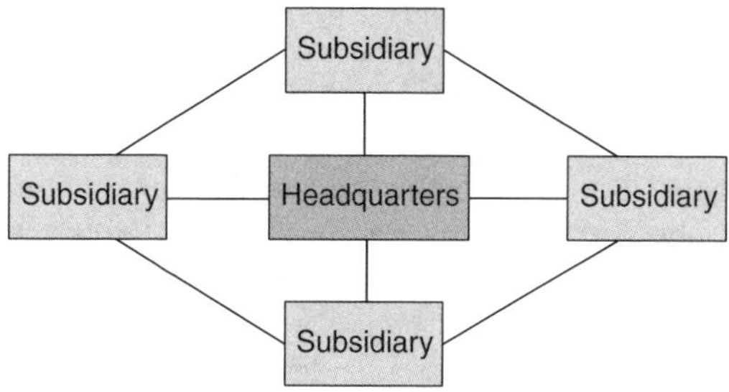

Figure 2.4   Organizational structure of the transnational company
Source: Based on Bartlett and Ghoshal (1990a) and Sydow (1993).

on market proximity, where market proximity is primarily an instrument for responding flexibly to international trade (Bartlett and Ghosal, 1990, p. 84). Market proximity makes learning processes involving all the organizational units in the business possible. Certain capabilities can be concentrated at selected locations, for example to exploit advantages of cost or expertise, whilst other resources and skills may not be maintained centrally and individual units cooperate to use them as needed. This means that the redundant structure of a transnational company can lower the susceptibility of the whole system to breakdown (Staehle, 1991).

The transnational company varies the role of its foreign branches, as company-specific adaptation is not necessary in all foreign markets. In some foreign markets the branches may sell globally standardized products; their role here is essentially to efficiently implement decisions made centrally. In contrast, in other branches differentiation is required. It may also be, for example, that some branches develop products which are then taken on by other branches, and in this case the headquarters hands over its leadership role in the system to the branch in question. One of the most important identifiers for a transnational company is that there is no clear assignment of roles within the system (Bartlett and Ghoshal, 1990a, p. 87).

A transnational strategy with its contradictory demands for differentiation and integration is implemented in an organizational model resembling an integrated network, characterized by 'predominantly reciprocating, cooperative relationships between organizational units with equal rights' (Sydow, 1993, p. 60). In addition it is also notable, more so than in other organizational models, for cultural integration in the form of shared values, visions, styles and philosophies. International human-resource management adapted to the requirements of the international company characterizes the personnel-related economics of this company model (Adler and Ghadar, 1990; Sydow, 1993, p. 60). The network typical of the transnational company is only used as an internal network structure. However, the network goes beyond the organizational boundaries of each company or the international group.

More precisely, interfirm networks are an organizational form targeting the realization of competitive advantage; they are notable for complex, reciprocal, more cooperative than competitive, and relatively stable relationships between legally independent but economically dependent companies (Sydow, 1992, p. 78). However, it should be noted here that economic dependence need not result in the foundation of a group. Important customers and suppliers (vertical relationships) are typically included in the interfirm network. Sometimes, however, horizontal associations to competitors can be maintained, as in the case of a strategic alliance (Bühner, 1989; Bronder and Pritzl, 1991, 1992).

According to Sydow an interfirm network can be seen as the result of differentiation across company boundaries and the integration of economic activities through the companies it contains, and as such represents a strategy of systematic rationalization (Sydow, 1993, p. 63). The interfirm network is created by a limited internalization of economic activities or it comes about as the result of an externalization of functions previously realized by the company or the group. Both the internalization and the externalization are based on the fundamental strategy of concentrating on core competence.

An interfirm network is regarded as a strategic network if it is conducted by two or more enterprises (Jarillo, 1988). Compared with other networks, strategic networks have a relatively formal interorganizational structure and are relatively open regarding integration and withdrawal of companies. Strategic networks are often also international networks, as they frequently extend beyond national boundaries.

The strategic network is roughly equivalent to the Japanese *keiretsu* model (Sydow, 1992, p. 38). Not only manufacturing companies, such as the automobile industry, conduct business in a strategic network; international traders such as Marks & Spencer or Ikea have also developed long-term relationships with their suppliers. International franchising systems may also be considered strategic networks.

For internationally active companies, the strategic network also represents a useful organizational model consisting of a structurally and culturally-based core with relatively tight links (for example, the transnational company itself) surrounded by a loosely connected periphery (strategic alliances and value-added partnerships, subcontracting).

The self-organizing processes triggered on the borderline between autonomy and control are, from a management point of view, ambivalent in nature. On the one hand they reduce the requirement for management input in the company running the network, on the other hand they add to the fragility of this kind of relationship between organizations.

In these network structures, senior management is less responsible for direct guidance and control but is more in charge of the 'context control' (Willke, 1987) of decentralized processes even though it is not proof to direct intervention. This context control which acknowledges in principle the autonomy and potential for self-organization by foreign subsidiaries can be effected both with staff integration and also by negotiation in which autonomy in particular but also the mechanisms for its control are defined between the parent and subsidiary companies (Sydow, 1993, p. 60). The integrated network model allows:

- different strategies in different markets to be pursued;
- switching from a local to a global strategy (and vice versa); and
- the organizational structures in the subsidiary company and the coordination and control tools of the parent company to be adapted to country-specific features (*ibid.*, p. 61).

Hedlund (1986) introduced the term 'heterarchy' into scientific discussion, a term which stresses the polycentric, self-organizing and, in respect of management and control, heterogenous character of this loosely linked structure in contrast to the strongly hierarchical structure of geocentric, global companies. Ideally, this kind of structure maps information about the whole in each of its parts. This increases functional redundancy, strategic flexibility and the capacity to learn in the organization of internationally active companies. It is also expected of these companies, more so than of others, that they play an active part in shaping their environment (Hedlund and Rolander, 1990).

The management of a transnational company is confronted to a particular degree by ambiguities and contradictions, which have their origin primarily in the necessity to adapt to local conditions and to integrate across the company. Neither the differentiation across boundaries nor overlapping integration can be implemented with organizational and structural measures alone in these kinds of internationally active companies (Buckley, 1994).

Management has the difficult task of integrating the different perspectives and philosophies that exist in the company and at the same time retaining its diversity. The goal of the company management is to build up the output and commitment of individual operational units, harnessing them for the whole company, and not to subject the foreign branches to centralized control (Bartlett, 1989, p. 459). According to Martinez and Jarillo (1991), foreign subsidiaries in a transnational company do not act autonomously nor are they fully dependent on the parent company. Foreign subsidiaries in this configuration are 'active subsidiaries', and viewed as strategic partners by headquarters. In the view of Martinez and Jarillo this type of organization makes the most demands on the simultaneous organization of local adaptability and companywide integration.

It should not be assumed from the description of the ideally typical stages of the internationalization process that each internationally active company goes through this process. It would also be wrong to assume that only the transnational company may be considered successful. It is much more the case that various country, industry and company-specific contingencies allow internationally active companies to evolve in different configurations and to be successful (Sydow, 1993, p. 62).

It should also not be forgotten that the coexistence of different configurations of internationally active companies is responsible for the contradictory results of sociological studies on the influence of the parent company on operational organization, concepts of qualification, ways of participating and staffing concepts in foreign subsidiaries (Heidenreich and Schmidt, 1991).

Collective internationalization strategy

Management in a company that does business on an international basis confronts problems that go far beyond those faced by management active only on a domestic scale. International management has to deal with a number of questions which national management does not have to consider (Bartlett and Ghoshal, 1985, 1989; Dülfer, 1991, 1997; Sydow, 1993). One of the most important questions for the management of an internationally active company is whether to move internationalization forward by investing directly in foreign markets, or whether an export strategy, perhaps even a collective internationalization strategy, might bring results. If the company decides on an export strategy, it must consider questions concerning the market, the competition and the culture. If management selects a direct investment strategy, it must decide which business functions (for example, setting up a branch sales office, acquiring foreign production locations, R&D) should be fulfilled in the foreign country (Dunning, 1993; Haak, 2001a).

The questions which international management must tackle can be assigned to different stages of the traditional management process: planning, organizing, staffing, directing and control. The question of whether raw materials should be acquired or personnel employed locally will affect planning, and remuneration and appraisal of managers employed abroad is affected by staffing and the corporate structures and culture (Staehle, 1999). Frequently, management approaches assume that planning has priority. The problem with implementing strategic plans is often only discussed on a scientific basis as an afterthought. Implementing a strategy in an internationally active company is always a process of not only intraorganizational but also interorganizational development – a fact which the literature on international management does not take sufficiently into account (Sydow, 1993, p. 48).

In more recent approaches the familiar management functions are also differentiated. However, plan-related conceptualization is replaced by a concept where all the functions have equal validity; instead of being in a linear sequence the management functions of planning, control, organizing, leadership and staffing are given equal weights in principle (Steinmann and Schreyögg, 1997, p. 8). Depending on the requirements of the situation in question, 'one or other of the management functions might enjoy priority' (Sydow, 1993, p. 48). The important point with this new conceptualization is 'that the strategy information is understood less as the result of formal planning but much more as an organized and self-organizing process' (*ibid.*, p. 49).

A large proportion of the problems of international management are solved within the framework of business and management studies. These are questions of strategy formulation, particularly that of why a company should do business on an international scale and the conditions under which a specific internationalization strategy is given preference (see for example Albach, 1981, 1992; Pausenberger, 1981; Lück and Trommsdorf, 1982; Macharzina and Welge, 1989; Welge, 1990; Welge and Böttcher, 1996; Dülfer, 1985). It should be noted, however, that questions of strategy implementation have been given scant attention in business and management studies (Sydow, 1993, p. 49).

In principle, companies doing business on an international scale have the option of pursuing their goals abroad through alliances as well as through the traditional internationalization strategies and direct investment. The opportunity to access the market and technology faster and the chance to share risk whilst remaining able to influence the alliance partner motivates companies to adopt the strategy of international collaboration. There are also other motives: lack of own resources to internationalize completely, avoiding additional overheads and barriers to market access.

Formulation of collective internationalization strategies is particularly important for global and transnational strategies (Cichon and Hinterhuber, 1989; Porter, 1985, 1986, 1990; Perlmutter, 1969). Currently more and more international companies are using 'an organisational form positioned between the market and the hierarchy', a collective internationalization strategy, the key manifestations of which (joint ventures, added-value partnerships, licensed production and so on) combine hierarchical features with those of the market (Sydow, 1993, p. 64).

Coalitions, strategic alliances, partnerships and cooperative ventures are conceptualizations which, in association with the development of a collective internationalization strategy, are on the path to quasi-internalization. The theory of international business infers the concept of internalization where this concept means 'the substitution of market trading relationships with hierarchical coordination'. Quasi-internalization does not assume, however, complete substitution of the market by hierarchy; nevertheless, purely market-related trading relationships are replaced by cooperative structures (Sydow, 1993).

Conversely, quasi-externalization focuses on the relaxation of previously hierarchical trading relationships, that is intraorganizational coordinated trading relationships. Company-internal hierarchical relationships are complemented by external market-related elements. To give an example: as a result of quasi-externalization a whole functional area which previously was attended to in one business (for example research and development, or certain production tasks) is now completely or partially carried out by a partner or by legally independent companies arranged in a network.

If we consider the level of international business activity, we see that the collective strategies for internationalizing a company are not new in principle, but have become considerably more significant as the speed of globalization has increased. In some respects, this organizational form has always existed as companies do international business by exporting goods, services or knowledge (for example by licensing). The strategy of collective internationalization which manifests itself in joint ventures, strategic alliances, value-added partnerships or increased international subcontracting is a strategic alternative to both export and to direct investment. More so than with other organizational forms of internationalization, the collective internationalization strategy allows multinational and global strategies or cost leadership and differentiation strategies to be pursued at the same time.

What is a collective internationalization strategy? There is no generally binding definition for the term, but, it can be described by the following characteristics which distinguish it from other forms of entrepreneurial internationalization:

- legal and economic independence of the business partners;
- voluntary and unforced collaboration;
- explicit agreement from the business partner regarding the cooperative venture, frequently in written form;
- *ex ante* coordination of business activity, agreed on both sides;
- a shared target; and
- partners collaborate constantly on the strategic levels agreed.

A further key towards defining the term collective internationalization is that it excludes *ad hoc* forms of collaboration; concrete discussions about long-lasting business relationships form a central determining element of collective internationalization strategies. Basically, the organizational forms of collective internationalization can be classified into those without shareholdings and those with shareholdings. Management and technical consultation contracts, licensing, subcontracting, joint ventures, turnkey systems, franchising and coproduction, to name but a few, are the most widely seen manifestations or forms of collective internationalization. There are no limits to business creativity, with unrestricted opportunities for innovation in the development of new organizational forms of these strategies (Haak, 2000a).

The most intense form of collective internationalization is the joint venture, which arises when two or more partners participate in a business, either by acquiring an existing company or by founding a new one. The classification of a joint venture as business collaboration depends on the extent of the shares held, as basically both partners need to have a say in management. Otherwise it would be considered a direct investment or a silent partnership. It should not be forgotten that collective internationalization strategies can include every element of the whole added-value chain of a business. Viewed in this way, it is possible to differentiate between international collective research and development strategies, acquisition strategies and production and marketing strategies.

The development and implementation of collective internationalization strategies frequently originate in the opening up of markets and sharper international competition in the course of globalization. Many firms are not capable of dealing with these challenges on their own, and for this reason they try to combine their strengths with those of other companies. In general, collective internationalization implies a long-term plan to create a union between companies to jointly pursue certain strategic goals. The partners are resident in different countries. Particularly central to the strategy is the definition of organizational domains, in other words, the form of collective strategy (joint venture, project, franchise and so on), specification of the target position amongst the competition, allocation and distribution of production and personnel, and definition of the degree of autonomy in agreement with the chosen business partner. It should be noted here that the strategy is affected by the perception and the interpretation of existing organizational relationships with the environment, and it in turn creates a framework for the interpretation of organization and environment. Here the term organization describes companies as sociotechnical systems which ideally bundle non-material and material resources to a unique competence (Wernerfeldt, 1984). In addition to a formal organizational structure, companies use a specific organizational culture to achieve the organizational goals (for example profit targets).

In traditional management studies, three levels of strategy are distinguished: corporate strategy, business strategy and functional strategy. Amongst other things, corporate strategy defines in which environment and in which networks a company should do business, which is important from the point of view of network research (Andrews, 1980). The business strategy defines how the company or its various sections deals with competition (for example, cost leadership or product differentiation). The functional strategy is responsible for the concrete development of the corporate and business strategies for each functional area.

Under discussion is the question of enhancing these three strategy levels with an interorganizational perspective covering a collective internationalization strategy pursued by several companies jointly (Astley, 1984; Bresser, 1989). In the context of internationalizing business activities with the faster expansion of globalization, this collective internationalization strategy is becoming increasingly important particularly with the creation of organizational forms such as strategic alliances, interfirm networks and third-country collaboration to achieve business goals in a global environment.

3
The Collective Internationalization Strategy: A Theoretical Approach

In this chapter the key points of scientific theory behind the different forms of collective strategy will be discussed. Central to the observations is a compilation and analysis of the evaluation methods and theories used in researching the phenomenon of collaboration. First of all it should be borne in mind that there is no usable theory which could serve as the basis of an explanation for different forms of collaboration; for example, the development and enhancement of strategic networks and strategic alliances. Sydow noted that an isolated approach would be unsuitable for even just adequate analysis and explanation of the many different forms of collaboration and the relationships between them in the real business world (Sydow, 1992). According to Sydow, using several theoretical approaches and models would permit more effective examination and better understanding of the different aspects and manifestations of the phenomenon of collaboration.

Theoretical approaches and models include the following:

- neo-classical theory;
- strategic concepts;
- transaction cost theory;
- principal agency theory;
- game theory;
- interorganizational theories.

The starting point for the following theoretical observations is neo-classical theory. I will then examine which explanations are offered by strategy-oriented approaches to and concepts of collective internationalization strategies, followed by a discussion of one of the models for the theoretical analysis of business collaboration most frequently used – the transaction cost approach. We shall also consider the principal agency theory, game theory and interorganizational theory.

Neo-classical theory

In industrial practice, one often encounters comparative cost accounting as an aid to making or enforcing decisions on vertical collaboration or integration, the decision parameter being:

- the demand function;
- the production function;
- the cost function.

Demand, production and cost functions only are considered in order to answer the question of whether a company should act alone or in collaboration to achieve optimum results. The neo-classical theory, which assumes perfectly balanced competition and markets, seems from the point of view of competition theory inappropriate for explaining the phenomenon of collaboration, not least because it excludes the problem of uncertainty (Backhaus and Meyer, 1993).

Furthermore, this theory, which is essentially oriented towards consideration of production costs, does not take into account criteria such as power, dependency and flexibility in a company, which are all of crucial significance for the structure and exchange of collective output (Picot and Franck, 1993). It also only distinguishes between the extremes of 'make' or 'buy', but neglects all other collective working methods in-between. The weaknesses and gaps in neo-classical theory mean it can make only a very limited contribution to an explanation for collective strategies. Neo-classical theory takes no account of concepts such as trust, loyalty, mutual obligation and solidarity, and when they are detected empirically they are considered as irrational behaviour on the part of the market actors. Other evaluation methods are needed to explain elements of collective strategies and their organizational manifestations. The neo-classical paradigm must be left aside; it is not helpful for considering collective strategies.

Strategic concepts

The enhancement of the deterministic concept of classical industrial economics with the strategic management approaches is due largely to the management researcher Michael Porter. The competitive strategies of individual company units become a deciding factor for economic success along with the structural conditions of the sector. Porter analyses collaboration strategies for their impact on the market as well as the competitive strategies that are central to his observations. Collective strategies are considered a means to the end of achieving a specific competitive position. Thus, for example, a collective strategy can make entry into a specific market segment easier, or by impacting on the structure of the industry create new competitive positions.

The discussion here deals mainly with strategic alliances and joint ventures. According to Porter and Fuller (1986), collective strategies have a number of strategic advantages:

- economies of scale;
- access to technology and expertise;
- reduction of risk; and
- impact on the competitive structure.

The benefits of a collective strategy are seen in economies of scale, access to the technology and expertise of the collaboration partner, in the reduction of risk to the company and in their impact on the competitive structure. Again according to Porter and Fuller (1986, p. 322), the costs or disadvantages of a collaborative strategy are:

- coordination costs;
- absorption of management capacity;
- erosion of the company's own competitive capacity with the lowering of barriers to market entry or unwanted escape of information; and
- the emergence of unfavourable negotiating positions.

Porter has not dealt with the theory of collaboration strategies in general. He concentrates on questions of vertical integration as one of the strategic options he has developed. Porter therefore sees 'long-term agreements', 'partial integration' and 'quasi–integration' as transitional forms in interfirm vertical collaboration with increasing degrees of integration. He refers to these transitional forms as opportunities to use both the benefits of integration and also at the same time to save some of the anticipated costs of vertical integration (Porter, 1990a, p. 397). Porter develops an orientation framework for vertical collaboration which summarizes the economic and administrative consequences of collaboration and hence of its different forms, listing the following aspects as important strategic benefits of vertical integration:

- cost savings;
- better knowledge of technology used in upstream and downstream processes;

- safeguarding supply and sales in terms of price, quality and quantity;
- equalization of power concentration;
- internalization of profits;
- improved differentiation of output;
- raising entry and mobility barriers;
- entry into a more profitable market level, and;
- protection against exclusion from the market.

Porter sees cost savings in a vertical integration resulting mainly from combined operations, internal control and coordination, the provision of integrated information, the lack of costly market transactions and stable business relationships. He also juxtaposes the economic benefits of vertical integration with a number of strategic costs, which result primarily from the following factors:

- increased fixed operational costs due to internal control and coordination and hence increased operational risk;
- less flexibility in changing suppliers and customers and the associated problems of quality, quantity and time;
- the generally high level of exit barriers;
- increased requirement for capital;
- decreased incentive to perform for integrated units; and
- different demands on the leadership of integrated units (Porter, 1990a, p. 378; 1990b).

It should be noted that strategy-oriented approaches to collaboration can be seen as essentially conditioned by the structure of the industry. The industry economy assumes the same perspective. Collaboration in the form of quasi-externalization is suitable from the point of view of industrial economics when external economies of scale could be realized, but the costs associated with a total externalization of functions should not be too high. Porter's theoretical point of view includes the strategy-relevant conditions in an industry from the possible perspective of collaboration, but it should also be noted that there are only rudimentary attempts to make any statement about the organization of the company and its management in concrete terms. Although more recent industrial economic and strategy-oriented research has made an important contribution towards illuminating the economic dimension of the company environment, it does not however consider the way economic processes are embedded in a social sense within sectors and the network-like structures which have developed between the businesses in them. Sydow (1992) considers that the potential relevance of industrial economics to knowledge and practice and the strategy-oriented approaches based on this tradition are limited as long as companies are treated as black boxes.

Transaction cost theory

Transaction cost theory derives in its basic form from the work carried out by Coase (1937) and was taken up and developed further by Williamson in the 1970s and 1980s (Williamson, 1990). Almost 30 years after Coase's conception of its basic structure, the theory was enhanced and applied to the discussion of long-term contractual arrangements, collaboration and alliances (Picot and Ronald, 1992; Alchian and Woodward, 1988). The transaction cost theory explains the transition from exchange of goods and services through markets to exchange of goods and services through hierarchies (companies). It provides an explanation for the emergence and the economic justification of companies, and is increasingly used to explain economic forms of organization and processes based on division of labour on a general economic level. The theory claims to explain why certain transactions in certain institutional arrangements are completed and organized with more or less efficiency. The central unit of scientific analysis is the transaction.

Transaction cost theory characterizes the institutional arrangement in which the exchange of goods or services takes place in two ways. On the one hand, the theory distinguishes the basic legal form of contract underlying the relationships of the exchange explicitly or implicitly; on the other hand it distinguishes the mechanisms on which the partners in the transaction agree so that possible unplanned changes to the cost or delivery side of the relationship can be dealt with. The costs are used as a deciding criterion for profitability. The costs used as this measure are those that the partners incur for the goods or services exchanged or for handling and organizing the transaction. At its theoretical core, this process in the transaction cost theory provides a comparison of the costs of alternative institutional arrangements for handling and organizing transactions. As it sees it, its aim is to answer the question of which types of transactions in which institutional arrangements can be completed and organized the most cheaply in relative terms (Williamson, 1985, p. 41).

An explanation of the two central terms 'transaction' and 'transaction costs' is particularly relevant to understanding this theoretical model. A transaction takes place when goods or a service are transferred over a technically separable interface. Transaction costs are a representation of the 'friction' of this transaction (Williamson, 1990, p. 1). Essentially, these are (Picot, 1990, p. 8):

- the costs of searching for information;
- the costs of negotiations;
- the costs of controlling the transaction;
- costs of monitoring the transaction; and
- costs of adaptation to changes.

Williamson also distinguishes between so-called *ex ante* and *ex post* costs. The *ex ante* transaction costs are incurred before the transaction takes place and are, for example, costs of the design of a product or of negotiating and enforcing an agreement. The *ex post* transaction costs arise after the transaction and can result from price negotiations or work to adapt the contracts. Essentially, however, transaction costs can be classified as information and communication costs. According to Williamson, it is not production costs and the technology used that determine the optimum form of organization, but primarily the transaction costs. Similarly, it is not the relative difference between the production costs, but the relative difference in the coordination costs which are crucial.

The efficiency criterion for the transaction cost theory is the sparing use of scarce resources. On the one hand the resources consumed in creating the goods or services being exchanged and on the other the resources consumed in handling and organizing the exchange are taken into account. The former is documented in the production costs, the latter in the transaction costs. Since the transaction cost theory compares the efficiency of alternative institutional forms of handling and organizing a transaction, it is based on the sum of the production costs and transaction costs as the efficiency criterion (Williamson, 1985, p. 22). It follows that the institutional arrangement in which the transaction costs are less is seen as efficient.

It is not always easy to give exact costs for the production of goods or services or to assign them to specific sources. It is particularly difficult to quantify the transaction costs which arise when an exchange is initiated and completed. It also seems difficult to assign the cost of monitoring individual transactions to the correct source; hence, the development of a way of accounting for transaction costs is still in the early stages. The central problem for the transaction cost theory is operationalization.

Another limitation of the transaction cost theory is that it is not necessary to measure production and transaction costs exactly. In principle, the theory is not interested in the exact amount that it costs to produce and transfer goods and services, but primarily wants to determine in which institutional arrangements a specific transaction costs more and in which less. This means that, frequently, approximate statements are sufficient to determine the relative profitability. Despite this, transaction cost theory cannot rid itself of the flaw that there is something arbitrary about the profitability in alternative institutional forms of organization. Only solving the central problem of operationalization will allow objective consideration. The decision for or against an alternative institutional form of organization could then be comprehensible with exact measurements. However, many other issues remain open. One of these is the systematic explanation of which factors determine the costs of handling and transaction in alternative forms of institutional organization? Only this would allow an exact specification of which form is better for which transactions, and for what reasons.

According to Williamson (1985, p. 52) three transaction characteristics impact on the cost of handling and organizing a transaction:

- the degree to which the transaction partner uses transaction-specific assets (asset specificity);
- the uncertainty associated with a transaction; and
- the frequency of the transaction.

The transaction cost theory also defines and differentiates alternative institutional structures on a theoretical contractual level, where the transaction is the central unit of analysis. Each exchange of goods or services is based on an implicit or explicit agreement, and in classifying alternative forms of contract Williamson draws extensively on an analysis of US contract law by MacNeil (1974, 1978). Like MacNeil, Williamson distinguishes between three forms of contractual agreement: classical, neo-classical and relational, which are fundamental to specific institutional arrangements. Transactions are completed via the market, via long-term contracts and in organizations (companies).

How does transaction cost theory deal with different forms of contractual arrangement? Let us look at the classical contract first. MacNeil characterizes this as a short-term contractual relationship which precisely defines the object and the conditions of the transaction. It is confined to the discrete act of the transaction. In the classical contract, the transaction partners complete their transactions in accordance with contractually fixed, *ex ante* rules and their obligations do not extend beyond the individual exchange process (Williamson, 1985, p. 69). Conflicts arising in this kind of transaction are solved by legal action.

The classical contractual agreement can be found in the institutional form of market exchange between two independent transaction partners.

The key difference between the classical and the neo-classical contractual agreement is that the costs and benefits that impact on the transaction are not completely anticipated by the transaction partners and are not precisely defined in the contract. The transaction partners expect that they will need to adjust the contract in the course of the exchange. When the contract has been agreed, more decisions are needed from the transaction partners on adjustment or in order to deal with conflict. The partners try to solve existing conflict by arbitration rather than in court. Neo-classical contracts are characteristic of many long-term agreements such as franchising or joint ventures, and long-term supply and sales contracts also come into this category (MacNeil, 1978; Williamson, 1985, 1991).

At the end of this continuum are the relational contracts which are again less discrete compared to the neo-classical contracts. They exhibit the greatest degree of openness compared to classical and neo-classical contracts in the *ex ante* definition of services mutually rendered. This contractual relationship is determined by long-term exchange dealings between the transaction partners which in the course of multiple transactions are integrated into a complex social relationship; conflicts between partners are frequently solved without involving the courts. Open-ended employment terms or business partnerships are typical examples of relational contracts (Williamson, 1985; MacNeil, 1974, 1978).

Note here that markets and hierarchies (companies) are the extremes on the continuum of economic organizations in the model proposed by transaction cost theory. In markets, the transaction is coordinated purely on the basis of price, which conveys the key transaction-relevant information. In market-exchange relationships, powerful incentive mechanisms ensure that the transaction is dealt with efficiently; deliverables and receivables are closely and directly linked and can be largely valued in monetary terms. The strong self-interest of the market actors is increased still further by competition. The unambiguous definition of the agreed deliverables and receivables offered by a classical contract means that agreeing, monitoring and enforcing the contract are all very low-cost.

In organizations (companies for example), or in other words in hierarchies, the transaction is based on directions from the company management. Ideally, the directions replace any market coordination. Production of goods and services in a hierarchy is much more costly than in a market transaction, the main reason being that the incentives applied internally to use resources efficiently are much less prominent than in a classical market-exchange relationship. Measuring performance presents another problem. Employees of an organization can try to perform less well than they agreed to or are paid for or exploit other input factors inappropriately to their own advantage. To limit the option of opportunistic behaviour of this kind, specific bureaucratic control and monitoring systems are institutionalized in hierarchies which also contribute to increasing price levels. Compared to purely market-exchange relationships, producing goods and services in hierarchies has a definite advantage in that it is easier to adjust the factors required for these goods and services to changes in the conditions prevailing in the market and in the competition. For example, if goods need to be made available in another form, quality or quantity via the hierarchy, the decisions required to bring this about can be made quickly and cheaply using the factors in the internal hierarchy of goods and services as all the input factors are within the remit of the owners of the organization. Conflicts which arise in the course of producing goods and services in a hierarchy can be resolved internally in the hierarchy and as a rule do not develop into court cases. A further benefit is represented by better information about the performance capacity and combinability of the various input factors.

However, taking into account the reality of producing goods and services and transaction processes, delimiting sharply between market and hierarchy (or organization/companies) is not meaningful; there is a seamless transition between the two basic structures, with a whole spectrum of institutional structures on the continuum between the two extremes. Collaboration in its many manifestations can be classified as a transitional form. It is the third form of economic production of goods and services and transactions. Accordingly, it is possible to identify cooperative elements at both ends of the market-hierarchy continuum. Cooperative ventures are created from the market situation when collaboration between companies intensifies; they emerge from internalization. Assuming a hierarchy situation, a limited outsourcing of functions or relaxation of the hierarchical structure results in externalization. Both internalization and externalization can be both horizontal (primarily competition) and vertical (primarily suppliers and customers). The transaction cost theory offers initial steps towards explaining horizontal collaboration. Overall, with its simplicity and the connection between market and organization theories, the theory seems to be suitable as an explanatory model of structures for collaboration between companies. Picot and Franck stress that transaction cost theory can include and analyse the whole spectrum of possible forms of integration, offering a general theoretical orientation framework for understanding cooperative relationships, although development is still rudimentary (Picot and Franck, 1993, p. 190; Fischer, 1993, p. 256). The theory is suitable for the analysis of vertical systems within companies and the vertical chain of suppliers and customers, and in the end this also means a vertical view of collaboration options and forms. Deciding in favour of in-house manufacture or outsourcing and explaining the degree of vertical integration realized have up to now been the main topic of research with transaction cost theory. In the 1980s and 1990s empirical investigations into different branches were carried out for the aluminium industry (Stuckey, 1983), textiles, the automobile industry (Baur, 1990; Walker and Weber, 1984; Monteverde and Teece, 1982), the aircraft industry (Masten, 1984) and information technology (Ulset, 1996; Mosakowski, 1991). There were also empirical investigations into the internationalization strategies of multinational companies. The focus here was on issues surrounding exports, licensing and direct investment (Gomes-Casseres, 1989; Gatignon and Anderson, 1988; Hildebrandt and Weiss, 1997) and the institutional structure of international strategic alliances (Garcia-Canal, 1996; Gulati, 1995; Osborn and Baughn, 1990; Parkhe, 1993) and joint ventures (Hennart, 1991; Kogut, 1988; Stuckey, 1983).

Although the transaction cost theory is a relatively young theory which in some respects needs to be further developed and become more specific, it has already made many positive contributions to the understanding of the structure of international cooperative institutions.

Principal agency theory

In recent years, the principal agency theory has established itself as a standalone theory. The theory assumes at its core a principal and an agent, where the principal is better informed than the agent. The subject of the research is the vertical coordination of decisions between the two contractual partners. At the centre of this theory is the institution of the contract and its role in exchange relationships between the principal and the agent. Typically the relationships might be between:

- employer and employee;
- purchaser and seller;

- owner and general manager;
- backer and general manager.

In all these constellations, a principal delegates to an agent specific tasks and decision-making powers for the purposes of realizing the principal's interests. This is done on a contractual basis and the agent receives payment for services rendered. The benefit to the principal of handing over tasks is that he or she can exploit the agent's specialized skills and information. However, it must be stressed in qualification that delegating can also cause problems. The less information the principal has about the motives, room for manoeuvre and performance of the agent the greater the risk that the agent might not act in line with the agreement. The theory assumes that the agent might well pursue his or her own interests to the detriment of the principal's. The principal has the basic problem of using a contract to ensure that the agent delivers in accordance with the agreement.

This problem forms the central theme of the 'Theory of Agency'. The theory examines the contractual structure of the relationship between principal and agent under the conditions of unequal distribution of information, and of uncertainty, taking risk distribution into account. The theory analyses typical problems in contractual relationships. There is also a discussion of the question of which mechanisms, such as incentives, control and information systems, will manage the principal's problems more efficiently. Important work on this subject has been presented by Laux (1990), Pratt and Zweckhauser (1985), Fama (1980).

The principal agency theory sees organizations as networks of contractually regulated order-based relationships. In this it describes a significant phenomenon which traditional research into organizations and neo-classical microeconomics neglects: the dependence of the production of goods and services on an efficient contractual structure of agency relationships. The importance of the theory is its capacity to present the important basic problems and decision calculations of the contractual partners in simple order and performance-based relationships. To a limited extent, the theory can also formulate recommendations on how to optimize the behaviour of agents by contractual regulations.

The basic model of the principal agency theory represents a relatively simple and precisely constructed theory, which is a key benefit for formulating hypotheses about coordination issues. Consequently, this theory has been deployed in many empirical studies. From the point of view of research into interfirm collaboration, however, the theory is only of limited use. The analysis of order-based relationships between organizations with the aid of this theory is still in its infancy, although the interfirm relationships in cooperative ventures can be reconstructed as principal–agent relationships. However, the theory takes no account of the social structure of organizations and cannot deal with the network character of collaboration (Sydow, 1992, p. 172).

Game theory

John von Neumann developed game theory in the late 1930s, and in 1944 he and his colleague Oskar Morgenstern expanded on it together (Neumann and Morgenstern, 1944). Fundenberg and Tirole (1991) in particular made a key contribution to the detailed analysis of game theory and its applications (Pena and Fernándes de Arroyabe, 2002). There have been frequent attempts in Economics to explain the emergence of business collaboration using methods of evaluation based on game theory. These approaches have in common that they pinpoint conditions under which better results can be achieved from performance with collaboration than can be achieved by competition. In contrast to the transaction cost approach, game theory does not take costs into account, but concentrates on the profitability of the cooperative venture. The terms 'prisoner's dilemma' and 'stag hunt' are used metaphorically to describe cooperative relationships (see Axelrod, 1991, for a closer examination of the prisoner's dilemma, and Haury, 1989, on the stag hunt). Samuelson has used the prisoner's dilemma to explain competitive behaviour in an oligopoly. He describes oligopolistic competition as a prisoner's dilemma and concludes from his observations that cooperative behaviour will predominate under certain conditions (Samuelson, 1975, p. 172).

From the point of view of collaboration theory, Axelrod (1991) has made a particularly important contribution to explaining it on the basis of game theory. In his research, Axelrod found that in an iterated prisoner's dilemma situation, where the duration of the game is not fixed, strategy is selected depending on the other player's behaviour. According to Axelrod (1991), collaboration comes about when the other player allows space for the development of reciprocal collaboration, and as part of his research he puts forward four rules which maximize the profit from the game when the prisoner's dilemma is iterated:

- avoid unnecessary conflict by cooperating as long as the other player does;
- provocability and reaction in the face of an uncalled for defection by the other;

- forgiveness after responding to a provocation; and
- clarity of behaviour so that the other player can adapt to your pattern of action.

Kreps (1990) also sees the emergence of collaboration between two players in an iterated prisoner's dilemma situation as a realistic option. Sydow's conclusion from his summary of evaluation methods based on game theory, seen from the point of view of collaboration, is that a cooperative strategy can also be effective where behaviour is opportunistic (Sydow, 1992, p. 231). A basic problem in game theory, however, is that it reduces reality to a few basic relationships; many important features are concealed by the abstract formulation. Game theory approaches assume egoistic, exploitative behaviour on the part of the players, whilst more recent work concedes that it is possible that the players might display a limited inclination to cooperate. It should be noted, however, that the explanatory value of game theory approaches remains very general according to Sydow (1992), and how collaboration is organized in concrete terms remains obscure.

Resource dependence, social exchange and the interfirm network theory

Many scientific investigations of interfirm collaboration are based on interorganizational methods of evaluation. Examples of work done in this area are by Benson (1975), Aldrich (1979) and Frazier (1983). This book cannot give a detailed description of all the important approaches to interorganizational theory, but good, detailed descriptions can be found in Sydow (1992) and Knyphausen-Aufseß (1995).

For the purposes of this book, it is important to note that interorganizational theories concentrate on describing and classifying interorganizational relationships. In this they differ in key aspects from the economic approaches to explaining the phenomenon of collaboration described above. Important theoretical approaches and their implication for the materialization of and reasons for collaboration which are presented briefly below are the resource-dependence approach, the social-exchange theory and the network approach.

Resource-dependence approach

In the past, the resource-dependence approach has frequently been used to explain collaboration. Work by Van de Ven (1976), Aldrich (1979), Scott (1987), and by Van Gils (1984) deserves particular mention here. The core assumption of the approach is the scarcity of resources; the company will only be able to acquire resources by exchanging with other organizations. The different forms of exchange that a firm is obliged to use, however, reduce its degree of autonomy. In order to limit the amount of autonomy lost to it, the company develops interorganizational relationships, which represent compensation for the loss of company autonomy. Avoiding, exploiting and developing dependencies of this kind which evolve with the necessary exchange processes are the main reasons interorganizational exchange relationships are defined and maintained. Power has a key role here and is seen to be a form of social influence. Power is the form of influence whereby a person, a position or the organization is given the chance to enforce a change of behaviour even against the will of others (Staehle, 1999, p. 398). In interorganizational relationships, the organizations endeavour to extend their influence over other organizations. Essentially, the important point here for the organizations is to control critical resources (such as staff, capital or technology) to maintain competitiveness. The organization can only meet its goals by controlling and monitoring these critical resources as appropriate. The organization has two basic strategies with which to achieve this: vertical collaboration, or vertical integration or acquisition.

The resource-dependence approach also offers explanations of why organizations enter into horizontal relationships. The approach assumes that companies enter into collaboration and coalitions with other users of a scarce resource in order to influence the power relationships in line with the organizations' objectives. It is also intended to avoid or at least limit excessive dependency on suppliers of a critical resource. It is a particularly positive aspect of this theory that it takes power, which is significant in economic practice, into account. Nevertheless, the approach does have some weaknesses. One weakness in particular is that it assumes that, ultimately, management will behave rationally; the approach cannot accommodate purely subjective decisions on the part of management. Unplanned or spontaneous actions are not taken into account as explanations or variables influencing the emergence of cooperative ventures (Sydow, 1992).

Social-exchange theory

Social-exchange theory offers a rather management-oriented explanation for the emergence of cooperative ventures. This theory can be understood as an individualistic concept which bases the creation of cooperative relationships only on the vested interests of the various actors in the organizations, that is, the companies. It defines exchange as a voluntary activity between two or more organizations for the purposes of better achieving objectives, and this voluntary exchange is carried out when the perceived benefits outweigh the cost of the exchange. In this process, three key determinants define the exchange relationship. The first is the partner's access to external resources, the second is the goals and functions of the participating companies and the third is the 'domain consensus' between them (Levin and White, 1961). The degree of domain consensus is determined by how far the goals of the partner are conflicting, overlapping or complementary. Posing the question of which factors should be considered relevant to the exchange between organizations finds existing power relationships and earlier exchange processes and the social context in addition to scarcity of resources, functional specialization and existing domain consensus (Cook, 1977; Staehle, 1999). Essentially, socio-psychological explanations for the emergence of social and personal networks are transferred to the level of interorganizational relationships. The great merit of the social-exchange theory is that it effectively takes into account the significance of social relationships in which the exchange between organizations is embedded. It is possible to conduct good investigations into symmetrical relations using this theory; however, for asymmetric relationships such as those that are typical in particular for vertical collaboration, research needs more theoretical approaches. The resource-dependence approach discussed previously is of use here (Sydow, 1992).

The interfirm network

The network approach was originally developed using the investment industry as an example, as it exhibits a particularly high degree of network-like connections between companies (Hakansson, 1982, 1987). At the end of the 1980s and in the 1990s, the area of application was widened to include strategic and international management. This approach is rooted in both social-exchange theory and the resource-dependence approach. According to the interaction-oriented network approach, market-oriented activities frequently gel to stabile while simultaneously changing interorganizational relationships. It is significant that cooperative ventures frequently emerge from relatively unimportant transactions, which initially do not require high investment nor a great deal of trust. For example, one of the most important facts about the network approach is that cooperative relationships between companies can be the outcome of both planned actions and spontaneous processes. A central conceptional element of the approach is represented by the interactions between the participants in the network. Interactions can be expressed in a technical, economic, administrative or social form, forming the foundation layer of stability and change in the cooperative venture as, over time, they consolidate on the basis of socio-economic relationships.

The interaction-oriented network approach takes on a particular character in the concept of the interfirm network (Miles and Snow, 1986; Sydow, 1992, 1995; Nohria and Eccles, 1992; Sydow *et al.*, 1995; Ebers, 1997). An interfirm network represents an intermediate organizational form of economic activity between the market and the hierarchy, 'which is characterized by complex, reciprocal cooperative rather an competitive a relatively stable relationships between legally independent, but economically usually independent companies' (Sydow, 1992, p. 79). If one organization represents a focal point at the centre of the network and controls the network from a strategic point of view, then it is called a strategic network (Jarillo, 1988). In this context, strategic means the proactive organization of a network which is determined mainly by market-oriented requirements and technological options and oriented towards the permanent development of competition-relevant potential. In contrast, regional networks are characterized by the geographical grouping of mainly small and medium-sized enterprises (Staehle, 1999, pp. 745–7). Networks are created when operational functions are outsourced or externalized or when collaboration with other organizations is intensified. Intensifying interfirm collaboration creates a network-like form of organization which is frequently referred to as a strategic alliance. The transitions between the strategic alliance form of organization and third-country collaboration are blurred. Neither the externalization nor the internalization of functions is driven on by the company so far as to replace the hierarchy with the market or the market with the hierarchy (Sydow, 1992, p. 105). The interaction-oriented network approach with its theoretical developments and practice-oriented approaches provides a comparatively good explanation of the evolution and organization of cooperative ventures. The network perspective developed in this approach can be recommended for the management of cooperative relationships.

4
Objectives and Motivation for Collective Strategies

Organizations are founded to achieve certain purposes and goals, and as goals impact on the structure and the behaviour of organizations (Mayntz, 1963; Perrow, 1970) they are accorded particular importance in analyses. When we speak of organizations with performance goals in this context, it transpires that they tend to hierarchical authority structures in their organizational orientation. Organizational regulation then serves to coordinate the members of the company so that the goal can be achieved efficiently. In addition to the significance of goals as factors determining the structure of the organization, they have, according to Porter *et al.* (1975) the following important functions:

- justification of actions toward third parties;
- information held by members and non-members about the purposes of the organization;
- code of practice;
- motivation; and
- a central measure for assessing performance.

Goals are understood to mean those of the organization (for example, the company) or those formulated by the members of the organization themselves regarding the conditions or conduct they wish to see in the organization.

Goals represent the variables according to which company activity orients and aligns itself. According to Meffert (1994), goals can also be interpreted as target conditions, which means they can also be seen as the triggers, motivation and benefit dimensions for economic activity. In their operationalized form, goals become measurement variables for determining the success of a specific action.

It should be noted, therefore, that goals in general describe a desirable state in the future which the organization is trying to achieve. According to Hauschildt (1977, p. 9), goals are statements with a normative character which describe a state of reality, always set in the future, desired by a decision-maker, to be worked towards by him/her or others. Where interfirm collaboration is concerned, goals are a constitutive element, and are a key feature of the phenomenon of collaboration. The real basis of business collaboration is the compatibility between the goals of its participants. Synchronous or complementary goals are a crucial prerequisite for the success of a collective internationalization strategy, forming the foundation for collaboration between participating companies.

All this means that it is important for the success of a joint venture into third-country markets that already in the prenegotiation stages the management of the participating businesses reconcile their goals in depth. Compromises will always be necessary when the future collaboration partners fine-tune their goals. The relative power positions of the negotiation partners determine to some degree which competing objectives prevail in the course of negotiations. For example, changes in the constellation of the competition or in the interests of management due to a new appointment at senior level can eventually result in changes to the detail of the goals or even possibly to a realignment of the whole venture. Conflict situations between the managements of the cooperating companies, adaptation processes or even dissolving the venture are conceivable consequences of incompatible development of subgoals.

The goals pursued in collective internationalization strategies are of a diverse nature. For the purchasing department of a company, price issues and increasing purchasing power will be the most important motivators for collective internationalization strategies and for the implementation of a joint venture. By combining the amounts purchased, it is possible to open up new, previously inaccessible markets or under certain circumstances maybe even avoid whole stages in the trading process. Therefore a key motive for a collective internationalization strategy can be the goal of reducing the price of purchased materials and services. In addition to cheaper purchasing prices, a company might be further motivated towards collective internationalization strategies if working with a partner provides a better level of information or establishes a stronger market position. In addition to this qualitative aspect, opening up access to resources held by the collaboration partner with the appropriate organizational implementation of the collective internationalization strategy should also be mentioned. State incentives or subsidies can also be a particular objective for collective internationalization strategies in purchasing (Contractor and Lorange, 1988).

In production, the goals of collective internationalization strategies primarily concern the more efficient use of production factors. In the final analysis, increasing the output capacity of a company has always been the goal of collective strategies. Efficiency targets in production are most frequently named for the implementation of collective internationalization strategies (Hamel *et al.*, 1989), as well as cost savings and the potential increase of output in growth markets. These efficiency targets are achieved with synergy effects on economies of scale or economies of scope when companies cooperate. Better use of underused production capacity and the reduction of overhead costs are also ways in which greater efficiency is achieved when companies work together. More profit from specialization is also cited as a goal of joint ventures (Contractor and Lorange, 1988; Steffenhagen, 1975; Gerth, 1971).

In sales and marketing, collective internationalization strategies aim to improve sales targets and hence the market position of a company in its target markets. Essentially, in the sales area of the company the goal is to increase the market share for products from horizontally linked companies or to increase a company's market power. Collective internationalization strategies in this area can impact on the competition, but when small and medium-sized enterprises join forces these strategies can also improve their competitiveness towards large companies, which has a positive effect overall on competition. Furthermore, collective internationalization strategies in sales might also achieve cost savings in sales-related areas such as advertising or merchandising or distribution.

If one considers objectives and motives for collective internationalization strategies independently of classification into functional business areas, one key motivator crops up in discussion again and again: power. Power-related goals frequently play a central part in collective internationalization strategies. According to Westphal (1991) three power dimensions can be distinguished in the structure of vertical competitive relationships:

- economic power;
- behavioural power;
- legally competitive power.

If the goal of a collective internationalization strategy is horizontal collaboration, then improving the power position in the market is in many cases the driving force behind a joint venture. The companies target increased market share or purchase jointly to achieve a more favourable supply or demand position. Earnings potential is improved because the power of the cooperative structure reshapes the existing relationships in the market quantitatively and qualitatively. Mahoney and Crank (1993) distinguish six political power targets that affect vertical collaboration:

- to reduce or maintain asymmetric information;
- to improve bargaining power;
- to assure access or build a barrier to entry to a market;
- to facilitate oligopolistic control;
- foreclosure of inputs; or
- to assure price discrimination for outputs.

A point to be made here about collective internationalization strategies is that the power-related goals above are in most cases not explicitly named by the management of companies participating in a horizontal or vertical collaboration. Sometimes, management keeps them secret as they are frequently not desirable from an overall economic point of view, if for example they could result in restricting competition, or be unacceptable to weaker collaboration partners who have to reckon with the loss of their autonomy or ability to compete.

From a strategic market point of view, there are numerous goals and subgoals for the implementation of a collective internationalization strategy. Lorange *et al.* (1992) distinguishes fundamentally between four market-strategic aims that could be achieved with collective internationalist strategies:

- to defend;
- to catch up;
- to remain; or
- to restructure.

Further goals that can be differentiated are expansion goals (Schrader, 1993; Hamel *et al.*, 1989), export goals (Harrigan, 1987; Morris and Hergert, 1987; Auster, 1987), capacity-utilization goals (Kelting-Büttner, 1991; Müller and Goldberger, 1986), flexibility goals (Bronder and Pritzl, 1992; Schrader, 1993; Prahalad and Hamel, 1990; Johnston and Lawrence, 1988), innovation goals (Mahoney and Crank, 1993), learning goals (Hamel *et al.*, 1989; Porter and Fuller, 1986; Backhaus and Piltz, 1990), quality goals (Porter and Fuller, 1986; Hamel *et al.*, 1989), safeguarding and risk-reduction goals (Schrader, 1993; Porter and Fuller, 1986; Bresser, 1989; Mahoney and Crank, 1993; Endress, 1991; Devlin and Bleackley, 1988; Morris and Hergert, 1987) and time-gaining goals

(Contractor and Lorange, 1988; Morris and Hergert, 1987; Backhaus and Meyer, 1993; Forrest, 1990). There are also social and personal goals.

Due to the heterogeneity of the goals and subgoals that can be shown for collective strategies, they have been grouped here into eight key objectives:

- to open up foreign markets;
- to make supply and sales more secure;
- to improve innovation and quality potentials;
- to realize economies of scale and scope;
- to reduce risk;
- to secure critical resources;
- to enable time and flexibility gains;
- to implement personal and social ideas.

5
Success Factors for and Problems with Collective Internationalization Strategies

Success factors

One of the pressing questions in international management is which factors affect the success or failure of a collective internationalization strategy. Using the theoretical approaches and models described previously, and also empirical investigations and experience from business practice, it is possible to predicate the positive and negative factors that impact on the success of collective internationalization strategies.

General statements about the factors affecting the success of collective internationalization strategies are of little use to operative management working in international cooperative ventures. It is imperative that statements about the general tendency are qualified by a detailed analysis of the situational context in which the strategy is to be implemented. The framework conditions relevant to the collective strategy can be divided into two categories to allow better analysis of the situational context: global and specific environment.

The global environment

Four key elements that have effective influence on the success of an internationalization strategy are:

- the development of economic, political and social framework conditions in the target country and in a regional and global context;
- the international and national competition and technology policies;
- the international and national industrial and market policies; and
- the transport, finance and communication structures.

When developing economic, political and social framework conditions, international management should note whether market boundaries change (for example in the People's Republic of China, the EU, NAFTA), or if new markets open up as changes are made to national economic policies. For example, China's entry into the WTO has changed key framework conditions for companies currently engaged or intending to engage in business there.

The political, economic and social conditions represent important prerequisites on global regional and country-specific levels and can facilitate but also obstruct or even prevent the organizational implementation of a collective international strategy. To quote just one example here, the People's Republic of China imposes very specific conditions on the organizational form of collective internationalization strategies in its economic area. The special economic and technology zones that have been set up place particular requirements on the way strategies can be organized. Due to legal and political restrictions, it is only possible to enter certain Chinese markets (for example car manufacturing and supplies, telecommunications, the agricultural industry) with a Chinese business partner. As a result, many German, Japanese and American companies have only been able to gain access to Chinese markets by issuing licences to Chinese companies. Furthermore, it is very important that international management evaluates precisely the social and political circumstances of their target country; social unrest or political excesses can seriously endanger the implementation of a collective internationalization strategy (sadly, there are numerous examples from history and daily affairs – for example in the Philippines or Indonesia).

International and national policies on competition and technology are also important factors influencing the success of a collective internationalization strategy. Examples of this are legal conditions (cartel laws) and the structure of national and international programmes for funding cooperative ventures in research and development (for example, the Sixth EU Research Framework Programme). International and national industrial and market policies also strongly influence the implementation of collective internationalization strategies. International and national funding programmes (for example, EU funding programmes for SMEs), as well as restrictions imposed legally or by economic policy in specific markets, have an impact on the effectiveness of collective internationalization strategies. In some cases certain forms of organization are not permitted. The fourth key element in the global environment, the transport, finance and communications structure, has a considerable impact on collective strategies. In particular, progress in communications technology allows and facilitates the implementation of internationalization strategies. For example, the deployment of information and communications systems beyond company boundaries enables the organizational form of economic activity known as 'virtual business' to be carried out (Griese, 1992; Scholz, 1994; Mertens, 1994; Sieber, 1998). Increasing the efficiency of financial, transport and communications structures has a very positive effect on the organizational implementation of a collective internationalization strategy.

The specific environment

The specific environment includes all aspects of the real industrial world around the company. An important factor is the competition situation prevailing in a sector, that is the intensity of the competition and the structural conditions. Competitive pressure that promotes collaboration can, for example, be triggered by the appearance of new competitors in the sector. The number, size and position of companies in a sector affects the implementation of a collective internationalization strategy. The methods for evaluating industrial economy and in particular the work by Michael Porter (1980, 1985, 1986) can be used to give a company-specific analysis of the factors influencing a collective strategy.

Scarce resources can be an important factor in the implementation of a collective internationalization strategy in a sector. A lack of resources for a potential collaboration partner may result in increasing willingness to cooperate in order to boost the scarce material with one or more partners. Other factors noted are technological development and its associated lack of security (Picot and Franck, 1993; Bucklin and Sengupta, 1993; Pfeffer and Salancik, 1978), market discontinuity (Mahoney and Crank, 1993), the number and quality of suppliers and customers (Mahoney and Crank, 1993), and the quality of input factors and the conditions that come with the participants. Crucial factors for the success or otherwise of a collective internationalization strategy for the participants themselves are their expectations of success in the joint venture (Moss Kanter, 1994), the basic attitude on the part of management to cooperative ventures (Bleackley, 1988), previous positive experience with cooperative ventures (Kelting-Büttner, 1991; Hakansson, 1989), the skills and personality of management involved in the cooperative venture (Staehle, 1999) and the real and assumed efficiency of each collaboration partner (Schubert and Küting, 1981; Staehle, 1999).

Other key factors in the success of a joint venture are the duration and the stability of existing business relationships. Trust and understanding for a business partner may have developed on the basis of a long-term existing successful relationship, and the positive experience provided by that collaboration will be assumed for future joint projects to form a positive foundation for the implementation of collective internationalization strategies. However, the company structure and philosophy, the corporate culture in its broadest sense, are also crucial factors (Schaude, 1991; Moss Kanter, 1994). It must also be assumed that in order to conduct a cooperative venture successfully, the areas are functionally compatible.

Corporate culture plays a particularly significant part in international collaboration. Culture as a theoretical construct has an important role in anthropology, in sociology and in management research and has accordingly been defined in many different ways. All the definitions have in common that culture is a system of shared values, norms, attitudes, convictions and ideals (Staehle, 1999, p. 498; Allaire and Firsirotu, 1984). Corporate culture is reflected in the conduct of management, in negotiating standards, in the ways conflict is handled and trust created, and in the perception and handling of time. If the employees in an international collaboration come from different cultural circles (for example, Germany and Japan – this will be discussed in more detail below), culture and company-specific methods of problem-solving become apparent and employees exhibit different styles of language, employ different methods of working and have differing preferences for achieving targets. Where there are greater discrepancies between corporate cultures, senior management of the companies involved needs to be particularly aware of this key factor, as it can impact on the success or otherwise of the collective internationalization strategy (Hofstede, 1980; Dill, 1986; Heinen, 1987; Porter and Fuller, 1986).

Alongside corporate culture, shared objectives have a positive effect on the successful outcome of a collective internationalization strategy. Harmonized targets are beneficial to the successful running of a joint venture, but one cannot assume that the goals of the partners are in reality congruent. The companies participating in the cooperative venture have frequently pursued different interests which under certain circumstances can work against the goals of the collective internationalization strategy. It follows that a collective venture can only be successful in so far as the basic goals of the partner companies allow. Goals should be discussed openly in the preliminary stages and in the course of the joint venture to deal with any ambiguities in the priorities of the partners.

As well as this precise agreement on goals, it is also important for the success of the venture that management is aware of where the boundaries for the collaboration are set. An unequivocal agreement on the resources to be made available to the joint venture and the limits of a potential future commitment should be mentioned here. Particularly in cooperative ventures between competitors, Hamel *et al.* (1989) caution against inadvertently transferring too much expertise to the partners. This runs the risk of undermining the core competence of the organization in the course of implementing the collective internationalization strategy in a joint venture, for example, and reducing long-term the competitive capability of the company. It is crucial that in the course of implementing the collective internationalization strategy instruments are defined which allow the companies to trade on the market separately after the collaboration has come to an end.

Collective internationalization strategies which are implemented with not just one partner, but with different partners make additional demands on a successful implementation. There can be interactions between different cooperative ventures which result from competitive relationships, and these should be anticipated by senior management in order to exploit the positive and to deal with the negative interactions as early as possible.

It is clear that the successful implementation of collective internationalization strategies is considerably influenced by the ways that partner companies participating in the interfirm collaboration adjust to it internally (Anderson and Narus, 1991; Schubert and Küting, 1981). They need to adjust their organizational structure to the prevailing conditions and to the task in hand, which has been defined between the business partners in the framework of the collective strategy (Lorange and Probst, 1987). This means that the form of organization and the degree to which it is organized should be structured according to the environment of the cooperative venture and the internal conditions, and developed in line with changes in the environment and the company. Taking practical points of view into account along with theoretical considerations, according to my interviews with Japanese and German managers in China and Japan (Haak, 2001b, 2003), operative management has only two real alternatives for organizing the internationalization strategy; either a simple structure regulated on a clear contractual basis, or a thoroughgoing collaboration with the creation of a separate joint enterprise.

If on implementing the collective internationalization strategy the partners in the undertaking choose a form of organization which will permit particularly active exchange, such as setting up a separate joint venture, the management should agree on a means with which to measure the success of the collaboration. Measures of success may be:

- profit targets;
- turnover targets;
- increased technological know-how;
- increased management know-how;
- additional added value (image for example);
- cost savings.

There is a need for regular monitoring, and the success of the venture should be measured and evaluated against the objectives defined in the collective strategy. Only this will enable management to introduce corrective action in good time, to make decisions which will put the venture back on the path to achieving its objectives. It is conceivable that management will decide to dissolve a cooperative venture, particularly if achieving targets with the partner company no longer seems realistic even after all possible corrective action has been investigated and would result in an unjustifiable strain on the parent company.

Lorange *et al.* (1992) recommends setting up a joint committee with overall regulatory and control functions to monitor the cooperative venture. The committee should also have the capability to impose appropriate sanctions on individual participants whose opportunistic conduct could damage the venture. Failure on the part of management to impose sanctions for bad conduct and potential exploitation of the cooperative venture will encourage perpetrators, which in the long-term would inevitably undermine the goals of the venture. Strategies to solve conflicts and clear definitions of liability when jointly made decisions arc not adhered to must be put in place.

Lorange and Probst (1987) see keeping the cooperative venture as flexible as possible as one of the crucial factors for the successful implementation of a collective strategy. This can be achieved by choosing a flexible form of organization. Against the background of dynamic and high-risk markets and the changing demands made on the participants in the venture, maintaining the flexibility of the form of organization resulting from the collective strategy is essential. Management must be able to deal independently with entrepreneurial freedom and realize a high degree of self-organization. Autonomy and flexibility, according to Bleeke and Ernst (1991, 1994), are key factors determining the success of a joint venture. Flexibility is here understood to mean the general ability of the venture to adjust both qualitatively and quantitatively to changes in the competitive situation; in other words, to form a fit between the environment and the company. This is the responsibility of the venture management and the regulatory and control committee.

The management of the cooperative venture and the management of the parent company face many challenges arising from the successful creation of a joint venture. These can range from staffing issues, through the form and degree of technology transfer, to the solution of cross-cultural conflict. Employees and employee networks which are usually organized horizontally between participating companies form the central base of the collaboration and guarantee, in the final analysis, realization of its objectives (Moss Kanter, 1994). Schaude (1991, p. 26) also stresses the special importance of the staff component, emphasizing quite succinctly that the people involved must be compatible. Smooth communication between the people involved in the collective internationalization strategy is an important factor in solving conflicts and for achieving the objectives of the cooperative venture. Schaude further emphasizes that stamina and commitment on the part of management are helpful in dealing with difficulties, a statement which is hard to deny (Schaude, 1991).

If the relationships between members of staff are characterized by mutual respect and expertise and if the managers involved have the required social skills, which might for example show up in clever handling of negotiations, then conditions are set fair for the success of the collective internationalization strategy. The interactions between managers involved and their capabilities, skills and knowledge are important in ensuring that a business collaboration works.

Management is presented with many additional and specific challenges, which go far beyond managing a company acting autonomously. The following criteria should be observed when selecting a member of staff to represent the company in the management of the cooperative venture: negotiating skills, assertiveness, an outgoing personality and willingness to assume responsibility. Based on his theoretical analysis of interfirm networks, Sydow (1992) sees the demands on the role of management changing. From a qualitative point of view the demands are growing as increasingly interdivisional and intercompany issues need to be dealt with and the collaboration generates more coordination work. Management in these cooperative ventures must take on more responsibility and have more general qualifications, such as political and diplomatic skills, in order to develop and maintain the relationships between the companies. Managers are required to balance diverging, frequently changing interests as management decisions can no longer be enforced via a hierarchical authority. The importance of human-resource (HR) management in the successful implementation of a collective internationalization strategy is highlighted, and particular demands are made of those in charge.

Endress (1991) stresses the ability to objectivize mutual interest and maintain a steady, factual distance towards all members as a key factor for the acceptance of a leader within the cooperating group. Operational practice makes clear the particular importance of the leader for the success of the collective strategy, and frequently the departure of an established leader results in friction or even standstill of the cooperative activities even though the framework conditions or the organizational structure of the venture have not changed.

Not only are the professional qualifications of management important, but also the willingness of management to cooperate can have crucial influence. Here, willingness to cooperate can be understood as the attitude of managers towards entering into a cooperative arrangement with other companies. Managers who have a fundamentally positive attitude to business collaboration will tend to prefer collaboration to complete integration. In Sydow's view, these psychological factors influencing the success of a cooperative venture are complemented by previous experience, cognitive reflection and subjective theory-creation on the part of the management itself (Sydow, 1992).

As well as a positive basic attitude on collaboration, similarity of values, mindsets, education, interests and technical terminology can have a positive impact on collaboration between managers from different parent companies. On the other hand, if the managers come from different levels and functional areas, divergent premises can make mutual understanding difficult. Furthermore, the capabilities and personal characteristics of managers who structure the cooperative venture should be matched to the specific intention of the venture and its associated tasks and challenges. A particularly supportive factor for the success of the cooperative venture is the continuity of management in senior positions. Frequent change of management is considered particularly negative for the productivity of the venture (Lyles, 1987). However, a change at leadership level can also bring a new positive impulse, but the adjustment and familiarization must be dealt with properly as productivity can fall during the transitional phase.

The reason why personal characteristics are so important in implementing a collective internationalization strategy is that collaborating with a partner in practice principally builds on existing management capacity. Drawing up the contractual basis, establishing initial contact and nurturing business and personal relationships to build up trust, frequent meetings and large amounts of communication, written and by telephone, consume a major proportion of the time budget. The personal suitability, professional qualifications, special motivations and the maximum possible continuity of the people involved in the collective internationalization strategy all have a considerable impact on its success.

Another important aspect crucial to the success of a collective internationalization strategy is the readiness of the companies taking part to contribute resources of a consistently high standard to the cooperative effort. On the level of HR management, this means that the necessary management resources must be provided by the partners in order to realize the collective strategy. In principle, the partners should be prepared to invest in the relationship into which they have entered. Particularly when problem situations need to be dealt with, it is important to have flexible access to sufficient resources such as staff with special qualifications or the use of advanced technology. If the parent company provides first-class resources for the cooperative venture, it will also demonstrate that it holds it in high regard, which will have a considerable positive impact on the motivation of participants and increase the likelihood of its success (Bucklin and Sengupta, 1993).

Trust is a central construct in the successful implementation of a collective strategy and represents the basis for successful collaboration. However, this trust need not develop into shared identity. It is sufficient if the partners can communicate openly and honestly. The literature on creating collaborations highlights trust again and again as a central requirement (Hakansson, 1989; Haury, 1989; Moss Kanter, 1994), with trust and commitment being key terms for creating a long-term partnership.

A central question in both management research and entrepreneurial practice is 'How can trust be built up in collective strategies?' What instruments does the management of an international joint venture, for example, have at its disposal for this purpose? Some conclusive statements can be found in the literature; for example, respect for the collaboration partner is crucially important to building up a basis of long-term trust. It is essential in this case to understand the situation of the collaboration partner and to acknowledge his or her contribution to the joint venture. Under certain circumstances when problems occur it can make sense to check one's own perspective by looking at the situation from the partner's point of view (Ohmae, 1989, 1990; Bucklin and Sengupta, 1993).

The role played by trust in the stability of business collaboration cannot be underestimated, but for the pragmatist of international management there is a problem in that trust does not come overnight. Trust between partners grows only very slowly with one partner making an initial effort. Research by Axelrod (1991) shows clearly that trust and reliability engender more trust. Another important point stressed in this work is that managers participating in a cooperative venture need not necessarily be friends for the venture to develop. Indeed, Axelrod (1991, p. 19) goes so far as to say that under specific conditions, collaboration based on mutuality can even develop between enemies. From the point of view of economics, the significance of trust is discussed to the effect that it can simplify complex control mechanisms and reduce the costs of control (Jarillo, 1988).

A solid basis for trust can only be created when the partners communicate sufficiently and provide each other with information relevant to the development of the cooperative venture. In the preliminary work for the venture, it should be ensured that as much information as possible is exchanged. According to Ohmae (1989) it is particularly important that managers involved in the collective internationalization strategy get together frequently to exchange information relevant to decision-making. This is the only way to avoid misunderstandings at an early stage and to achieve consistent agreement about how the cooperative venture should develop. However, it should not be forgotten that too many meetings can lead to 'conference fatigue', the response to which might be a drop in motivation or even cause some participants to absent themselves. The art of management is in establishing the correct frequency for collaboration meetings under the prevailing circumstances. Between meetings, management can be kept informed about developments in the collective internationalization strategy in writing.

Another aspect of the success of a collective strategy, closely associated with the issue of communication and information, should not be underestimated; this is the size of the management group taking part in the organizational implementation and development of the collective internationalization strategy. As the size of the group increases, problem-solving by direct personal contact is replaced by codes of behaviour, usually written, as orientation points. Negotiation processes become tighter in their form and content, and as the size of the group increases formalized processes complement or replace informal exchange. The result is the tendency to lose flexibility. The danger of encroaching bureaucracy increases, and the relationships between members of the cooperative venture become more impersonal. The relative significance of the individual and his or her perceived ability to have any influence is reduced. Managers in the group lose motivation, and consequently there is frequent reference to the need to keep the group as small as possible (Haury, 1989). It cannot be said prior to the implementation and development of a collective strategy what size of group generates the optimum increase in productivity for the collective internationalization strategy. The social and professional qualifications of managers, their experience with cooperative ventures and working in groups and the unforeseeable dynamic interactions between managers in the situational context determine the optimum intensity of the relationships. The important point is the willingness of management to adapt the size of the group to the requirements of the developing collective internationalization strategy and its organizational manifestations in the target countries.

Effective conflict management is also important, as conflicts can be seen as an integral component of any collaboration; conflicting goals inevitably cause tension and problem situations. Conflicts can also arise on many other levels, particularly when one of the partners accuses the other of opportunistic conduct. The negative impact of conflicts on collective internationalization strategies can, however, be reduced by the way management handles them. For this reason, effective conflict management is one of the key prerequisites for the successful implementation of a collective strategy. Which tools are used for conflict management depends largely on the type of conflict.

Let us now look at a second level of understanding and management of collective internationalization strategies: the problems associated with them.

Problems

Many conflicts and problems can arise during the implementation of a collective internationalization strategy, and may assume magnitudes that can result in the failure of the collective strategy. Consequently, the ways that collaborating companies handle conflict and detect and solve problems play an important part in the success of a collective strategy. Conflicts and problems are given as reasons against collective strategies both in the literature (for example in Contractor and Lorange, 1988) and also in practice. Conflicts between companies implementing a collective strategy may result when problems with collaboration become concrete. In order better to understand the causes of conflicts and the ways of handling them in collective strategies we first look at their nature. First of all, they manifest themselves on three levels:

- at the company-environment level;
- at company level (for example between management and owners);
- at group level, such as between senior staff and their subordinates.

The causes, subjects and progression of conflicts are so many and so various that there is little point in attempting a definition of conflict as a construct. However, a description of the situation which is frequently described as conflictory will aid the understanding of conflicts. According to Filley (1975) conflictory situations often have the following characteristics:

- mutually exclusive goals and means;
- at least two people or groups are in an interaction;
- the interaction is aimed at influencing or oppressing another person or group in order to allow the goals of the first person to be achieved more easily;
- there are inconsistencies in the related actions and reactions between the persons or the groups.

Using this description of a situation as a basis and taking different aspects into account, it is possible to illustrate different forms and types of conflict, which are well-documented and analysed in Krüger (1972), Rüttinger (1977), Dorow (1978) and Katz and Kahn (1966). There is particular interest in the causes of conflict. One cause put forward is that companies represent a 'sovereignty association' which is the source of many hierarchical conflicts and struggles for redistribution (Dahrendorf, 1959). The cause of functional conflicts (coordination and collaboration) is the fact that companies are fundamentally based on division of labour and specialization. Furthermore, the people who work in a company have their own goals and needs, so that conflicts can arise between the informal and the formal manifestations of a company.

According to Duncan (1975), Dorow (1978), Staehle (1999), DuBrin (1974) and Dessler (1976), the causes of conflict can be grouped as follows:

- one person/group dominates another person/group;
- low-status person/group gives higher-status person/group instructions;
- differences in the perception of an issue or a situation;
- competing goals, interests, attitudes;
- imbalance in the mutual dependency between person/group;
- adjacent person/group works according to divergent rules;
- split responsibility of persons/groups;
- company structures with unclear, ambiguous responsibilities, competence and work areas;
- reorganization (for example, merger, staffing cutbacks, development of the organization).

The conflicts arising from these causes are mainly perceived as interruptions to the running of the organization (company); classical management authors see the ideal of harmony, consensus and collaboration realized in the smooth-running, well-coordinated and well-managed company. Conflicts in and between companies, such as those arising for example in the organizational implementation of a collective strategy, are seen as troublesome, as dysfunctional for the efficient running of the organization and therefore to be suppressed or avoided.

Many authors assume wrongly that conflicts are avoidable and their primary cause is the personal shortcomings of members of the company (Kelly, 1970; Hellriegel and Slocum, 1986). It was Coser (1956) in particular who broke away from this exclusively negative view of the phenomenon of conflict. He examined the aspects of conflict that are positive for a person, a company and society. People and groups need both phases of harmony and of conflict for their productive development; change in companies and change in business structure virtually presuppose conflict. Dahrendorf (1972) even finds the driving force for positive social change in conflict. An exclusively positive or negative evaluation of the phenomenon of conflict does not seem meaningful, and many research results indicate that both functional and dysfunctional consequences for the organization and the individual are associated with conflict. Grunwald and Lilge (1982), Hellriegel and Slocum (1986), Robbins (1974), Walton (1987) and Glasl (1980) have made particularly important analytical contributions to management research on this subject.

The positive aspects of conflict can be summarized as follows (Staehle, 1999):

- conflict may stimulate new ideas and arouse new creative processes;
- increase group cohesion (might also have negative affects);
- release tension, revealing new and clarified situations;
- represent prerequisites for organizational change, as dissatisfaction with the prevailing norms leads to conflicts;
- result in the development of new activities and energies which have a positive effect, particularly on the competitive situation.

However, the positive consequences, as already mentioned briefly, are juxtaposed with many negative effects of conflict. Conflicts can cause the following (Staehle, 1999):

- stress and dissatisfaction in the individual/group, whereby it should be considered that functionality for the company can mean dysfunctionality for the individual/group;

- instability and confusion from the point of view of the company;
- functional disruption to the running of the organization;
- disruptions to communications and collaboration;
- distorted perception and stereotyping as the result of declining interaction;
- decline in reality and increase of emotionality.

If we now look at conflicts in implementing the collective internationalization strategy, we see that a certain amount of conflict is an unavoidable component of all exchange relationships and does not necessarily have negative consequences for the strategy (Ruekert and Walker, 1987). The successful mixture of a degree of conflict and business efficiency cannot be determined *ex ante*. Investigations show that both excessively low (lack of ideas, little creativity and powers of innovation) and also excessively high levels of conflict (stress, intrigues, communications breakdown) are associated with low business efficiency. In contrast, a medium level of conflict seems to have the effect of increasing efficiency. When a medium level is reached depends on the situation and the individuals or groups involved. Management can influence the level of conflict with a target-oriented information policy.

Conflict of interests and congruence of interests occur together in collective internationalization strategies in principle because the independence of the partner remains intact in the organizational implementation of the strategy and the goals and interests of individual economic units are pursued as a priority. It is not possible to regulate in advance to avoid conflict in the course of a cooperative venture. Over the course of time, conflicts arise when, for example, individual participants try to improve their position in the joint venture within the framework of implementing the collective internationalization strategy. Another trigger for conflict in the collaboration can be the unilateral increase in contribution by one partner or the relative increase of power which leads it to expect a greater share of the output of the cooperative venture when the agreement is renegotiated or restructured. Causes of conflict in collaboration between companies can be incompatible information and management systems and differing conduct, norms and values (Sydow, 1992). A major cause of conflict between partners in implementing a collective internationalization strategy is fundamental lack of trust (Anderson and Narus, 1990; Steffenhagen, 1975).

It was further established in empirical studies that the probability of conflict varies with the closeness of the relationships (Ruekert and Walker, 1987). When there is little interaction between partners in the collective internationalization strategy, much more conflict can be expected than when they work together frequently and resources flow freely.

Anderson and Narus (1990) refer to the positive aspects of conflicts in collective internationalization strategies. In their view, finding a joint solution to conflicts has a positive impact on the collaboration, indeed even strengthens the relationship of the partners. The joint solution of conflicts is evaluated as a success of the cooperative venture. This success forms an important component of the self-image of the cooperative venture and creates an orientation point with which management can assess performance. Conflict can trigger innovative behaviour or create more new structures which are perceived as an appropriate response to the problem. Emerging conflicts dealt with quickly by appropriate conflict-management techniques can allow the company to adjust faster to changes in its environment, for example. The success of inter-firm collaboration cannot be measured directly by the appearance or non-appearance of conflicts.

Looking at different phases is quite useful for understanding the phenomenon of conflict in collective internationalization strategies. Conflicts arise in different phases of the lifecycle of a cooperative venture. Tröndle's (1987) theory-driven study of conflict probability and intensity associated with the lifecycle of a cooperative venture shows that in its initial stages the probability and intensity of conflict occurring is high as the partners need to reconcile differing interests and goals.

In the growth phase, working together has become more the norm for companies, and the likelihood of conflict is reduced as revenue increases. There are few synergy effects in the mature phase of the venture, and as it degenerates and revenue drops the probability and intensity of conflicts increases again. Both partners might consider a relaunch strategy at this stage. The precondition for this is, however, that goals continue to be compatible and the opportunities for using synergy effects have not yet been exhausted and that the partners are seeking to benefit from new potential. If a relaunch of the venture is not attempted or is not successful, then its dissolution is the inevitable result in the theoretical model of the lifecycle.

The negative examples of failed organizational forms of interfirm collaboration have a detrimental effect on the implementation of collective strategies. Seeing cooperative projects fail deters other businesses from deciding to cooperate. Another important aspect which prevents cooperative ventures forming in the early stages is the self-image of a company. This is expressed particularly in the attempts by many small and medium-sized companies to maintain entrepreneurial independence. In family-run companies, the rigid perception of independence on the part of the company leadership and reasons of tradition present an obstacle to the implementation of a collective strategy as company activity is internationalized (Ohmae, 1989). In a tradition-rich company, interfirm collaboration can be seen as a break with tradition, possibly also as a betrayal of the successful principle of independent management, which may have been borne out for decades.

Other difficulties and problems in the organizational structure of interfirm collaboration in implementing a collective internationalization strategy are frequently observed in the wide differences between the corporate cultures and functional procedures dictated by the structure. Differences in company structures and administrative procedures can be problems for interfirm collaboration. Cooperative ventures always have problems if output cannot be improved, and the benefits of cooperating must be obvious to all participants. As negotiations, knowledge and technology transfer between partners and many other factors generate costs for the parent companies, the objectives and the benefits to the companies participating must be unambiguous and repeatedly brought to their attention over time. This is the only way to retain the commitment of the parent companies so that the collective internationalization strategy can continue.

A central requirement is a continuous flow of information about all the important aspects of the cooperative venture. Again, this is the only way to assign tasks and responsibilities clearly to each partner and to delimit and distribute costs and factors for success. If the flow of information is poor, and it is not possible to assign tasks and responsibility properly, much intercompany and intracompany conflict could result which would impair the performance of the cooperative venture. This can again lead to doubts about the benefits of the collective strategy for the parent companies. Although from a theoretical point of view, clear assignment and delimitation of tasks and responsibilities appears desirable in order to keep the likelihood of conflict as low as possible, in practice it is frequently very difficult to calculate how costs and results should be distributed.

One level which has not been considered as much as it deserves in the scientific debate so far are the psychological factors for the managers involved in the implementation of a collective strategy. Resistance from within the company, from the management itself, which could work against rational consideration of cooperating needs to be examined in detail. The management's fear of losing control could be a powerful driving force for not seeking a collective internationalization strategy at all. Empirical studies have shown that the desire for autonomy acts as a check on the implementation of collective strategies. The limitation or even loss of power when decisions are taken by the partner are a psychological barrier obstructing interfirm collaboration (Lorange, 1992).

Possible loss via resources and decisions should be seen as a key problem in collective strategies (Lyles, 1987). The causes of conflict for international collective strategies may therefore be seen in the following levels:

- the economic level;
- the personal level;
- the psychological level; and
- the social level.

Handing over decision-making in the course of establishing and developing a business collaboration is equivalent to losing power and suffering insecurity about roles in the company and in the cooperative venture. For entrepreneurs or managers with strong leadership personalities, this is associated with emotional negative moment that should not be underestimated. If decision-making capacity is not transferred to the management of the cooperative venture, the probability of success for the collective strategy is reduced.

Resistance to passing on information and to making decisions in interfirm collaboration, as mentioned previously, can have reasons other than rational economic ones. They frequently arise from emotional backgrounds which develop from personal antipathy or conduct in participants which is not compliant with their roles. Occasionally, the mutual dislike of managers involved in business collaboration can be so strong that only a staff reorganization can ensure continuing success in the cooperative venture. Insufficient communication and lack of trust between participants are seen as central interpersonal problems, frequently resulting in the failure of the collective internationalization strategy (Kelting-Büttner, 1991; Schaude, 1991).

Psychological and sociological factors in conflict are usually not detectable at first sight and are consciously or unconsciously concealed and suppressed by the people affected, but from the point of view of efficiency they dominate the success or failure of a collective internationalization strategy. They form the motivational basis for the actions of management, although most managers do not think about them in concrete terms. Frequently, one looks for legal, economic or organizational reasons when the implementation of a collective strategy fails, although these are frequently only the product of psychological and social problems in the background. For example, sociological obstacles resulting from differing education, values and different technical terminology (Endress, 1991).

A sophisticated conflict-management system is helpful in the successful design of a collective internationalization strategy. However, the options offered by conflict management from the point of view of the dynamics and complexity of social and psychological phenomena should not be overestimated. Despite this limitation, there is a positive glut of publications on the subject of conflict management with more or less empirically based recommendations (DuBrin, 1974; Hellriegel and Slocum, 1976, 1986; Kast and Rosenzweig, 1985).

In summary, at this point, I would like to illustrate the most important recommendations for encouraging conflict – presented in Robbins' (1974) interactional approach – and for handling conflict, offering some assistance and orientation for the implementation of collective internationalization strategies. Conflicts are handled by:

- smoothing over,
- creating a shared enemy,
- creating a shared superordinate goal,
- accepting the criticizer into the group or organization,
- removing the causes of the conflict (remuneration, staff changes, specialization, changes to duties and responsibilities and so on),
- negotiating (bargaining, looking for and implementing compromises),
- third-party assessment (arbitrator, ombudsman, trusted person and so on).

Conflicts are created by:

- announcing changes,
- encouraging competition between managers involved in the inter-firm cooperative venture,
- encouraging an open, relaxed climate to ensure free-flowing communication and information (expressing opinions and so on),
- specialization and differentiation of power, roles and status, selectively passing on information to management and other decision-makers,
- disseminating uncertainty and playing off formal and informal groups against one another (differentiation in remuneration and incentive systems) (Staehle, 1999).

In addition to ways to create and mitigate conflict, to conclude this section I would like to summarize the measures intended to prevent conflicts arising in the first place. The following factors are recommended:

- encourage communication and interaction between managers and groups participating,
- rotate group members and move management between the parent company and the cooperative venture,
- avoid profit and loss situations between managers and groups, and
- reward, in the widest sense, the actions on the part of management and groups which increase the overall efficiency of the cooperative business and stabilize and develop the joint venture.

6
Implementation of Collective Internationalization Strategies

The Japanese company as a learning organization: learning through collaboration

Faced with increasingly dynamic and globalized conditions in international competition, Japanese management is currently looking for new ways to increase the competitiveness of their companies. The strategies that held firm in the boom years are no longer of any help. The collective internationalization strategy, particularly in its organizational manifestation of third-country collaboration, represents a way of enabling business learning processes. It is not a state that is responsible for business success, but a process – the process of learning; learning is important for the implementation of a collective strategy.

So, learning should be considered the crucial factor in the successful implementation of a collective internationalization strategy. Do the right conditions prevail in Japanese companies to carry out learning processes and to use them to achieve business goals? What, however, do we mean by learning? What does individual and organizational learning mean for a company or, more precisely, what is a learning organization? What are its characteristics and how do they manifest themselves in Japanese companies?

For answers to these questions we shall look at Japanese companies from a learning perspective and select, from the many different levels of observation, two aspects which are central to competitiveness under globalization:

- Organizational learning through:
  - technology transfer, or

- knowledge transfer

for example using automation technology; and

- Organizational learning through *kaizen* (as a process of constant improvement involving all member of the organization.

First, however, let us turn our attention to the theoretical basis of the learning organization and consider first the terminology. In an attempt at definition, we find that learning is a pattern and change of conduct resulting from experience which enables organisms to react appropriately to situations on the basis of previous and continuing experience (Brockhaus, 2002). Learning assumes perception; if something is not perceived, it cannot be learnt. Another characteristic is that learning cannot be observed; we can only 'compare the conduct of a person before and after certain events (for example, practice, experience) and conclude that something has taken place in the person which we refer to as learning' (Staehle, 1999, p. 207). Accordingly, 'learning can be defined as a relatively persistent change in (long-term) behaviour' which 'represents the outcome of practice and experience, and learning processes necessarily presuppose a memory which allows perceived information to be retained and reproduced on command' (*ibid.*).

Human beings have the ability to reflect, to think about their actions, which is not the case for organisms in general. They have the ability consciously to change, vary and, if they wish, enhance their behavioural options. However, to do this they need a certain motivation; a fundamental interest must be present so that humans put themselves through the effort of learning. Learning psychologists agree that learning requires reinforcement, or activation. There are a large number of theories of learning reflecting different attitudes to the purposes and goals of human learning to offer explanations of the learning process. In particular there are the cognitive and social theories of learning and the stimulus–response theory, which can be referred to as classic (see Bergius, 1972; Luthans, 1985; Luthans and Kreitner, 1985; Brandstätter *et al.*, 1978; Latham and Saari, 1979; Bandura, 1969, 1977, 1986, 1990; Gist and Mitchell, 1992 for more information).

Theoretical approach

Leaving aside learning at an individual level and looking at organizations or companies in their entirety, we see that organizational learning is not identical to individual learning. Furthermore, it would go too far to explain organizational learning as an aggregation of individual learning processes (Fiol and Lyles, 1985; Wiegand, 1996). Nevertheless, theories of human learning offer an initial approach to the problem of the learning organization. Piaget's (1985) concept of learning, which assumes the individual but focuses on structures (stages of development) behind changes in individual behaviour, and not the change to individual behaviour, presents a way of understanding the phenomenon of the learning organization (Pautzke, 1989). According to Piaget's process model, organizational learning can be interpreted as the development of a stock of knowledge shared by all members of an organization. The essential differences between learning processes in an organization and in individuals are that the former has developed more or less person-independent learning models and systems.

Shrivastava (1983) distinguishes between six fundamental organizational learning systems:

1. The one-person organization;
2. Mythological learning systems;
3. Participative learning systems;
4. The information culture of an organization;
5. Formal management systems;
6. The bureaucratic system.

System 1 is a one-man institution. In this case one person (for example an independent businessman) is the crystallization point for all the learning processes. Shrivastava also distinguishes between mythological (2) and participative (3) learning systems. The latter is, for example, a group or team formed for *ad hoc* problem-solving. If we take a car factory as an example of an organization, a participative learning system could be the setting-up of a quality circle to improve manufacturing quality in the final assembly stages – a basic example of the Japanese company as a learning organization, which will be discussed in detail later. Mythological learning processes are expressed in stories, narratives and myths about the organization, even in the culture of the organization which serves as a depot of knowledge. Shrivastava defines the information culture of an organization (4) as an organization-specific learning medium in informal communication channels. Formal management systems (5), found for example in strategic planning processes or in the traditional management information systems, represent other separate learning systems in an organization. The final learning system in Shrivastava's list is the bureaucratic system (6), which consists mainly of rules, programmes and codes of behaviour to prescribe precisely the conduct for specific situations. Rules move individual decisions, which are frequently taken in uncertainty, to a higher level without individual learning processes and conflicts. Due to their regulated nature, decisions are easier to trace back and their depersonalized character completely frees them of individual arbitrariness. In contrast to the formal management system, the bureaucratic learning system is extremely rigid and only slightly flexible (Kieser *et al.*, 1999).

Looking at all six learning systems together, an increasing depersonalization of the learning process becomes apparent from the first stage of development (one-man institution) to the final stage of the bureaucratic learning system. To be more precise: it is no longer an individual who is learning, which is essentially the case in the one-man institution, nor a selected group in the organization in the way that senior management (the Board) might represent the whole organization (vicarious learning), but the accumulated knowledge of the whole organization that undergoes a change. Using this systematic classification, one can refer to a continuum of learning levels which starts at the basis of individual learning, that one learns for oneself, through learning for organizations, for example through very senior management or certain management groups, to learning by the organization itself in the form of management systems such as total quality management, and bureaucratic structures (Staehle, 1999, p. 915).

Knowledge can be lodged with individual employees in an organization as individual knowledge, and can be lost to the organization if that member leaves (see also Albrecht, 1993). On another level, an organization's knowledge can be collected in documents, kept in files which hold actions, measures, decisions and business procedures. This can be the case in business plans which make development paths and goals comprehensible for members and non-members of the organization (Hansen, Nohria and Tierney, 1999). Organizational knowledge can also be held in material objects (for example, tools, machines and plant), which then serve members as guidelines for their working process (Neuberger, 1997).

For example, the arrangement of tools and machines implicitly contains information for the operators on the sequence of the work process (Argyris, 1990). According to Argyris and Schön (1999), organizations represent information on tap in the sense that they embody strategies to carry out difficult tasks which could also have been carried out in different ways. Organizational knowledge is tied to the sequence of processes and procedures (for example, the sequence determined by the automation technology in a mechanical process – drilling, turning, cutting) and represents solutions to the various problems (for example producing a steel shaft to customer specifications) that exist in the execution of a manufacturing process.

Organizational knowledge about the execution of tasks can manifest itself in very different forms (Bach and Homp, 1998). Possible forms are belief systems underlying actions, prototypes from which actions are derived or rules of procedure for action, similar to a computer programme. Argyris and Schön (1999, p. 28) represent this knowledge through so-called theories of action, an approach which has the advantage of including action strategies as well as the values which determine the selection of strategies and the assumptions on which they are based. Their theory of action can take on one of two forms: 'espoused theory', which comes to the fore when a specific pattern of activity needs to be explained or justified, and the 'theory-in-use' which is tacitly present when the pattern of activity is carried out. The 'theory-in-use' is constructed from observing the patterns of interactive behaviour amongst the members of an organization in so far as their behaviour is determined by formal and informal rules for joint decisions, delegation and membership (*ibid.*, p. 29).

The theories-in-use in organizations are implicit rather than explicit, as rules for collaborative behaviour and decisions frequently are. Workplace descriptions, formal strategies and formulation of goals and organizational plans representing the formal documents of the organization are an expression of the espoused theory, which is frequently not identical to the routine and real patterns of activity in the organization. The theory-in-use declares its identity over the course of time, so that historical views of organizational development are of great value to the understanding of the current organization. In a large, stable Japanese organization such as Matsushita, for example, which is active all over the world, its products or the social position in Japan show that changes have taken place over time. Products have changed and so, possibly, have the functions which Matsushita has for Japanese society. However, if we look at the development of the theories-in-use at Matsushita, which for example are apparent in the patterns of promotion, forms of control exercised by the company, training systems and types of conflict handling, it can be seen that the theory-in-use has changed very little in comparison to the products. The theory-in-use as expressed in the company philosophy of *kaizen* (the process of continuous improvement) offers a good point from which to understand organizational learning processes.

According to Albrecht (1993) and Lullies *et al.* (1993), the way in which a company makes use of its knowledge and manages learning needs a holistic conception. It takes on the task of aligning the information carriers (individual, social, technical or organizational) with the strategic goals of the organization (Bach *et al.*, 2000; Bea, 2000; Bullinger, 1998; Classen and Becker, 1999; Davenport, 1996). However, it should not be forgotten that the generation of strategic goals depends on existing organizational structures and stocks of knowledge, but also affects the structures retroactively so that we must call it a reciprocal set of conditions (Heimerl-Wagner, 1992). Collective internationalization strategies are also exposed to these sets of conditions, with the partner company representing an additional set of conditions affecting the drafting and design of the collective strategy. Giddens' (1988) general thinking on the duality of structure aids understanding the interactional relationships of strategy and structure. Organizational structures are always the production of human action and therefore of strategy, and at the same time they are a medium for human actions and the associated learning processes; as such they permit, but also limit strategy. In collective strategies this process does not take place on the level of the single organization, but on an interorganizational level when the interactions between the partners' structures and strategies start to take effect.

It is clear that the concept of organizational learning is suitable for managing individual and organizational collections of knowledge as the different learning levels and learning processes are systematically linked to the concept of organizations as knowledge systems. It is also clear that a necessary condition for organizational learning in hierarchically structured organizations is the sharing of a knowledge base (Garratt, 1990; Geißler, 1996; Hanft, 1996). The knowledge base can be shared in the organization itself, within the framework of the collective internationalization strategy, and also between organizations. According to Duncan and Weiss (1979) it is only possible to speak of organizational learning when the knowledge base developed is one shared by all members of the organization. The key point here is the fundamental change to collective shared patterns of behaviour or the interpretation schemata accepted by the organization. It is for this reason that Argyris and Schön (1978) coined the term 'theory-in-use', as described above – the day-to-day theories according to which decisions are made and which determine the actions of individuals in organizations.

How do organizational learning processes take place in a company? It is above all the divergence between the expectations and the results of actions that correct the theories-in-use in an organization. Argyris and Schön call this 'single-loop learning'. According to Argyris and Schön, organizational learning takes place when individuals in an organization are faced with a problematic situation and investigate it on behalf of the organization. Employees find inconsistency between the results they expected from their actions and the actual outcome. Investigating this may mean that they modify their image of the organization or their understanding of organizational phenomena, and rearrange their activities so that actions and results are again congruent. This changes the theory-in-use of the organization.

However, in order to be entered into the organizational base, such learning must become embedded in the images of the organization which exist in the heads of its members and/or in the epistemological artefacts (diagrams, memories, programmes) in the organizational environment. It follows that by single-loop learning, Argyris and Schön mean instrumental learning which results in the organization performing better in its work and which changes strategies for action and the assumptions underlying these strategies so that the moral concepts of a theory-in-use remain unchanged (Argyris and Schön, 1999, p. 31).

To illustrate, let us take a worker at Hitachi Seiki assembling a machine tool who discovers a defective component. He can pass this information on to the production manager who, in his turn, could change the product specifications and manufacturing methods with the goal of improving quality to remove the fault. Strategy would be changed so that the performance of the machine-tool manufacturer Hitachi Seiki remained within the framework of the existing moral concepts and norms. The basic concept or the norm itself, the quality of the component, remains unchanged. According to Argyris and Schön (1978), single-loop learning processes can be split into four basic phases:

- looking for errors (discovery);
- looking for new solutions (invention);
- implementing the solution (production); and
- evaluating and generalizing from the results for the organization overall (generalization).

It is only when the existing interpretation schema and the values and norms valid in the organization for the removal of errors and negative deviation (performance gap) have failed repeatedly that the organizational framework of activity is revised. Argyris and Schön call this double-loop learning, meaning a form of learning which results in a change of values of both the theory-in-use and the strategies and assumptions (1999, p. 36). For our previous example in the Japanese company Hitachi Seiki, this form of organizational learning would go hand in hand with changes to the manufacturing norm and the product quality, thus changing the orientation framework of the daily actions of the organization members.

The final way in which an organization learns according to Argyris and Schön involves investigations through which an organization improves its ability to learn through both single-loop and double-loop learning. Following Bateson (1985), they move to a meta-level in the sense of learning in order to learn. The results of this learning process result in fundamental restructuring of the character of individual learning and/or the learning systems in an organization. This kind of learning system, which is associated with massive restructuring, assumes that out-of-date and incorrect knowledge and behaviour have been previously unlearnt. According to Nystrom and Starbuck (1984, p. 59; Staehle, 1999, p. 917) there are three different ways in which managers can unlearn individual theories-in-use:

1. Listen to contradictions; this includes, for example, acknowledging other, possibly different opinions in the organization.
2. Think in alternatives; for example, look at diverging scenarios for organizational development to be able to assess and understand the company better in future.
3. Experiment; that is, try out new ways of responding and new ways of thinking to create opportunities for unlearning traditional behaviour and trains of thought.

As well as the findings of Argyris and Schön, another factor central to answering the question of how organizations learn concerns the dissemination of new knowledge. This presupposes, however, that the knowledge is communicable, can be agreed on and integrated (Staehle, 1999, p. 917; Duncan and Weiss, 1979). Wiesenthal (1995) goes a step further towards answering the question. He calls for the inclusion of abrupt and wide-reaching change in the existing conceptions of organizational learning. Looking at the different concepts of the learning organization it becomes clear that unlike in traditional organizational development, which sees change as an exceptional situation, it is seen as normal for learning organizations (Scheurer and Zahn, 1998; Schreyögg, 1998). The theory of *kaizen* fits in here – the continuous improvement of structures and systems involving all employees as a basic company task. This normal case of on-going problem-solving and learning ties up management resources continually and requires a minimum structure and long-term regulations within which this process can take place. In the course of organizational learning processes, structures which have become rigid over time are tested for their coordinating efficiency and, where a performance gap is found, a negative deviation, they are changed to ensure that the goals can be achieved efficiently. If it is found, for example, that an autonomous venture will not enjoy lasting success, it is possible to select organizational changes in the form of proceeding collectively. From the learning point of view, the change appears as a process integrated into the daily working routine; there may be no functional specializations familiar from the traditional organizational development (Papmehl and Siewers, 1999; Reber, 1992; Senge, 1999).

In considering learning in Japanese organizations, or to be more precise Japanese companies, we first have to look at the Japanese system of management more closely. Is it more likely to encourage organizational learning and, if so, in what form? Which learning systems are used in essence and how widely? Are Japanese companies, based on their traditional management system, able to determine negative deviation owing to an autonomous company? Indeed, can they deal with negative deviation by undertaking the necessary steps to carry out and implement a collective internationalization strategy?

Organizational learning through technology and knowledge transfer

To examine the Japanese company from a learning point of view, we return to the two central modes of learning mentioned earlier – organizational learning through technology and knowledge transfer, and organizational learning through *kaizen*, and shall first consider the former.

If we look back at the organizational learning processes in Japanese companies, it becomes clear that their success worldwide over the last few decades has been linked in no small part to the transfer of technology and knowledge and associated advances in learning. One of the crystallization points for successful development has been automation technology. Successful transfer and development of sophisticated automation technology from the USA and Western Europe were important prerequisites for the economic and production technology-related 'triumphal march' of Japanese companies after the Second World War. With the transfer of technology and knowledge, organizational learning processes took place which permanently altered the organizational structure and competitiveness of Japanese factories. The process of developing and adopting automation technology in Japan was crucial to the rapid rise of Japanese companies in the decades following 1945.

Taking over and improving technology from the United States and Western Europe, increasing productivity through new ways of organizing labour and automation technology, a countrywide programme to improve quality based on the ideas of the Americans Deming and Juran, and a high degree of flexibility in the manufacturing process, were key elements as the Japanese made rapid progress through advances in organizational learning. Many Japanese companies from different industries were integrated in company networks, providing an excellent mechanism for any advances in learning in one company to be passed on to others.

On an individual level was the commitment and willingness to learn on the part of Japanese technicians, engineers and managements particularly in electrotechnical and mechanical engineering operations, and in the research laboratories for manufacturing science. Improving existing conditions and realizing knowledge in practical applications characterizes organizational learning in Japanese companies (Fürstenberg, 1972). Technology and knowledge transfer, market-driven industrial integration of innovative automation technology and new forms of labour organization have all been features of technology management in successful Japanese companies (Renkel, 1985).

Research into manufacturing science in Japan after the Second World War, particularly during the economic boom that started during the early 1950s, was determined by increasing automation (Dolezalek, 1956). The use of innovative automation technology in changing production processes strongly affected the work of production management and machine-tool designers (Dolezalek, 1960, p. 1). The rapid rise of Japanese industry prepared the ground for a systematic transition from automated machine tools, standard machines or specialized machines, to the automation of the whole production process. Learning processes at both the individual level and for the whole organization enabled the organizational change, which was integrated in the economic boom. They could even be said to have been mutually dependent (Schüppel, 1996).

Immediately after the Second World War, Japan was occupied with building up and designing new economic structures (Freedman, 1988). From the economical and technological points of view, reconstruction of the economy took priority (Itô, 1992). Shortly after the war, price controls, subsidies and rationing of raw materials were among the most important industrial-political tools used by the government to support coal mining and steel production (Vestal, 1993).

The most important factor in the dramatic development of the Japanese economy was the rapid upturn in industry until the early

1970s (Tsuruta, 1988, p. 50), which was essentially supported by mass production and automation technology (Park, 1975). The reforms during the American occupation had also been significant for the continuing dynamic development of the Japanese economy (Waldenberger, 1994, p. 23). The fall-out from the deconcentration measures was the disentanglement in terms of finance, organization and staffing of the 10 large economic conglomerates (*zaibatsu*), creating the key conditions for competition which supported the rebuilding and boom phases until the beginning of the 1970s (Beason and Weinstein, 1994).

Furthermore, demand from abroad for Japanese goods stimulated and accelerated the economic development of the early 1950s (Abegglen and Stalk, 1986). The development of the Japanese machine-tool industry was particularly affected by a dramatic event in world politics – the outbreak of war in Korea on 25 June 1950, which in the tension surrounding the Cold War resulted in an increase in global demand. Orders received from the USA over many years had a particularly far-reaching impact on Japanese mechanical engineering, and this boom in demand contributed to the recovery and stabilization of the Japanese economy which at the beginning of the 1950s had still been unsteady (Itô, 1992, p. 11).

After a short phase in which the growth rate slowed slightly after the Korea boom, mainly caused by falling private investment, the period of investment boom which brought *kôdo seichô* (rapid growth) began in 1956–57. The high level of investment was oriented towards the development of heavy industry, with the intention of increasing production capacity and to drive on modernization and rationalization in production. Economic policy was set to growth (Chalmers, 1982). The real annual growth rate of GDP in Japan in 1955–60 was 8.6 per cent, 10.6 per cent in 1960–65 and in 1965–70 it peaked at an average of 11.2 per cent (Itô, 1992, p. 45; Keizai Kikakuchô, 1994, pp. 46–7). Even though the high growth phase in the Japanese economy until the first oil crisis in 1973–74 was not entirely without fluctuation, economic expansion in the 1960s was astonishing, particularly when the destruction caused by the Second World War is taken into account (Hemmert and Lützeler, 1994, pp. 23–44).

Until well into the 1950s the same processing companies that predominated before the war were in the majority; the textile industry for example. However, along with the primary industries, the assembly industries (Waldenberger, 1996) such as car manufacturing, mechanical engineering and particularly machine-tool engineering became the mainstays of the boom. There was an especially high requirement for automation in those sectors of industry, and exchanging ideas with national and international research into manufacturing technology carried and drove on Japanese efforts at automation (Spur, 1991, p. 16). It was in those sectors that the basic learning and transformation processes took place that enabled the successful introduction of automation technology.

The advances in learning and knowledge in Japanese companies in the key industrial sectors were boosted by the Japanese state, which encouraged learning by transferring technology and knowledge from abroad (Renkel, 1985). It supported both existing and new sectors with tax concessions and cheap loans, and foreign currency was allocated specifically for the import of raw materials and sophisticated machine technology. The domestic market was closed to imports and direct investment, in order to 'on the one hand protect the developing domestic industry' and on the other hand the isolation made it easier 'to import technology because it reduced the ways in which a foreign company could share in the Japanese market to the licensing of technology' (Waldenberger, 1998, p. 47). New knowledge was rapidly disseminated in companies via the quality circle, for example, which became the foundation and instrument of organizational learning processes as learning and knowledge were removed from the individual to a broad organizational base. The members of the organization shared the same existing knowledge base and used methods they had drawn up together to develop it, a key condition for organizational learning (Garratt, 1990; Geißler, 1996; Hanft, 1996; Ducan and Weiss, 1979).

In Japanese industry, investments were used primarily for rationalizing and modernizing production systems which followed demand in the machine-tool industry (*Nihon Kôsaku Kikai Kôgyôkai*, 1982, pp. 81–3). As the supplier of the means of production, machine-tool construction provided the technological basis for development of other industrial sectors. The Japanese car industry profited most from advances in technological learning in the machine-tool industry, illustrated by the learning artefacts and precision-designed automatic machine tools.

Just after the Second World War, national industry was the main source of impetus for growth and specific production-related demand in the Japanese machine-tool industry. Only later, at the beginning of the 1970s, did West European and American companies gradually become significant customers for Japanese machine tools (Collis, 1988). Before that, in the 1950s and 1960s, basic technological gaps had needed to be filled with the import of sophisticated machine-tool technology. From 1957, Japanese industry became important as a source of demand for the German machine-tool industry, and in 1961 and 1962 it even represented its largest group of buyers (Haak, 1997, p. 130). German technology and processing knowledge were bought in. It was not just a case of company-specific learning aimed at mastering new production methods, but of passing on knowledge to suppliers to enable them to develop sophisticated technology as quickly as possible. Technology and knowledge transfer, with the main production company in the interfirm networks (*keiretsu*) 'nannying' suppliers to Japanese machine and automobile manufacturers, which in the 1960s were still very underdeveloped, represented an enhanced form of organizational learning. Collective strategies were therefore already being realized in those early stages, stabilizing the development of Japanese companies and forcing learning between sectors – an illustration that the structure of the Japanese economy has been defined by collective strategies.

Buyers in the big Japanese general trading houses (*sôgô shôsha*) found a broad range of advanced technology in the Federal Republic of Germany in the 1960s. Application-oriented design solutions together with sound research into production technology and high quality were the basic strengths of German machine-tool construction.

Increasing demand for machine tools as Japan's economy developed was one of the most important stimuli for tackling new learning processes, which were frequently associated with technical innovation in machine-tool construction. The import of the latest machine-tool technology, particularly from Western Europe and the USA, the close collaboration between Japanese machine-tool companies and their suppliers and the long-term collaboration with university researchers into production science provided the Japanese machine-tool industry at the end of the 1960s and the beginning of the 1970s with the basic technology and knowledge needed to meet the growing demands of national and international markets (Fischer, 1979).

Due to the economic framework conditions of those years, efforts to automate manufacturing in Japan with conventional machine tools were concentrated mainly on applications in large-scale series production and mass production. Automation of the manufacturing, particularly in the automobile industry, was driven on by the development and implementation of modular systems (Spur, 1979) as the economic boom created huge demand. Several machines, essentially highly productive specialized machines, were linked together according to the flow principle into transfer lines. Workpiece handling was automated and several manufacturing procedures grouped in one station (Spur and Ebert, 1993, p. 28). Such transfer lines represent artefacts of organizational knowledge, the change in automatic manufacturing equipment being linked to organizational learning. An organization learns and in the course of learning changes its technological artefacts in order to be able to react properly to internal (for example, employee qualifications) or external (for example, market demand) requirements. In the 1950s and 1960s the dominant arrangement in Japanese industry was the rigid linking of manufacturing equipment characterized by automatic transport of the workpiece through simultaneously controlled feed mechanisms at a fixed speed determined by the longest workcycle (Chokki, 1986). Fixed transfer lines were used first mainly in the automotive industry with its large volumes for each workpiece; crankshafts and cam shafts, valves, axles and gear boxes for example were all produced on fixed transfer lines at this time.

Since the late 1950s, electrical control systems had formed the core of a transfer line (Griffin, 1955; Kennedy, 1954), which meant that the development of the lines had also become dependent on progress in the electronics industry. Technological innovation on the part of Japanese machine-tool suppliers became a dominating factor, and the control systems became the subject of increasingly in-depth research and learning by American, Western European and Japanese engineers (Spur, 1991a, p. 498). The technological realization of rigid and later flexible transfer lines (Adler, 1988, p. 36) was supported and made possible by the rapidly developing supplier industry which was given particular impetus in Japan by the specific forms of *keiretsu*. The electrotechnical industry in Japan also drove on the development of automation technology (Asanuma, 1989).

When machine tools were deployed in automatic transfer lines the main task of the control system was to repeat unchanging sequences of movement quickly and precisely, mass producing goods of uniform quality without human intervention (Mommertz, 1981). The automatic manufacturing process was provided by a control system tailored to the technical production conditions, involving mechanical, electrical, pneumatic and hydraulic control components (Simon, 1957).

Whereas the introduction and promulgation of the transfer line was primarily the result of requirements of mass and large-scale serial production, numerical control had been used on machine tools in the late 1950s and during the 1960s mainly for one-off parts and small-scale series production. Previously, mechanical, electrical and hydraulic tracer control had been used with templates as fixed programme media. The impact of numerical-control (NC) technology in machine-tool engineering in Japan resulted in just a few years in completely new types of machines. Designers and manufacturing engineers were asked to provide new solutions, and numerical-control technology became the engine of production technology overall (Simon, 1969).

The origins of computer-controlled automated manufacture lie in the development of numerically controlled machine tools in the USA. Numerical control as a successful innovation and basic technological paradigm goes back to the digital machine-tool control system invented by Parsons and developed with the Massachusetts Institute of Technology (MIT) (Kief, 1991). (The fundamental idea of controlling a machine tool with numbers, that is numerical control, evolved in the manufacturing process for rotor blades; see for example Hirsch-Kreinsen, 1989, 1993; Spur, 1991.) In 1952, the technological concept of numerical control (NC) became known in Japan for the first time when Professor Akira Takahashi of Tokyo University reported on the development of numerically controlled machine tools in the United States. Shortly after this, Japanese machine-tool companies, the electronics industry and universities and state institutions started researching this new area of production technology intensively. The first result of these joint efforts was the numerically controlled revolving hole-punching machine launched by Fujitsu in 1956 (Hoffmann, 1990).

More developments emerged in rapid succession. As early as 1957 the Tokyo Institute of Technology announced the completion of a numerically controlled lathe for experiments and further investigation, and soon after the machine-tool manufacturer Makino Milling Machine developed the first Japanese vertical milling machine with numerical control in collaboration with Fujitsu. In these early stages, the numerically controlled lathes from the company Ikegai and a jig borer designed by the Mechanical Engineering Laboratory at the Ministry of International Trade and Industry (MITI) (now the Ministry of Economy, Trade and Industry (METI)) as part of a three-year research project represented further important steps forward. In 1958, Hitachi Seiki designed a hydraulic numerically controlled milling machine, also in collaboration with Fujitsu, two of which were supplied to the Heavy Industries Nagoya Aircraft Plant (Hitachi Seiki, 1991, p. 16).

From the late 1960s, rapid advances in computer technology and electronics in the USA and Japan played a crucial role (Behrendt, 1982, p. 19; Park, 1985). Learning was taking place on more than a national level, with Japan relying on integration into international research in manufacturing science to safeguard its organizational learning processes with knowledge and technology transfer.

Although the Japanese manufacturers of numerically controlled machine tools still had to struggle with high development costs and serious quality problems at the beginning of the 1960s, the trend reversed at the end of the decade. Market resistance was gradually overcome, demand for flexible manufacturing technology grew rapidly, and the Japanese and then later the American and West European markets became receptive to numerically controlled machine tools from Japan. Technicians, engineers and managers in Japanese machine-tool companies and research establishments realized their advances in learning from knowledge and technology transfer in standalone products. It was these products that underpinned Japan's outstanding competitive position in world markets in the 1970s and 1980s.

One of the key advances in learning and knowledge for the Japanese NC machine industry was the development of the electrical and electrohydraulic servo motor by Fujitsu and FANUC (Fujitsu Automatic Numerical Control) (Schröder, 1995). The great advantage of servo motors compared to conventional drive technology is that they allow the design of more precise, more reliable, more powerful but primarily comparatively cheaper numerically controlled machines. These could also be manufactured in larger series and accounted to a great extent for the huge success enjoyed by the Japanese machine-tool industry (Brödner, 1991). However, it was not only in drive technology, which is all-important for production, that Japanese engineers became so proficient so rapidly; they also caught up with American and Western European development in control-system design. Between 1965 and 1969, Japanese machine-tool factories launched the first NC control systems with integrated minicomputers (Spur, 1991a).

The rise of FANUC can be seen as an example of a Japanese success story during the phase of automation technology. FANUC started life in 1972, hived off from its parent company Fujitsu, who played a significant part in the development and distribution of NC technology in Japan. As early as 1956, as a consequence of a strategic decision by the Fujitsu management, the company was concentrating on computers and control systems, and the business began to encourage long-term development in production technology which only became financially successful 10 years later. The idea of developing an NC control system at Fujitsu was due primarily to Dr Seiuemon Inaba, who also had a key role in its execution. The development presented Inaba's research and development team with a considerable number of technical problems, the first being the construction of computer circuitry. However, after 10 years of development, they succeeded in producing a low-cost, efficient numerical-control system. The FANUC 260 for point-to-point position and linear path control was coupled to three electrohydraulic motors, and its launch at the end of the 1960s in Japan triggered a considerable sales boom (Schröder, 1995, p. 147; Spur and Specht, 1990).

In the late 1960s and early 1970s, Japanese research and development concentrated mainly on application research and on putting the new numerical-control technology to use in processing industries. The first machines were deployed in mechanical engineering, in automobile production and in the electronics industry. However, it was only with growing experience and advances in problem-solving and learning processes that Japan's own discoveries of new technologies became important for production technology in Japanese companies.

Technology and knowledge transfer from Western Europe and the USA in the early years of automation technology was implemented in many different ways. The Japanese mechanical engineering industry within the framework of collective strategies made intensive use of the opportunity to acquire patents and licences and to enter into collaboration agreements with leading technology companies in the mechanical engineering sector and the electronics industry (Nonaka, 1990). Collective strategies with European and American companies not only facilitated technology transfer, but also made it easier to enter foreign markets. Integrating Japanese scientists and engineers in international research into manufacturing technology was also crucial for the advances in organizational learning brought about by technology and knowledge transfer. To all intents and purposes, Japanese management and engineers fared well with collective strategies, and as such strategies coincided with structures receptive to learning, they represented the crucial factor for successful technological and economic development in Japanese industry following the Second World War.

Since the mid-1960s, the impact of automation, computer technology, flexibilization and decentralization of manufacturing processes has lead to a fundamental change in the way industrial businesses work and in individual and organizational learning processes. The new forms of operation are those which have aimed to reduce the functional division of work by integrating tasks. With computer support in the factory, particularly with the use of computer numerical control (CNC) machines, there have been new opportunities for socio-technical work-system design since the end of the 1970s and the beginning of the 1980s. It only became possible to establish different forms and varieties of group work as rational alternative forms of organizing labour in Japanese factories, or to be more precise in automated manufacturing processes, with the wider use of computer-assisted manufacturing equipment. Technological changes and individual and organizational learning processes have been mutually dependent (Adler, 1988), with the result that job enlargement, job enrichment and change of job location may be realized simultaneously as a principle of design.

The use of CNC systems had far-reaching consequences on the options for designing manufacturing processes. Organizations learnt and modified structures needed to fulfil tasks, and CNC systems made it possible for preparatory work on the manufacturing process to be removed from production planning and returned to the worker and the actual place of production. On the basis of this outstanding development in technology, demands to abandon the division of labour increased. The aim of these attempts was to reduce division of labour from 'as much as possible', in accordance with Taylor's principles, to 'as much as is required' in future. The work process was to be carried out by employees who were as highly qualified as possible and with full content and wide-ranging autonomy.

Japanese companies were very receptive towards NC and CNC technology. It is interesting to note here that in those companies, as compared with German companies, the requirement for advanced and continuing training associated with the introduction of new NC technology represented only a small obstacle. One reason was that manufacturers of control systems and machines ran intensive training and support programmes when NC was first developed, with customer employees being trained and supported over six months. Particularly in the introductory phase, engineers from the manufacturers were on hand to guide customers through the first application steps and to help with troubleshooting.

Furthermore, when starting their careers with a company, Japanese manufacturing engineers were first employed in processing where they frequently became highly qualified at user level. When a new employee was taken on, the part of the company in which he would work was not at that point clearly specified; he or she would need to be flexible enough to change direction in the company (rotation system) to absorb new information and learn new accomplishments and skills. This involves primarily individual learning to cope with new challenges in working in the company. Personal rotation takes place in formal management systems and tried and tested bureaucratic structures, and is a form of learning removed from organizational learning unless the employee shares the knowledge he or she acquired in the previous position with the new group (participatory learning). According to Duncan and Weiss (1979) this creates a basic prerequisite for organizational learning – developing a knowledge base shared with other members of the organization.

There is a further aspect in taking on new employees to join regular staff that is important for our examination of the Japanese company as a learning organization. Many Japanese companies are linked in personal networks with schools and universities which have a long tradition of supplying them with job candidates (Woronoff, 1983; Useem, 1996). Hence recruiting is based not just on qualifications and the personal characters of candidates, but also on which school or university they attend(ed). This implies an evaluation of the employees who previously came from these schools and universities, who throughout their career have a permanent but not explicitly formulated responsibility for the chances of future candidates from their alma mater getting a job. Before an applicant can enter a company, preselection takes place on the basis of the values and standards accorded to each educational establishment in order to find junior staff that fit perfectly into the corporate culture, and require little socialization on the part of the company itself.

The ideal trainee for a Japanese company accepts as smoothly as possible the theories of action necessary to carry out the work The new employee in a company constructs a theory-in-use from observing the patterns of interactive behaviour between employees; behaviour defined by formal or informal rules for joint decisions, delegation and membership. The selection of candidates from specific education establishments with desirable moral concepts and standards seems particularly promising for learning the theory-in-use, but asks less of management in learning and adaptation, thus increasing efficiency of the organization in achieving company targets.

Given Argyris and Schön's contribution to the discussion of the learning organization at the meta-level (deutero learning), the traditional method of recruiting Japanese trainees seems somewhat problematic: improving learning on the single-loop and on the double-loop level, which goes hand in hand with serious restructuring of the individual and organizational learning systems, requires that out-of-date knowledge and conduct be unlearnt. According to Nystrom and Starbuck (1984) there are three ways in which managers can unlearn their own theory-in-use, thus contributing to the improvement of the system overall: listening to contradictions, thinking in alternatives and experimenting. However, with the conformity and homogeneity of personnel recruitment in Japanese companies, these abilities seem doubtful.

The Toyota production system, which combines advanced automation technology and forms of organization, is an expression of both learning through technology and knowledge and the process of continuous improvement of structures and systems referred to as the corporate philosophy of *kaizen*. The term 'Toyotism' which is heard frequently in the context of the Toyota production system and is equated with it, has established itself mostly as the opposite, but sometimes as an extension of or complement to 'Western Taylorism' and 'Fordism' in scientific discussion and in industrial practice. Similarly to Fordism, the Toyota production system is mainly used in large companies which have concentrated on mass production. Its distinguishing features are lean management and lean production (Boesenberg and Metzen, 1993; Clark *et al.*, 1992; Scherm and Bischoff, 1994).

The lean production approach originated with Eiji Toyoda and Taiichi Ôno. In a well-known study (Womack *et al.*, 1990) by the Massachusetts Institute of Technology, published in 1990 under the title *The Machine that Changed the World*, Toyota's factors for success are named as:

- technology leadership;
- cost leadership; and
- time leadership.

The two concepts of lean management and lean production as part of the corporate approach and basic company strategy, view the factory as a whole system, a work system overlaying the individual workstations and the workshop. Essentially, Toyotism concerns the developmental mainstays of manufacturing science: manufacturing technology and work organization. It tries, whilst avoiding any form of waste, to combine the benefits of manual production – Taylor's central interest in rationalization – with the advantages of mass production. The roots of Toyotism lie in:

- Taylorism;
- Fordism;
- German production engineering research; and
- American management science.

Development of the revolutionary production methods of Toyotism has been fed by the stock of experience and development of Taylorism (including standardization of work processes and timed control of production activity) (Staehle, 1999, p. 23), of Fordism (traditional assembly lines, optimum arrangement of man and machine) and German production engineering research, specifically machine-tool engineering. The most important feature of Toyotism is the abolition of storage. Together with work organization and manufacturing technology, internal and external production logistics were given a key role in corporate success as Toyotism became more widespread.

Lean management and lean production were developed for the manufacture of passenger cars at the Toyota Motor Corp. factories, and the system was also used by suppliers to the automobile industry. This production system is not restricted to Japan; it is has also been effective in achieving notable improvements in productivity and quality in other economies (Schmitt, 1998; Yui, 1999). Essentially, the key factor is organizational learning which requests from the advances in manufacturing technology and work organization, improved product quality and careful use of resources. Other features of this organizational learning system are low storage, shorter product development times and low staffing levels. In addition, especially at Toyota Motor Corp., involving assembly workers in the permanent quality control system and the continuous process of improvement (*kaizen*) (Shimizu, 1988), has resulted in production errors falling dramatically and costly post-processing being minimized.

Organizational learning through *kaizen*

Kaizen can be interpreted as the Japanese management philosophy which involves every employee in continuous improvement of structures and systems (Hayashi, 1991). The starting point for this philosophy is the recognition that each company is confronted with many problems, and that these can be solved by establishing a corporate culture with two main features: each employee can with impunity point out errors and identify problems, and solutions for the weaknesses identified can be found if employees work together (Yamashiro, 1997; Imai, 1993; Abegglen and Stalk, 1985).

Through *kaizen*, problem-solving tools are developed with the primary intention of continuous improvement in the interests of the customer. Quality assurance, the just-in-time philosophy, comprehensive productivity monitoring, suggestion schemes and much more are all linked together under the umbrella of the *kaizen* philosophy (Nonaka and Takeuchi, 1997; Sebestyén, 1994). *Kaizen* promotes process-oriented thinking, as the intention is to improve corporate processes in particular so that goals can be achieved more efficiently. Following Argyris and Schön, this process-oriented thinking is equivalent to organizational learning. The starting point is that the organization acknowledges a problem. For example, employees in a multifunctional project group (Hyodo, 1987) might find after systematic investigation that there is a discrepancy between the results they expect and the actual outcome of their actions. They examine the matter and try to rearrange their activities so that their actions and results are again congruent (Nonaka and Takeuchi, 1997). The organization members' theory-in-use is modified if the discoveries leading to the solution of the problem are fixed in company-specific artefacts such as a change in the manufacturing organization and in new work programmes. In other words, the organization has learnt. A key element of this problem-solving process specified within *kaizen*, where negative deviations (performance gaps) are recognized, is repeated analysis of an existing set of facts (Nonaka and Takeuchi, 1997). Taiichi Ôno, former Vice President of Toyota Motor Corp., gives a vivid illustration:

Question   Why has the machine stopped?
Answer   The fuse blew because it was overloaded.
Question   Why was the machine overloaded?
Answer   Because the bearing had not been correctly lubricated.
Question   Why was the bearing not correctly lubricated?
Answer   Because the oil pump isn't working properly.
Question   Why is it not working properly?
Answer   Because its axle bearing is worn.
Question   Why is it worn?
Answer   Because dirt got into it (Imai, 1993, p. 75).

Looking at the company to find the causes of problems and the reasons for negative deviation and identifying solutions is the core thinking behind *kaizen*. In order to diffuse the philosophy of continuous improvement further throughout the company, product teams at the level of work organization and personnel management were put together within Toyota under Ôno's leadership. In these teams, each group member was able to carry out all the stages in production. Group members were responsible for work distribution, working together to find ways to optimize the production process (Hyodo, 1987; Nonaka and Takeuchi, 1997; Ernst, 1999). At regular intervals, with the support of engineers, quality circles were set up. These represent a central element of the learning organization, in finding problems (negative deviations) which might then lead to a revision of the organizational framework of action.

At the concrete level of the flow of parts in the production process, Ôno developed the well-known just-in-time system. This has been represented in the literature in many different and occasionally contradictory ways, but its determining features are group technology, the *kanban* system, short set-up times, harmonization of the production process and quality assurance (Görgens, 1994, p. 15). This astonishingly simple and economically attractive idea was that in each stage of the process only as many parts are produced as necessary to cover the immediate requirements of the next manufacturing stage. Empty containers were returned to the previous processing stage which was the automatic signal to produce more parts. Essentially, this just-in-time system is oriented towards intracompany and intercompany processes, and would be impractical without the conscious organizational implementation of collective strategies.

Another modification to work organization which affected the whole production process at Toyota was the grouping together of design and manufacturing engineers in teams, and the encouragement of group-based success. Learning and knowledge boundaries within the organization were abandoned and the knowledge available at different hierarchical levels and the associated methods for solving problems were put on a broader plane. As a result, development times for new car models fell dramatically and product quality again improved. This structural change represented a considerable advantage from the marketing policy point of view; it was possible to respond quickly to changes in customer requirements and work intensively and cheaply in a number of niche markets.

Organizing a team as an independent and accountable company unit initiates learning when negative deviation is identified, and makes knowledge available to team members to carry out their work. Each team member has the ability to carry out many, in some cases different, types of work within the group and the resulting redundancy creates a very flexible company (Hyodo, 1987). With shared knowledge bases, team organization forms the basis and is a catalyst for organizational learning in Japanese companies (Ducan and Weiss, 1979). In these companies, quality is at the centre of the product and process-oriented efforts towards improvement and innovation within the *kaizen* philosophy. Economic success only comes when the customer is convinced of the quality of the product, and the high quality of Japanese products and the quality management systems in Japanese companies are considered exemplary today. This has been achieved through integration in multi-structured interfirm networks. In other words, it is the organizational implementation and design of collective strategies – whether just-in-time, in international research and development, or in seconding staff between companies in a network – that has put Japanese companies in a position to maintain their competitiveness and build on it.

Originally, the development of production-oriented quality procedures derives from American ideas and industrial applications.

Following the Second World War, these American achievements were methodically developed into Total Quality Control in Japan. Organizational learning was enabled by technology and knowledge transfer (for example, automation technology) and frequently formed the basis of further independent development (NC and CNC technology and technical manufacturing applications), which again made possible organizational learning through changes to knowledge bases (knowledge integrated in technology, for example manufacturing processes) in the organization.

Organizational learning through the companywide and cross-company process of continuous improvement is one of the key characteristics of Japanese companies. The endeavour to achieve a zero-error strategy in Japanese production plants as part of the total quality management system, which means that a defective part is not only rejected but the cause of the error is also removed, is an expression of *kaizen*. In response to the technical problems with products and production which arose in the interplay between American, Western European and Japanese methods and applications, the system today concentrates on continuous improvement not only in production, but as a management concept around activities throughout the whole company. For instance, Japanese production workers, marketing experts and design engineers work together in groups to identify problems, find solutions and develop better technology in order to remove a previously investigated negative deviation. The improvements drawn up are then applied not only to this working group, but also become valid for other working groups via central integration and coordination, using works managers for example. The improvement becomes obligatory for all members of the organization, becomes a new standard and also a long-term theory-in-use for employees new to the company. The search for improvements to products, processes and systems applies not only to the company itself, but creates a bridge to interfirm collaboration as part of the collective strategy.

The high degree of standardization in the formal management systems of Japanese companies brings about successful learning in groups that is of benefit to the whole organization; that is, it enables organizational learning. This knowledge is also passed on to or shared with other companies via collective strategies. New knowledge circulates through companies in the same networks very quickly. The highly-regarded *kaizen* concept, the Japanese leadership philosophy which still remains valid even under the currently prevailing 'low-growth' conditions, has proved to be an effective method for learning particularly in the area of production, and enables progress in a combination of individual, organizational and interorganizational learning situations. In order to answer the question posed at the beginning of this chapter, Japanese companies have always tried to be learning organizations in their efforts towards continuous improvement and to integrate missing technology and knowledge on an organizational and particularly on an interorganizational level. The collective strategy and its many forms of implementation make up a core component of the Japanese economic system and represent one of the most important parameters in the economic success enjoyed by Japanese companies since the Second World War.

Collective internationalization strategies in Japanese industry

In the context of internationalizing business activity, the collective internationalization strategy is becoming increasingly important particularly in forming international cooperative ventures, strategic alliances and networks. As we have seen, international cooperative ventures provide an opportunity to initiate internal learning processes in companies and to share in the learning successes of other companies. Differences in organizational structure, business systems, management philosophy, market-entering strategies and particularly in international personnel management, can be beneficial to companies linked in a collective strategy provided they are understood correctly (Dathe, 1998).

Management in international company collaboration faces particular ambiguities and contradictions which arise primarily from the need to adapt to local circumstances and from companywide integration. Neither cross-border differentiation nor overall integration can take place purely on the basis of the organizational structure in this configuration of companies engaged in international business (Sydow, 1993; Abo, 1989). The management of companies cooperating on an international level has the difficult task of integrating existing divergent perspectives and philosophies, but at the same time allowing differences to remain in order to use learning to improve the competitive position. The goal of the company management in an international cooperative venture will be to build up the performance and commitment of individual units and harness them for the whole company, and not to standardize the differences with centralized control mechanisms.

Reciprocal technology transfer plays a key role in successful learning (Spur, 1998a), and international business collaboration represents one of the central strategic management options for taking on increased pressure from competition. This is the point at which collective internationalization strategies crystallize (Perlitz, 1997a; Bea and Haas, 2001). Frequently, companies cannot deal with the demands of opening up a market and dramatic development in technology alone. Joining forces with other companies is an obvious way to push forward any restructuring necessary and to cope with internationalization. Success is not only determined by internal company strengths, but, in the era of globalization, increasingly by the nature of relationships with other companies and organizations (Balling, 1998).

International companies have the option of internationalizing through direct investment and export and also through cooperating with companies abroad. Companies are strongly motivated towards collective internationalization strategies by the opportunities of faster access to markets and technology, and of a partner to share the risk whilst maintaining a certain minimum influence over their partners (see Campbell and Burton, 1994).

Business collaboration can in principle be appropriate for every stage of the value-added chain. From research and development through production to marketing and services, there are many possible ways. It just requires entrepreneurial creativity. It is no exaggeration to say that the structure of Japanese industry is defined by business collaboration. Vertical and horizontal groups (*keiretsu*), to which most of the big companies in the country belong, are considered typical features of the Japanese economic system. Individual companies establish long-term membership of a *keiretsu* by seconding staff and exchanging information on a regular basis, and by intertwining capital (Hemmert, 1999). This collaboration continues on foreign markets, which can often be seen in large projects or in coordinated sales strategies. In the literature, business collaboration is frequently represented as the antithesis to competition; however, the Japanese system is peculiar in the simultaneity of collaboration and competition. Its economic reality can be illustrated by a comparison with team sports: members of the same team also compete to a certain extent between themselves, although the main concern is to maximize team performance.

Cooperative activity between Japanese companies and what can now be called the classic joint ventures between Japanese and foreign companies for the purpose of opening up markets have a certain amount of tradition. It is remarkable that Japanese economic policy particularly favours international collaboration with strong support. For example, the Japanese foreign trade authority promotes the idea of Japanese–foreign business collaboration with events and publications and helps companies to find partners.

Under certain conditions, international cooperative business ventures can receive financial support in the form of loans from the Import Bank of Japan or the Overseas Economic Corporation Foundation (OECF), which in October 1999 were merged into the Japan Bank for International Collaboration. The Japanese government has entered into loan insurance agreements with several countries, including Germany, to cover the risks of third-country projects in international business collaboration under certain conditions.

A closer look at the development of joint ventures between Japanese and foreign companies shows that despite political and economic backing, there was a dramatic fall in the number of Japanese–foreign joint ventures outside of Japan from the second half of 1995 to mid-1999. In the first six months of 1995, Japanese industry entered into approximately 800 joint ventures with foreign companies in international markets. In the first half of 1999, according to figures from the Japan External Trade Organization (JETRO), there were just 300 new joint undertakings (JETRO, 1999). The main reason for this drop has been the crisis in the Japanese economy, which in many companies has resulted in radical restructuring. International cooperative ventures are being put to the test as they tie up capital urgently needed for company reorganization. Growing liquidity problems in Japanese companies are determining the trend towards caution in concluding new joint-venture agreements (Inkpen, 1995). The motives for international business collaboration cited by Japanese companies, such as sharing costs and risk, access to external resources and new markets and exerting an influence on competition, apply as they did previously, but safeguarding the continuing existence of the company now takes priority. The restructuring process will still take some time.

Asia has lost significance for Japan as an economic area; in the light of the economic crisis there, this is hardly unexpected. In 1994, 58 per cent of all international collaboration (joint ventures and collaborations on technology) was located in Asia; in 1999 it was only 21 per cent, whereas the North American region increased its share from 26 per cent to 50 per cent. Even in Europe there were more joint ventures and technological collaborations in the first six months of 1999 (274) than in Asia (248) (JETRO, 1999).

Asia's weak position, particularly in technology-related collaboration, cannot be explained by the crisis alone. It is also the result of the long-term strategic orientation of Japanese industry in this area. It is not joint technology-oriented development that now characterizes Japanese involvement, but cooperative ventures to open up and penetrate markets. Consequently, international business collaboration in this region is essentially a case of the Japanese side providing the know-how, and as a rule the technology, particularly production technology. The Asian side frequently offers the relationship and information network of expatriate Chinese citizens which spans the whole of Asia, the labour, and in some cases additional risk capital.

Currently, North America and Western Europe occupy centrestage for Japanese management. This is particularly obvious for collaboration on technology, where the foreign partner's strength in technology is an important motivation for Japanese companies to cooperate according to a survey by JETRO. The Japanese are pressing for intensive international collaboration in the areas of communications, biotechnology and chemistry and pharmaceuticals (JETRO, 1999).

In 1996, North America's share in all cooperative activity on technology with Japanese companies was 36 per cent, which had increased to 57 per cent by the first half of 1999. The changes in Europe went even further. Just between 1996 and the first half of 1999, technology-oriented collaboration with Japanese companies more than tripled. Around 25 per cent of all technology collaboration with Japanese companies was in Europe, and just 15 per cent in Asia. Recent years have been a shock for Japanese industry, which had become accustomed to success, and whether this shock will have a therapeutic affect depends crucially on Japanese management's ability to learn. It is its task to initiate change in Japanese companies. Strategic management needs to take the warning signals of recent years seriously, to interpret them correctly and to introduce creative changes and learning processes; this could be a difficult, and sometimes bitter process. It will be the responsibility of Japanese management to introduce the next steps towards company-specific restructuring and towards internationalization to meet the demands of globalization. Learning, with its strategy and corporate-culture-related significance, is both the crucial key factor for organizational change and the major driving force behind the emergence of international business collaboration.

Japanese industry has for decades shown the West how learning may be transformed into creative and successful management concepts (Abegglen and Stalk, 1989). The constant commitment to improving the status quo and the will to realize what is learnt in industrial applications characterize this process (Dirks, 1995). If Japanese management reflects on its strategic strengths, then collective internationalization strategies, essentially international business collaboration, will again make their powerful contribution to the internationalization of Japanese companies.

Since 1996 the economic regions of North America and Europe have been increasingly in the focus of internationalization through collective strategies. The trend towards technology-oriented collaboration will continue in the coming years, when it will also become apparent whether it will stabilize towards the West. If the current upturn in Southeast Asia regains strength, then it is conceivable that Japanese companies will return to creating and penetrating new markets in international collaboration, possibly to the detriment of technological collaboration in the West.

Collective internationalization strategies of Japanese companies in advanced technology

As shown in both the preceding sections, collective strategies play a central part in economic life today, particularly in collaboration between industrial companies. This might be due to cost benefits in different areas of the world, or to a partner's technological core competence in the value-added chain. Some of these cooperative ventures can be compared to fleeting friendships, which last until one partner has extracted sufficient benefit from the collaboration. This can happen, for example, after a bridgehead has been established in a previously unexplored market or market segment, and related to this not a few managers have been faced with the problems associated with creating and operating a joint venture in the highly-praised growth market in China (Inkpen, 1995; Child, 1998, 2000). Other forms of collaboration can, however, mark the start of long-term collaboration which stabilizes in joint research and development, for example, or in a world-wide secondment of personnel. These are then particularly successful collective internationalization strategies which act as guiding lights to other companies.

There is almost no data available for current and future collective strategies in international Japanese companies in the fields of advanced technology. From the point of view of economic analysis, the picture is incomplete and fragmented.

It is clear that under the pressure of globalization, corporate success largely depends on an ability to carry out product and process innovations more efficiently, more flexibly and above all faster than the global competitor (Perlitz, 1997a). The speed at which new, innovative products enter and penetrate markets are key factors for success in growth markets (Abegglen and Stalk, 1989). To take an example at random from the many possible forms of collaboration, joint international research and development are becoming increasingly important as markets become more demanding and competition increases for Japanese companies (Hemmert, 1997, pp. 84–106).

Technology-oriented, economically motivated collaboration at different levels of the valued-added process can therefore also be interpreted as an attempt by Japanese industry to confront the problems experienced by individual companies trying to make an impact on a market by forming groups (Dirks, 1995). Collaboration within the framework of traditional interfirm networks with partners in the same group of companies is a phenomenon that has been known for a long time in Japan. It has been discussed thoroughly for years and from the point of view of economic and management science has been well-researched (Hemmert, 1999, pp. 55–8). On the other hand, a new and only inadequately examined trend has appeared over the last few years – technology-oriented alliances of Japanese and foreign companies.

What are the focal points of business collaboration? An initial look at the total number of Japanese cooperative ventures with foreign partners in advanced fields of technology in mid-1999 reveals the dominance of information technology and biotechnology or pharmaceuticals. For the five years 1994–99, there were a total of 655 information-technology partnerships with foreign companies (38 per cent). This was followed by environmental technology with 440 (25 per cent), biotechnology/ pharmaceuticals with 402 (23 per cent) and new materials with 238 (14 per cent).

However, events are dominated by another aspect: Japanese companies are clearly oriented towards North America, as demonstrated by the large number of technology-oriented cooperative ventures in American industrial companies. Of the 1,735 international partnerships in technology documented by JETRO (mid-1994 to mid-1999), 907 or 52 per cent were in North America, 395 or 23 per cent were in Asia and 359 or 21 per cent in Europe. Those regions where technology is weaker, Oceania, Middle East/Africa, Central and South America and the former Soviet Union and Eastern Europe had altogether merely 74 or 4 per cent.

The fact that Japanese–American collaboration dominates is not a great surprise, nor is it unexpected that its focus is technology, following as this does a general trend in the leading industrial nations. Much more interesting is the closer examination of the driving forces for the rapid rise of technology-oriented international collaboration in the late 1990s. Between 1997 and 1999, the increase in industrial collaboration in the areas of information technology, biotechnology/pharmaceuticals, environmental technology and new materials doubled.

Over the period 1997–9 particularly in the up and coming sectors of information technology and biotechnology/pharmaceuticals, the number of cooperative ventures between Japanese and foreign firms increased exceptionally quickly. A look at the development over the last five years of the 1990s indicates that the causes of these conspicuous growth rates merit a more detailed examination. At the end of 1995, fewer than 100 new technology-oriented cooperative ventures were added in the fields of information technology, biotechnology/pharmaceuticals, environmental technology and new materials. In the first half of 1999, over 300 new arrivals in those areas were documented by JETRO, and over 150 new industrial partnerships were in the area of information technology alone. There was a similar development in the extremely dynamic biotechnology/pharmaceuticals sector, although at 100 the number of new partnerships in absolute terms was lower. However, in comparison, note that in the first half of 1995 there were fewer than 50 newcomers.

The reasons for the sharp rise in international collaboration in advanced technology sectors are many and complex. Japanese newcomers in these research-intensive fields clearly hope that by working with technology leaders, often with competitors, they will find a way to access the technology and the market cheaply and quickly. A further point which might explain the enthusiasm for collaboration also deserves consideration: high-tech projects require high levels of capital.

The development of new products and advanced manufacturing technology and opening up and penetrating new markets requires a considerable amount of capital that few Japanese companies relying on their own productivity can currently supply. It is becoming harder and harder for individual companies to keep up on their own. Biotechnology and pharmaceuticals, environmental technology and new materials are all costly fields and even in information technology the signs of the times are pointing to collaboration. Combining efforts in research and development can free up urgently needed capital for corporate restructuring, for reengineering, and for speeding up the process of internationalization. The emphasis is on meeting the now perceptible pressures of globalization with international alliances. This is not all: safeguarding the company's existence is frequently sufficient motive to leave behind the protection of tried and trusted Japanese networks and to enter into international cooperative research ventures (Haak, 2000b, pp. 113–16).

However, there is more. There is another factor driving Japanese companies towards international collaboration: the time factor. Innovations in products and processes, technical expertise and its industrial applications achieve faster and wider global diffusion; the time factor is becoming a new strategic factor in competition, as advanced technologies are promulgated at top speed. Companies retain technological monopolies for a short while only. In order to survive worldwide competition in economically promising and sophisticated markets for technological products and processes, Japanese companies are being asked to provide new research and development concepts. International collaboration in new, pioneering technologies are a form of strategic realignment for Japanese companies. They want to become faster and more effective to use the opportunities on global markets and exploit the international competitive advantage that comes from technology leadership.

Also from a manufacturing science point of view there is much in favour of a cooperative venture; it's not easy for a company on its own to speed up the production of ideas, the prerequisite for any future innovation. The development of new products and advanced production processes, the discovery of new methods, procedures and principles require creativity and a sound education but also market-oriented knowledge and specific experience in different subject areas (Spur, 1998). Having ideas is mainly associated with entering into new areas of science or application, which also requires stronger links to areas that have not yet been explored in this context. An example is machine-tool engineering which received astonishing impetus to develop through the interaction between mechanical engineering and electronics. Technology transfer between cooperating partners not only involves several disciplines and expert knowledge from overlapping fields, it also requires realization of prototypes, management and application knowledge and the rapid acquisition of new qualifications.

Joining forces for a differentiated research potential allows companies to concentrate quickly on tasks in hand. Basic research, applied and innovative research and technology transfer are all intertwined. Combined creativity in a company in an industrial cooperative venture generates a broad area of development for technological implementation. Western partners can use the strengths of Japanese companies in searching for innovation and technology transfer, and Japanese partners gain access to basic and applied research via their Western partners.

Phase jumps in technology are rare; progress in new technologies usually evolves. Revolutionary technologies require longer innovation time – numerical-control technology is a good example here – and usually require follow-up work and more effort than the invention itself (Spur, 1991a). The costs of this are reduced by cooperating on research. There is a clear trend: Japanese industry is not staking its future on the fragmentation of its company research and innovation, but on focusing precisely on the technologically and economically powerful partners they seek out from all over the world (Okumura, 1998).

This is particularly apparent in the fields of biotechnology and pharmaceuticals and in the equipment, software and e-commerce aspects of information technology. In this area, Japanese companies are looking increasingly for collaboration with innovative and financially sound companies doing business on an international basis. However, when a collective strategy is realized with Japanese companies, an appropriate balance of technology transfer and technology protection is called for, which may be difficult for strategic and operative management. Analysis of core business competence and the value-added chain reveals sensitive corporate knowledge. Within the framework of managing the cooperative venture, senior management often needs to decide at which stage of the value-added chain moveable and embedded knowledge should be protected in order to deal with an unplanned drain of know-how at an early stage (see especially Granrath, 1994, p. 191).

Undoubtedly, there is a strategic necessity for Japanese companies to enter into more collaboration with leading international technology companies; Japanese management must accept the change in circumstances. The increasing complexity of research work is forcing them to greater interdisciplinarity, to use the specific expertise of other practitioners of research and development. Both the Japanese and foreign sides should aim to establish cooperative research in advanced fields of technology on a partnership basis. However, business collaboration can strengthen a partnership towards other companies but at the same time weaken one partner at the expense of the other (Dathe, 1998). Innovative approaches to collaboration which take into account the strengths and weakness of the partners should be worked out. This also means creating mechanisms which ensure an overall improvement in efficiency whilst maintaining specific interests and conserving the interests of all participants.

The Japanese supplier network system in transition: a challenge for collective strategies

The Japanese supplier network system is in transition and, consequently, so are the collective strategies between suppliers and customers that have been in place for many years. In 2003, thirteen years after the bubble economy burst and six years after the Asian crisis, Japanese industry still offers a sobering picture as described briefly in the introduction. Japanese companies are having to struggle with many problems, still suffering the effects of overdrawn investment in production capacity, and are finding it hard to cope with the consequences of globalization. The long recession, economic deregulation, and the partial opening of the Japanese consumer and capital goods markets have brought fundamental change to the system of close ties between end customers and suppliers. More intense competition on national and international markets, increased flow of trade and not least the emergence of new, lively competition in Asia are all factors in the disbanding of traditional supplier structures in Japan.

Japanese suppliers define themselves rather as members of interfirm networks than as individual organizations with strategic goals. A large proportion form *keiretsu* together with other mutually linked companies. (Literally, *keiretsu* means series or order, and describes groups of associated companies whose members maintain traditional business relationships, frequently consolidated by mutual shareholdings; but see also below and Itô, 1992, pp. 181–9.) The industrial landscape in Japan is dominated by a few large *keiretsu*, made up of many companies active in the most important sectors. Management autonomy and the independence of each company are respected, but the companies formulate an overall strategy jointly. As a rule there is a bank, a general trading house and one or two industrial companies at the centre. The large *keiretsu* are made up of 200 companies altogether which have shares in thousands of small and medium-sized enterprises (Bosse, 2000, pp. 139–46).

The companies integrated into such groups are offered preferential opportunities for buying and selling. Without a doubt, this represents discrimination against companies that are not members, making it difficult for foreign companies in Japan to access the market (Okumura, 1998, pp. 60–1). Most of the misunderstandings regarding groups of associated companies in Japan and their effect on competition arise largely from imprecise use of the term *keiretsu*. There are no fewer than three meanings that should be clearly distinguished. First of all, it means groups of companies from different sectors; secondly, distribution networks of manufacturers of consumer goods; and thirdly it means the production-based supplier networks in industry which are discussed below (Hemmert, 1993).

The vertically integrated industrial supplier networks which are organized around a manufacturer are characterized by an asymmetrical power relationship. They form a pyramid with a manufacturer at the top and numerous supplier companies arranged in different levels underneath. One of the best-known examples is the Toyota Motor Corp. production system, which has more than 10,000 sub-companies. The small companies are usually completely dependent on the umbrella company (Toyota Motor Corp.). The advantages of this kind of vertical arrangement are in the exchange of information and joint product development with the associated technology transfer. Toyota's tried and tested supplier system is one of the reasons for its record profits 2002 (fiscal year April 2001–March 2002). Nissan also succeeded in getting out of the red in which was not least due to structural changes in its supplier system. The weak state of the Japanese economy continues to put suppliers further under pressure, and radical changes to the supplier system cannot be avoided.

Investment, the central mainstay of the economy, is slowing down, domestic consumption is stagnating and exports are suffering from the economic downturn in the USA and in neighbouring countries in Asia. The high level of public debt and the many imponderables and uncertainties surrounding the real financial status of Japanese banks all aggravate the situation. The difficult economic position means increased competition in Japanese supplier industries which, not so long ago, had been able to count on business ties developed over decades to ensure that they could sell their products to their partners. For various reasons suppliers have lost this security, and changes to basic conditions in the course of globalization are now also making themselves felt in Japan. In recent years the big ultimate buyers in Japan have moved large parts of their production abroad. Changes to exchange rates, rising wage costs and liberalization of Japanese legislation mean that Japanese direct investment abroad has increased since the 1970s, a trend which has accelerated over the last few years.

In the early stages of Japanese internationalization, attention was focused on access to natural resources, working in markets which were protected by the import substitution policy, and on securing cheap labour for export production (Yoshihara, 1978). The rapid rise of the yen following the Plaza Agreement of 1985 led to a new wave of Japanese investment abroad. Since the early 1990s, due to increased demand in the Asian economic region, rising labour costs in Japan, more high flying by the yen and demands from Asian guest countries to localize, a reorganization of regional production networks of Japanese companies has been observable. The main feature of this reorganization is the shift of high added-value products and production processes with increasing reimport to Japan.

Japanese suppliers have lost a considerable part of the domestic market. In addition, ultimate buyers have been urging their supplier companies, which were frequently in the same *keiretsu*, to follow them abroad. In many cases this has been due to quality problems with local producers. Those Japanese suppliers with a more solid capital base followed their customers in order to safeguard their leading position in the supplier system. They also entered into collective strategies with Western companies to move into technology leadership positions (Haak, 2000c, pp. 64–8). However, in recent years new competitors have appeared in the economic arena. Previously, it was almost exclusively Japanese competitors from other *keiretsu* who engaged in serious competition with Japanese suppliers, but now, for example, companies from China (Haak, 2001b, pp. 46–51) and Malaysia, both able to offer lower costs and the required standards of quality, have appeared on the scene as potential partners for Japanese buyers (Takahashi *et al.*, 1998).

However, yet another trend is accelerating the disbanding of the existing supplier networks with their collective strategies of many years. Although it was unthinkable a few years ago, big foreign companies have for some time now been buying into Japanese companies or even taking them over completely. High-profile examples such as DaimlerChrysler AG and Mitsubishi Motors Corp., and Renault Group and Nissan Group have received coverage in the international press.

The goal of the alliance with Renault (started March 1999) who acquired an equity stake in Nissan, was to set up a powerful bi-national group within a balanced partnership focused on performance. The plan to strengthen equity ties and the strategic management structure will accelerate the development process. The success of the alliance depended first and foremost on the recovery of Nissan, over and above the complementary strengths of both groups and the huge potential for synergies. The action plan from Nissan produced extremely rapid results, and the group returned to profit in 2001. Joint work carried out within the alliance advanced in step with strategic cooperative ventures in engineering, manufacturing, sales and especially in purchasing.

The competitive environment to which Japanese suppliers are now exposed has changed as foreign companies bring a not insignificant proportion of their own supplier networks into the relationship and set new standards. This is breaking up the ties between suppliers that have developed over decades, calling into question established collective strategies. Trust and experience in partnership collaboration and personal and financial ties between *keiretsu* companies have been weighty arguments for retaining existing network structures, but neither DaimlerChrysler nor Renault take account of Japanese sensibilities, announcing sweeping cost-cutting measures for many different areas within the Japanese companies. Such Anglo-American rationalization has had serious consequences for Japanese suppliers as they have had to respond to the pressure on costs.

Not only the huge involvement of foreign competition is worrying suppliers, there is increasing competition within domestic markets in Japan as the lengthy recession has a detrimental effect on demand. As ever, it is the supplier firms that act as buffers in the 'crisis of the giants' with its dwindling orders and staff lay-offs (Bromann, 2001, pp. 15–16).

'Restructuring' has become a fashionable word in Japan. With it, Japanese management associates a series of measures that involve many strategic realignments: concentrating on core competence (Dirks, 1999, pp. 65–8) in the product and service area, and tightening up purchasing and sales are part of it as well as introducing and reinforcing performance-related principles in management and pay. In the past, ensuring growth by continuously increasing sales and market shares was the leading strategic principle, indeed the company philosophy (Abegglen and Stalk, 1985, pp. 5–8). The constant principle emerging from efforts towards new strategic restructuring is to put in place and maintain thinking in terms of cost and profit in Japanese companies. Establishment of the 'new thinking' shows up particularly in the procurement practices of the ultimate buyers. One taboo has already been broken: abandoning partners of many years' standing in favour of cheaper suppliers – the dissolution of interorganizational ties that were established in the course of collective strategies.

The response of Japanese suppliers to these demands is promising. They are concentrating on the high-tech, knowledge-intensive parts of processes with a high proportion of added value – in a nutshell on mastering technology and knowledge as a survival strategy. Only this process will make Japanese companies interesting for potential collaboration partners.

Suppliers offer essentially two options. Technology leadership can be achieved with a *pioneering strategy* whereby each new technological challenge is accepted and a new product or production process introduced as quickly as possible. This can also be achieved with the so-called *exploitation strategy* which aims for a leading position in the market over the whole life-cycle of a technology (Spur, 1998a). However, suppliers often take a third route: finding new areas of business. This can go hand-in-hand with product and customer diversification. Offering extra work steps can also make the company more attractive to its existing customers. Identifying potential customers, target-oriented scrutiny of market development and addressing future customers in a professional capacity are all tasks with which companies were previously unfamiliar. Independently acquiring information about markets or competition is new territory for many Japanese companies. Japanese suppliers will have to lose much excess baggage in the twenty-first century, but transition process in collective strategies that bind Japanese suppliers in their networks has been started. New, creative collective strategies are needed to enable them to survive international competition under the changing political, economic and social conditions in the course of increasingly dynamic globalization.

German management and international business collaboration

German managers, particularly in small and medium-sized enterprises active in Asia, have some reservations regarding collective internationalization strategies. The problems that can arise in the search for and selection of partners and the costs involved in the early stages of negotiating and coordinating cooperative ventures make many German companies wary of collective internationalization strategies. Reacting flexibly and quickly to changes in market conditions and to new competitors becomes more difficult when responsibility and decision-making powers have to be shared with a partner also involved in Asia (Hilpert and Taube, 1997).

German management sees additional problems and risks in collective internationalization strategies with Japanese companies. The different mentality of Japanese managers to whom they would have to adjust as part of a joint venture is just one problem out of the many they anticipate. Difficulties arise at the beginning of a potential cooperative venture in the search for information about the Japanese partner company. How does one access this information? Who offers low-cost and reliable information about possible collaboration partners? If information is available, how should it be interpreted, since German companies are not familiar with the market or the competition environment in Japan and other economic regions in Asia. Acquiring information about a Japanese partner's strategic plans and interpreting them correctly in the light of economic development and the competitive situation represent difficult steps at the beginning of a potential collective internationalization strategy.

Despite these misgivings on the part of German management, which arise particularly at the beginning of a partnership with a Japanese company, business collaboration is often chosen as the way into the Japanese market and other markets in Asia. Reasons why Japanese and

German companies venture into different markets together are, from the management point of view, primarily operational bottlenecks, which show up in scarcity of resources (staff, expertise, capital) and also in insufficient knowledge of the target country and its traditions. Further, German management does not have the political or economic contacts which local partners frequently bring with them. There is a whole series of very successful Japanese–German cooperative ventures which direct all their business activities not only towards Germany or Japan, but towards other markets as well, particularly in Asia (Haak, 2001b, 2002b, 2003; Hilpert and Taube, 1997; Deutsch-Japanischer Wirtschaftskreis, 1997).

Investigations carried out into the Asia-Pacific region in the 1990s by the ifo Institute for Economic Research and by the Free State of Bavaria in Germany illustrate how willing German companies are to collaborate with Asian partners. The results of the study, which are documented in part in Hilpert and Taube (1997), make it clear that German industrial companies are prepared to realize collective internationalization strategies with Asian partners in production. Such collaboration with local partner companies represents a possible option for many German companies to implement a collective internationalization strategy. However, they seldom choose to go into production with American or Japanese companies in the East and Southeast Asian region.

Most German companies carried out their own sales and marketing in the 1990s in the Asia Pacific region. If they did cooperate on the level of sales and marketing in a target country, then it was primarily with local companies. Japanese or North American companies, although often astonishingly well-positioned in Southeast Asia, were only very rarely considered as business partners for German companies. Where the distribution channels of Japanese trading houses were used, then this happened most frequently via branches in Hong Kong, the Philippines and Thailand; products in these cases were mainly mechanical engineering products. There was also collaboration in trade in capital goods with Japanese trading houses. Strategic alliances between German and Japanese partners were realized mainly in the chemicals industry, mechanical engineering and in transport.

The tradition of business collaboration in Japan

As shown in the previous chapters, the Japanese economy is characterized by horizontal and vertical interfirm networks (*keiretsu*) as seemingly immovable components of its structure. Membership of a group is expressed in interlinked capital investment and continuous exchange of information and personnel between its companies. When a business activity is internationalized, the companies in a group frequently proceed together and so the internationalization process in the form of collective internationalization is a phenomenon long-known in Japan.

Collaboration is often highlighted as an identifier for the Japanese economic system, and realizing collective strategies does not therefore represent a serious problem for Japanese companies. They enter into cooperative ventures with other Japanese companies at home and abroad and with foreign partners at home. Prime Minister Koizumi made foreign investment a personal crusade in a statement from the government at the beginning of 2003. He wants to make Japan more attractive to foreign companies, in order to double the number of factories in Japan within five years. In association with this, there will be more company partnerships between foreign investors and Japanese companies, for currently Japan presents a rather unassuming picture in this respect. In proportion to its economic power, Japan only has a marginal role as a target for foreign investment. Measured against Japan's gross domestic product, foreign direct investment in 2001 was only 1.3 per cent.

Japanese companies have only little experience with strategic alliances and third-country collaboration, so these organizational forms of collective internationalization strategy represent a new phenomenon for the Japanese economy. Industry did not turn its attention to them until the late 1980s and the *Keidanren*, the Federation of Economic Organizations, discussed the fusion of Western and Japanese management systems at the beginning of the 1990s. Later in the 1990s, with globalization progressing rapidly, international alliances became a trend in corporate engagement.

There were many mechanisms to promote Japanese foreign alliances. At the end of March 2003, the expert commission appointed by the Japanese government presented its report on encouraging foreign companies to become involved with Japan. A key move was the dissemination of information about Japan as a location for investment, and about Japanese companies that would be suitable as potential collaboration partners for foreign investment. It was also intended to make it easier to enact foreign takeovers and mergers by changing corporate law, for example, and to allow foreign companies more access to previously closed areas of business. In addition, the administrative procedures for foreign investors were considerably simplified.

The Japan External Trade Organization (JETRO) will probably become the central coordinating body for foreign companies. A central contact point will be set up for foreign investors which will liaise with individual Japanese ministries to simplify and accelerate the administration. Another focus is the improvement of working and living conditions for foreigners in Japan. This concerns the residential and entry status of specially qualified engineers and scientists and the improvement of conditions for foreign doctors wanting to practise in Japan, for example. All these measures are aimed at making the Japanese economy and particularly Japanese companies more attractive for investment.

JETRO is continuing to promote the idea of Japanese–foreign business collaboration at various events in Japan and abroad. A large number of publications and electronically assisted administrative procedures and communication with companies abroad give further support to the idea of collaboration. JETRO also helps Japanese and foreign firms to identify and make initial contact with partner companies. Under certain conditions, Japanese and foreign companies can receive loans with guaranteed support from JETRO. The Japanese government has signed loan insurance agreements with Germany, France and Great Britain, which mean that the total risk in third-country projects is covered by one national export insurance. The condition is that the Japanese content must amount to at least 30 per cent of the total order.

Research into Japanese–foreign third-country collaboration by the ifo Institute for Economic Research for the period January 1994 to June 1996 found a total of 385 ventures. Most Japanese business partnerships in this period were with American companies (106), followed by Hong Kong (48), Taiwan (48), Germany (28), Great Britain (28), South Korea (20), France (19) and Singapore (13). There were more cooperative ventures in third countries with companies from the Netherlands (9), Malaysia (8), Thailand (8), Indonesia (7), Italy (7), China (6) and Sweden (6). The sectors in which this form of collective internationalization strategy was found most frequently were chemicals (61) and in electrotechnology/ electronics (60). These were followed by automobile construction and parts suppliers (48), steel and non-precious metals (33), mechanical engineering (28) and textiles (15). The most important economic regions for Japanese–foreign third-country collaboration were Asia (292) of which almost half were in China (Hilpert and Taube, 1997).

A closer look at business collaboration between Japanese and other Asian companies reveals that, as a rule, for this form of joint venture the Japanese company provides the technology and/or the expertise (management knowledge), whilst the other Asian companies contribute the relationship and information networks of overseas Chinese that frequently span the whole of Asia and often provide risk capital for the organizational realization of collective strategies. A comparable process takes place in American and Western European companies in their alignment towards the Asian economic region. Business collaboration between Japanese and American and European companies in third countries for the purposes of opening up the Asian market in particular is found less frequently. Nevertheless, their numbers are increasing, whilst Japanese–Asian third-country collaboration is tending more to stagnate.

The crucial reasons why Japanese companies decide on third-country collaboration with a Western partner were established by JETRO in a survey: Japanese companies are primarily interested in the technological competence (38%) and marketing capacity (36%) of the partner. Other motivations were strategic standpoints (28%), capital (26%), the image or brand name of the partner company (10%) and the goal of minimizing risk (10%) (Hilpert and Taube, 1997, p. 25). JETRO also examined German–Japanese third-country collaboration, but data collection was stopped to save costs in 2000. Only incomplete information is therefore available, so that researchers have to use the work by the ifo Institute for Economic Research (Hilpert and Taube, 1997), the JETRO records that are not available to the public, but which were made available for the purposes of this book, and other relevant sources (documents from the Deutsch–Japanischer Wirtschaftskreis (German–Japanese Economic Group), the Deutsches Institut für Japanstudien (German Institute for Japanese Studies), newspapers, journals, company files, interviews with experts in this field).

Third-country collaboration

Third-country collaboration as an expression of a company's collective internationalization strategy is notable for the fact that both partners based in their own countries do business in a third country. In the following we consider an alliance between Japanese and German companies which both want to do business in a foreign market. (On the other hand it could equally be a Japanese–German third-country collaboration with a foreign partner company from the third country, forming three-sided form of third-country collaboration; and they might well be joined by other partners.)

Third-country collaboration can be differentiated on the basis of the shareholding, although shareholding is not always necessary. They may also be distinguished on the basis of their duration; some are of a short-term nature whilst others are set up with longer-term collaboration in mind. Another criterion is the concrete form taken by the scope of activities. Some of these ventures include all the business activities in the partnership, whilst others cover only some company functions which will be carried out in the third country jointly (for example building up a shared distribution network, developing a specific technology).

There are various motives for third-country collaboration (Deutsch–Japanischer Wirtschaftskreis, 1997). The initial consideration is often to gain competitive advantage that a company on its own cannot realize by entering into a partnership for the chosen target country (third country). Examples of key advantages achievable with third-country collaboration are better use of company-specific resources, knowledge of the competition and of the market, and technology-related considerations (Haak, 2003). Another key reason for third-country collaboration may be a company's lack of resources which might manifest itself in insufficient capital investment, but which frequently also shows up in too few employees to allow international expansion. Partners in the third-country collaboration then serve to fill a gap in human resources. Insufficient funds often force companies to cooperate with a foreign partner in opening up a new market, for example, or in searching together for raw materials for production in the home countries of the partners (Deutsch–Japanischer Wirtschaftskreis, 1997).

If for example a German company has in its possession a technology (for example processing technology) which the Japanese partner does not have, but it has no financial resources with which to become active in the third country, then the German firm can contribute the technology and the Japanese company the necessary capital to the venture. Another case might be where a lack of capital in a Japanese partner leads the Japanese management to contribute its knowledge of the target market and the German partner to provide the capital to open up the market (Deutsch–Japanischer Wirtschaftskreis, 1997; Hilpert and Taube, 1997; Haak, 2001b, 2003).

Insufficient knowledge of the market in the third country can also result in third-country collaboration. Local partners in the third country can reduce the cost of the collaboration, allowing more resources for working on markets in other areas. Another reason might be to allow further expansion of the production programme. Third-country collaborative ventures are particularly interesting for the internationalization of partner companies when they all benefit from synergy effects (Deutsch–Japanischer Wirtschaftskreis, 1997; Haak, 2001b, 2002b, 2003).

Two indicators are used to classify third-country collaborative ventures. On the one hand, the international collaboration in the third country can be based on contractual agreements, in which case no new independent companies result from the collaboration. On the other hand, the international collaboration may result in independent company unions which are active in the third country, for example in China. Strategic alliances are positioned between the two; they can be based on a contractual agreement or result in the founding of a company in third countries (Haak, 2002b).

Third-country collaborations are frequently created on the basis of sales and delivery contracts. A German company that plans to internationalize its business activities in Asia has the problem of how to set up its launch onto the various target markets in Asia (Haak, 2003). Each market operates under specific conditions and the German company needs to accommodate these requirements. Frequently, export is the first step towards internationalizing business activities, and the context of an export-oriented internationalization strategy, partners are sought with sufficient knowledge of the market in the target country. Japanese mediator organizations, which function as independent units in the target country, can then act between the German company and the customer in the foreign country. Large Japanese trading houses could be the partners in these collaborative ventures, in which case a contract is made between the German producer and the Japanese trading firm which establishes the specific activities for the third-country collaboration in the target country. In this context, one can also talk of indirect export. This form of internationalizing business activities is frequently the preliminary stage to proceeding independently in the target country at a later date (for example, a company will build up its distribution network in the Asian target country or found a subsidiary). Notice will then be given on the contractual third-country collaboration or it might expire. Japanese–German third-country collaboration can also arise as a result of technology contracts, where there is a distinction between licence, expertise, technical help and advisory contracts (Haak, 2001b, 2003).

Japanese–German third-country collaboration in East and Southeast Asia

In principle, Japanese management is prepared to work with German companies in third countries – it is in their interest. Japanese interfirm networks (*keiretsu*) are showing a tendency to break up, and a strategic realignment is taking place in the Japanese general trading houses (*sôgô shôsha*) with the result that Japanese companies are looking for new company partners with whom to open up and dominate long-term the attractive but high-risk Asian markets (Haak, 2002b, 2003).

Due to the excellent reputation that German technology and German quality enjoys in Asia – we are focusing here especially on East and Southeast Asia – Japanese management is particularly interested in German companies as partners. This applies not only to traditional industries such as mechanical engineering and plant construction, and vehicle manufacturing, but also to young industries with potential for the future such as telecommunications and environmental technology (Haak, 2002b, 2003; also Hilpert and Taube, 1997). This is true not only for large companies such as Siemens AG, Bayer AG, Volkswagen AG, BASF AG and so on, which are securing their market position with extensive direct investment, but also for many medium-sized German enterprises who have entered the East and Southeast Asian markets in recent years and made a name for themselves with their excellent products and manufacturing technologies (Haak, 2002b).

Basically, Japanese management hopes that cooperating with German companies in East and Southeast Asia will bring an increase in the efficiency of existing activities or create new potential. Discussions with representatives of Japanese companies that work with German companies have revealed that four basic targets can be identified.

1. The fundamental goal of increasing profits from business activities in East and Southeast Asia, mainly by entering the market faster, using the expertise provided by the German partner and by complementing their own product range and acquiring financial help from both German government institutions and directly from the partner company.
2. Lower costs through economies of scale and avoiding duplicated investment by entering the different East and Southeast Asian markets together and exploiting cost benefits by division of labour beyond the specific target market.
3. Targets to reduce risk by investing less capital and saving resources for other internationalization activities or for restructuring companies in Japan.
4. Gaining prestige by working long-term with internationally well-known and admired German business partners (Haak, 2003).

The resources available to a Japanese company represent a deciding factor in determining the options for realizing commercial alternatives in the internationalization process. Resources are relevant for two reasons in cooperative strategies: firstly, the company's own resources form a supply pool for the potential partner, and secondly the company needs the resources in order to exploit the benefits from the cooperative venture for its own ends. The key factors – capital, expertise, competence and time – show clearly that Japanese companies are trying hard to enter into cooperative ventures with German companies in East and Southeast Asia (Haak, 2002b).

Currently, capital investment is one of the factors limiting internationalization of Japanese companies. Even large internationally active Japanese companies are not in a position to enter the market with a 100 per cent subsidiary, and acquiring or founding a new company abroad with the aim of setting up a fully-owned subsidiary is even more out of the question for small and medium-sized Japanese enterprises. Frequently, however, companies are forced to enter East and Southeast Asian markets and production locations due to their obligations to deliver in the *keiretsu* even though they actually need to use their capital for restructuring in Japan (Haak, 2001b). The investment made by small and medium-sized Japanese companies in East and Southeast Asia is not only limited by a lack of capital, but direct investment is considered to be a risk. Medium-sized enterprises are only prepared to invest a substantial proportion of their capital if the associated risks remain manageable. Japanese management assumes that collaborating with a German company in East and Southeast Asia, especially in China, can reduce the risk of entering the market, particularly if the option of a step-by-step approach to the cooperative venture as experience increases is considered (Beamish, 1988, 1998).

If, for example, the goal of the venture is to enter the Chinese market, a collaboration strategy is the best solution to the problem of capital, even if a German partner already has the required knowledge of the market which could be used and, ideally from the Japanese point of view, it does not need to build up its own marketing organization. Different emphasis in expertise frequently provides the reason for Japanese–German collaboration in China, where German and Japanese management might both bring specific knowledge of markets in the Chinese economy. A company's competence, as well as its expertise, plays a crucial role for joint ventures in China (Haak, 2001b, 2003).

Competence, in contrast to expertise, is understood as the capabilities of a company, which as a rule cannot be captured in written form. Interpreted more broadly, it can also mean corporate culture, in this case Japanese and German corporate culture which might possibly merge into a new corporate culture in a joint venture with China as the target country. By combining the strong points of their corporate cultures, the German and Japanese parent companies might create an outstanding competitive advantage, but one should not lose sight of the considerable difficulties in bringing together two different corporate cultures, which could result in the failure of the cooperative venture. As yet there is no answer to the question of how to implement a new corporate culture into which the culture of each of the companies in the cooperation can merge. Currently we know more about the difficulties created when two different cultures meet than we do of ways to engender new and successful corporate cultures.

Competence should not only be understood as part of the package on offer from the company partnership, but also as the willingness of a company to enter into a cooperative venture. With direct investment only, a company can make its competence available to the subsidiary with no other influences. The prerequisite for this is, however, that the appropriate management qualities are available in the company. In a company with hitherto no experience abroad, direct investment without any knowledge of the market and the conditions overall represents a relatively high risk. For Japanese small and medium-sized enterprises, cooperative strategies reduce the risk as the German partner's competence optimizes the pooled resources.

Under the market conditions prevailing in China, with product development becoming faster, the time factor is playing an increasingly important role in the profitable marketing of a product. Particularly in the case of high-tech products, the time it takes for research and development costs to amortize continues to decrease. Empirical investigations show that if a market launch is delayed by 10 per cent, company profits may be reduced by around 25 to 30 per cent. The conclusion for both Japanese and German companies is that a company with a new technology is forced to market it on a global scale as quickly as possible; they do not have the time to build up their own marketing channels in foreign markets. Japanese–German third-country collaboration might achieve a competitive advantage if each is able to share the established distribution structures of the other (Haak, 2001b, 2003; Hilpert and Taube, 1997).

7
Characteristics and Motives of Japanese–German Third-Country Collaboration in East and Southeast Asia

Changes and challenges in the region

Let us begin this chapter with the economic region: Asia, more precisely East and Southeast Asia, the focus of the following discussion. East and Southeast Asia, understood here as the geographical region stretching from the Kuril Islands in the north to the Indonesian archipelago in the south, is still considered today as one of the less advanced regions of the world compared to Western Europe and North America from an institutional point of view. Particularly in direct comparison with Europe's spectacular progress in achieving integration over recent years, East and Southeast Asia still presents a very narrow spectrum of regional organization and collaboration (Buzan and Segal, 1994). Using Europe as a reference point seems difficult as the regions have completely different premises, but it helps to understand the changes and challenges in this region.

Europe and East and Southeast Asia are characterized by completely different political circumstances (Ardent and Pflüger, 1995). Immediately after the Second World War, Europeans began to reappraise the past and draw far-reaching political and social conclusions which still now determine the actions of the European states. Particularly France and Germany, but also the Benelux countries and Italy made efforts early on to achieve a new order in Europe with the goal of safeguarding human rights, democracy and the rule of law. These states came to the conclusion that European integration would promise more success in the achievement of this goal and in preventing totalitarian and authoritarian tendencies than would isolated efforts within a narrow national framework. In a Europe still suffering at first-hand the effects of the dreadful experiences of the Second World War, union was also considered an effective way of keeping Germany under long-term control.

In the East and Southeast Asian region there has been no comparable cross-border political or historical reappraisal with all that that implies economically, socially, corporately and culturally. On the contrary, East and Southeast Asian states are observably in a process of national self-assertion, which manifests itself not least in a high regard of their national sovereignty. These states are therefore not prepared to cede national rights to supranational organizations. In addition, there is still a great deal of political resentment towards Japan, as there has not yet been a comprehensive reappraisal of its past as a martial and colonial power (Böhn, 1992; Platz and Rieger, 1996). These subjects have been aired politically and addressed publicly in Japan only lately, when for example on the occasion of the 50th anniversary of Japanese surrender on 15 August 1995, the head of the Japanese government at that time, Murayama, expressed his regret for the horrors of the Second World War, and in recent excursions into foreign policy on the part of the current Prime Minister Koizumi.

Even though in many states in East and Southeast Asian, flexible pragmatism seems to be the order of the day, and there is less concern with accounting for the past in routine business, Japan's historical legacy remains an obstacle to a far-reaching process of integration (Pohl, 1994). There are also reasons other than history for the low level of integration in the region, originating in the socio-cultural, religious, political and economic differences between the countries. Politically, the region spans democracies such as Japan, South Korea and Taiwan, authoritarian regimes such as Indonesia and the Philippines and totalitarian states such as China and Cambodia (Binderhofer, 1996; Dürr and Harnisch, 1986). Japan has had a democratic constitution since 1947, but democracy in other states in the region (for example South Korea, Taiwan and the Philippines) is still very much in its infancy and, in Western European understanding at least, not at all sound. Political unrest in recent years in Indonesia and the Philippines, the treatment of the opposition in Malaysia and the violation of human rights in many East and Southeast Asian states (for example in Laos, China, Myanmar and Cambodia) make integration of the states and political contact between them extremely difficult.

The religious situation in the region is also heterogenous: Muslims in Indonesia, Buddhists in Thailand, atheists or Confucianists in China,

Christians in South Korea and in the Philippines, and Shintoists in Japan are just a few examples (Bechert and Gombrich, 1995; Edsman, 1976; Weggel, 1989). No other region of the world, Latin America, Europe, North America, nor even Africa can boast such variety. A clash between different Asian ideals and social models originating in the political, social, religious and historical areas of conflict is not impossible (Huntington, 1994). For example, the ASEAN states still harbour considerable resentment towards China, which with its economic development over the last 20 years has been able to resume its role as a major power (Hilpert and Haak, 2002). The rise in the Chinese defence budget and Peking's claims to the Paracel and Spratly Islands which are also claimed by ASEAN members are indicators of future conflict. The Taiwan issue is also far from being clear and military threats by the People's Republic of China in the Taiwan Straits are putting a further strain on moves towards regional integration.

There are other economic and political factors that stand in the way of regional integration. Economic growth in the Asian countries is based largely on successful exporting, and Japan is very worried that increased regional integration in East and Southeast Asia would partition off the trading blocks EU, NAFTA and the potential East and Southeast Asian block from each other and create exclusive groups (Hilpert, 1993). If this partitioning does come about, external trade in the East and Southeast Asian region would develop into a zero-sum game, as all the exports and imports would be taken by countries in this region. Growth supported by exports would therefore no longer be possible. Japan in particular, which has already been plagued with serious economic and structural problems for more than 10 years, would, as a largely export-oriented country, suffer. The growth engine of export, already weakened, would fail and the difficult situation in Japan, which stagnating domestic consumption is doing nothing to help, would become even worse. Against this background, attempts by Japanese economic and foreign policy-makers to use APEC (Asia-Pacific Economic Cooperation) as an instrument and to promote the liberalization of commercial policy which is also desired by the WTO (World Trade Organization) are understandable.

Another economic problem is the widespread protectionism in the region. In each of the countries, which are all at very different stages of economic and social development, the amount of protectionist activity varies. The introduction of a free-trade zone in the region would result in profits from the increase in trade flowing mainly towards the more prosperous countries. Those countries have always had relatively open-trade connections and would suffer only small losses in the reduced income from duty (Hilpert, 1993). This background makes sense of the recent free-trade agreement between Japan and Singapore, which on the basis of their per capita gross social product are two of the richer countries of the region, and clearly leaders. Singapore leads in Southeast Asia as a metropolis of service and trade, and Japan in East Asia as the second largest industrial nation in the world.

Even if the reasons given do not exactly accelerate formal integration in East and Southeast Asia, there have been, signs that development in the region is quickly making up ground, particularly in the last ten years, focusing mainly around ASEAN (Association of South East Asian Nations). ASEAN was created in 1967 in Bangkok (Rüland, 1995), where the five founding states were Indonesia, Malaysia, the Philippines, Singapore and Thailand. Brunei became a member on 8 January 1984, Vietnam on 8 July 1995, Laos and Myanmar on 23 July 1997 and Cambodia on 30 April 1999. The founding statement, the Bangkok Declaration of 8 August 1967, gave the three fundamental goals of the association:

1. 'To accelerate the economic growth, social progress and cultural development in the region through joint endeavours in the spirit of equality and partnership in order to strengthen the foundation for a prosperous and peaceful community of South-East Asian Nations;
2. To promote regional peace and stability through abiding respect for justice and the rule of law in the relationship among countries of the region and adherence to the principles of the United Nations Charter; [and]
3. To promote active collaboration and mutual assistance on matters of common interest in the economic, social, cultural, technical, scientific and administrative fields.' (http://www.aseansec.org/history/asn_his2.htm)

These goals would indicate that the focus of the joint policy is economic and cultural. However, evaluating ASEAN against its own targets shows that its achievements in these two central areas of policy, economics and culture, might be considered meagre. When ASEAN was founded, it was impossible not to take historical circumstances into account; after the takeover of Indochina, the fear of more communist attacks in Southeast Asia worsened. This fear became manifest when in 1971 in Kuala Lumpur, four years after the foundation of ASEAN, ZOPFAN (Zone of Peace, Freedom and Neutrality) was launched as a security policy concept; here, neutrality signified mainly the absence of influence of foreign states in the region (Feske, 1991). To overstate the case, in its initial stages, ASEAN was an anti-communist association looking for wide support from the West (Schütte and Lasserre, 1996, p. 13).

The foundation of ASEAN should, however, also be seen in the context of an early wave of 'Third World regionalism'. In Southeast Asia, indeed in the whole of Asia, ASEAN was the first subregional cooperative association to include neither established nor newly industrialized countries, but developing countries exclusively. Buzz words such as 'south–south cooperation' or 'new world economic order' associated with fantastic ideas about dissolving asymmetrical distributions of power between the rich countries of the North and the poor countries of the South defined the spirit of much development and regional political discourse (Rühland, 1995).

Nine years after Bangkok, regional integration received a new impetus, motivated primarily by security policy. On 23–24 July 1976, the first meeting of the Heads of Government of the ASEAN states took place on the Indonesian island of Bali. At this first ASEAN summit, an agreement, the Treaty of Amity and Cooperation in Southeast Asia, TAC, and a framework agreement on an action programme (the Declaration of ASEAN Concord) were signed. A closer look at these documents reveals:

- 'An agreement on mechanisms to deal with conflict peacefully;
- the explicit renunciation of threats or the use of violence;
- the establishment of a 'High Council' to deal with conflict by regional trials;
- the intention to carry out major projects jointly;
- mutual guarantee of duty relief by creating a Preferential Trading Arrangement, PTA;
- the establishment of a central ASEAN secretariat in Jakarta.' (Stahl, 2001, p. 25)

A year later, regional cooperation was strengthened, particularly as regards economic policy. At the second ASEAN summit of 4–5 August 1977 in Kuala Lumpur, the Association responded to the difficult economic situation worldwide with comprehensive resolutions including a rice reserve, an oil regulation programme and a swap arrangement where there were problems with the balance of payments. Intensive collaboration with neighbouring states and with the European Community were also decided upon.

During 1976 and 1977, the direction for regional integration was essentially laid down, but no significant changes took place for several years. The third ASEAN summit did not take place until 10 years later, from 14 to 15 December 1987 in Manila. However, this was disappointing in so far as no further steps towards integration were taken, although limited progress was made in key points such as institutional reforms, integration of economies and economic policies and joint defence.

Another five years passed before the fourth summit was held in Singapore in 1992. ASEAN aims were widened to include the Singapore agreement. In the three central documents (1. Singapore Declaration; 2. Framework Agreement on Enhancing ASEAN Economic Cooperation; 3. Agreement on Common Effective Preferential Tariff (CEPT)) the states in the Association agreed to widen collaboration in matters of security, to strengthen the ASEAN institutions and to set up a free-trade zone in Southeast Asia – the ASEAN Free Trade Area (AFTA) – which would reduce duty step by step over 15 years to 0 to 5 per cent for all industrial goods and remove non-tariff obstructions to trade (Erdmann and Kreisel, 1994; Freiwald, 1996).

The economic success of the Southeast Asian member states, illustrated in the 1970s and 1980s by average growth of 7 per cent annually in the national gross domestic product, was only the result of regional collaboration in that the joint security policy ensured political stability (Uhlig, 1992). It was mainly the efforts of individual member states of the association that were responsible for the growth and less so the agreements within the framework of the ASEAN Free Trade Area.

Part of the success story of ASEAN is that after years of effort to create a nuclear weapon-free zone in Southeast Asia, at the fifth summit conference in Bangkok in December 1995, the Treaty on the Southeast Asia Nuclear Weapon-Free Zone (SEANWFZ) was finally implemented. The signatory states declared themselves willing to renounce the development, the construction and the purchase of atomic weapons. However, it should be noted that still up to the present day, each state is free to accept ships or aircraft equipped with nuclear weapons from other states in their own sovereign territory, which is not completely in line with the theoretical concept of a nuclear-free zone.

The path towards peace and stability in Southeast Asia which started in 1992 in Singapore continued with the ASEAN 2020 vision which was agreed at the informal summit in Kuala Lumpur in December 1997. The following is a précis of the declarations of intent and the goals: peace and stability in Southeast Asia with peaceful resolution of conflict; the development of a partnership for dynamic development and reduction of economic differences between states; and the establishment of an association of humane societies. The 'Hanoi Action Plan' and the 'bold measures' agreed at the sixth ASEAN summit on 16 December 1998 in

Hanoi primarily targeted an economic revival of the region following the crisis in Asia in 1997–98.

These agreements may be characterized more or less as an *ad hoc* programme intended to return the states to steady growth. It is considered that economic growth is the necessary prerequisite for modernizing the countries and creates the necessary framework conditions to allow all the ASEAN states to make up ground. At the end of the 1990s, the economic objectives were given priority over efforts to achieve integrated security. At the third informal summit in Manila in November 1999, this trend was underlined when no more objectives for security policy integration were set. However, at the 34th ASEAN foreign minister conference in Hanoi in July 2001, the positive progress of the ASEAN forum, particularly the ASEAN Regional Forum (ARF), in the security dialogue for East Asia was highlighted and the significance of ASEAN for security policy integration was further reinforced.

In the 35 years that ASEAN has existed, it has been more successful in security policy than in economic policy. Early on ASEAN was concerned to find a way to calm the initially very tense relationships between member states. Whereas from the beginning of the European integration process, regional exchange of goods together with the political motives for integration were of great importance (particularly for Germany: Europe was its most important market after the USA), in Southeast Asia it was more the decisions on security policy which had an integrative effect. Peace in large parts of Southeast Asia, long-awaited particularly in Vietnam and Cambodia, represented one of the most important mainstays for the dynamic development of the economy in ASEAN countries and their integration in the global economy.

Key impulses for favourable economic development in the ASEAN countries were provided particularly by Japan, as an advanced industrial state. In the mid-1950s, Japan began its dynamic rise to becoming the second largest industrial nation in the world, proving spectacularly that it was possible to make up ground in industrialization. Japan was elected as a model for economic development by Malaysia amongst others. 'Look East' was one of the key slogans which the Malaysian Prime Minister Mahatir Mohammed frequently used in his modernization propaganda, shunning the Western development models in favour of recipes for success from Japan. Even though the Japanese business models became less celebrated in the 1990s, Japan's leading economic position in East and Southeast Asia is undisputed. With only 7.5 per cent of the population, Japan made around 60 per cent of East and South Asia's gross domestic product in the end of the 1990s.

Japan's leading role in the region can be illustrated with the 'flying-geese' model. The model describes the regional economic interdependencies of East and Southeast Asia, resembling a staggered chase in which Japan is pursued by the newly industrialized economies (NIEs) – Hong Kong, South Korea, Taiwan – these by the ASEAN states, and the ASEAN states by China. The countries all entered the phase of industrial development at different points in time: in Japan this was in the 1920s and 1930s, in the NIEs it was in the 1970s, in the ASEAN states it was during the 1980s, and for China it was the end of the 1980s. This has resulted in a dynamic mix of development in East and Southeast Asia which did not stop completely in the Asia crisis in 1997–98, but was merely interrupted.

The flying-geese model further assumes that countries in a certain stage of development can only produce those products which are appropriate for the capital and technology with which they are equipped. Technologically more complex products and the necessary means of production associated with them must be imported from countries in front of them in the model, and therefore at a higher development level. In a countermove, countries that are not yet quite so well-developed export more labour-intensive products into more-developed countries as they can manufacture them more cheaply with their lower wage costs and associated outlay (Böhn, 1992; Brucker, 1990; Halberstam, 1991; Pohl and Weggel, 1994). As a country develops, the availability of capital, human resources and technology improve so that it can manufacture higher value products and control the appropriate production processes itself (Schütte and Lassere, 1996). As the wage costs in that country are still relatively low, however, it gains competitive advantage over the country at the next higher level of development and is able to force it out of its traditional product ranges. However, as the country in its turn is forced out of production in some areas by countries on lower development levels, there is a shift in each position in the model overall. Each country therefore has its own fixed place within the model with the prospect of going through the same development processes as countries on higher levels. Due to the different developmental stages and the associated competitive advantage for each country, division of labour over the region is pronounced. Associated with this is the intensification of intraregional trade and intraregional direct investment, which again is growing much faster than the exchange of goods and capital with other regions.

In the flying-geese model, Japan should always be out in front with the leading economic role in East and Southeast Asia. However, the condition for this is that technology transfer from Japan to the other East and Southeast Asian countries only takes place with a definite time offset. If, for example, the NIEs were able to use modern information systems to catch up with Japanese industry more quickly, Japan's position out in front would be under threat. Therefore, it would seem more sensible from the Japanese point of view to keep the management of their industrial 'transplants' in the other countries in the region Japanese, and only outsource those areas of the company not involved in the development of new products or manufacturing technology. This would keep the industrialization and development process in East and Southeast Asia largely dependent on the development process in Japan, unless European and American companies strengthen their involvement in the region should their strategic situations or economic objectives change.

Comprehensive economic integration in the region will eventually reduce the heterogeneity of the countries and make Japan's strategy of maintaining its leading role much more difficult. One should also not forget the 'little tigers' – South Korea, Taiwan, Hong Kong and Singapore – which since the 1960s have shown impressive development in industry and services and have made their influence felt in East and Southeast Asia (Gaffga, 1996; Brucker, 1990; Hilpert and Haak, 2002). In addition, China's boom since the early 1980s has brought an enormous economic dynamic to the region. Both in international business and in international economics, it is widely recognized that the current rise of China has wide implications for the international economic and political order in general, and for the East and Southeast Asian region in particular. The states in the region are facing the challenge of an economically and politically successful China, which with its low sales prices and improving product quality, is set to become a major competitor in global manufacturing markets, including the Japanese domestic market, which is quite a worrying prospect for Japan's economic and political elites. On the macro level, China is challenging Japan as East and Southeast Asia's centre of economic gravity in terms of production and markets. In the 1990s, China initiated a new phase of regional business cooperation (Hilpert and Haak, 2002). And although this new trend was mainly launched and promoted by Japan and Australia, ASEAN played a key role in a formal sense.

From the point of view of ASEAN, there have been primarily two trends which have given efforts towards multilateral cooperation and integration new urgency: the American retreat from the region (unification of Vietnam, withdrawal of the American military from bases in the Philippines in 1992) left a power vacuum which gave rise to old and new concerns and fears regarding the hegemonic ambitions of Japan and China. Furthermore, from the point of view of ASEAN, at the beginning of the 1990s global tendencies to form political trade blocs increased. Southeast Asian states saw here the danger of losing important export markets in North America and Europe (Maull and Nabers, 2001), which would be equivalent to losing one of the central catalytic functions for increasing industrialization or in more general terms for the modernization it required. For the ASEAN member states, symptoms of this bloc-building tendency were particularly apparent in the European Union's plans for a single domestic market and in the formation of NAFTA.

How did ASEAN respond to these changes? From the economic policy point of view, the association relinquished its reservations on the concept of East Asian–Pacific economic cooperation. In 1989, it agreed to the foundation of APEC (Asia-Pacific Economic Cooperation), which was promoted by Australia (Hilpert, 1992a). 1992 can be seen as a turning point in terms of both security policy and the economy. At the fourth ASEAN summit in Singapore, discussion on security policy was widened as part of the ASEAN Regional Forum as was the attempt at economic cooperation within member states based on a free trade zone – the ASEAN Free Trade Area (AFTA).

In the context of this development, institutionalized political integration emerged in both economic and security policy. Developments included APEC mentioned above (founded 1989, 1991 summit); and the East Asian Economic Caucus (EAEC), which began in 1991 as the East Asian Economic Grouping and since 1997 has been organized as the ASEAN +3 meeting initially for foreign ministers and then as an annual summit for the heads of state and governments of ASEAN member states, with China, Japan and South Korea (Korhonen, 1998). Furthermore, there is KEDO (Korean Peninsula Energy Development Organization), founded in 1996 (Harnisch and Maull, 2000) and ASEM (Asia Europe Meeting), also since 1996.

What brought about these East Asian cooperative processes? It seems that with the exception of KEDO, they were triggered by economic involvement at regional and transregional levels (Maull and Nabers, 2001). Transnational and multinational companies from Japan with their internationally networked company structures (*keiretsu*), overseas Chinese companies in trade and investment, and also Korean conglomerates (*chaebol*) and internationally active Taiwanese groups drove forward the forms of horizontal and vertical division of labour in East Asia (Schütte and Lasserre, 1996, pp. 65–90). In addition to company networks, the role of other networks – scientists, politicians, journalists and business associates – should not be underestimated in their efforts to breathe life into and drive on regional cooperation and integration. Since the 1960s, a number of unofficial discussion forums have emerged, where scientists, business associates and journalists talk to government representatives about cooperation issues in East and Southeast Asia. The most important forums are the Pacific Economic Cooperation Council (PECC), which led to the foundation of APEC and above all the Council for Security Cooperation in Asia-Pacific (CSCAP), which complemented the ASEAN Regional Forum in the area of security policy.

On the whole, economists still dispute the value of informal business integration and the tendencies towards political cooperation and integration (regionalization) in East and Southeast Asia. For instance, ASEAN is frequently held up as an example of the success of interstate cooperation outside of Europe; however, a number of experts doubt the durability of these relationships. Some scientists tend to decry the organizational forms of collaboration on security and economic policy that have emerged over the last 10 years as talking-shops and grant them only little influence in the increasing stability in East and Southeast Asia, and particularly in the ASEAN states (Maull and Nabers, 2001). Other authors, on the other hand, including acknowledged international economists, stress the enormous capacity to learn of the countries in East and Southeast Asia which the impressive economic growth rates over the last few decades have proven. They argue that East and Southeast Asia on the basis of this proven capacity for learning and the development of regional cooperation with formal integration could catch up with the West and possibly overtake it (Bergsten, 2000).

However, it is difficult to share this optimistic assessment. A striking example is the Asian crisis, which started in July 1997 with the devaluation of the Thai baht and only gradually died away in 1999, clearly showed the structural problems with interstate cooperation in the region. The economic and internal political difficulties experienced by most of the founder members of ASEAN during the Asia crisis, and the expansion of ASEAN at the end of the 1990s to include three very troubled members, Myanmar, Cambodia and Laos, created an additional burden for the cooperative negotiations of the Association. New regional and transregional cooperation processes must be put on a broad and solid basis so that crisis events in the region can be dealt with. Without international help, the Asian crisis would not have been overcome so quickly.

Whilst in Europe, for example, the level of integration rose considerably with the agreements in Maastricht, attempts at integration in East and Southeast Asia happen on a much lower level. The conditions for the region becoming a single integrated area are already unfavourable given the heterogeneity discussed above. In Europe, almost 2,000 years of shared culture and geographical proximity have produced an almost homogeneous entity in comparison to East and Southeast Asia, and in recent years European integration has been balanced. Despite the North–South divide that exists in the European Union, the range of economic power is much smaller than in East and Southeast Asia, where the political, cultural and economic differences must be seen as a serious obstacle to integration in comparison to Europe. A single currency, even it were to be seriously considered by the East and Southeast Asian states, is a long way away. And a yen-bloc would not be acceptable to many countries for historical reasons. In addition, there would be no point in having a single currency without China as the second most important commercial and industrial power in the region and without the economic potential of the overseas Chinese (Hilpert and Haak, 2002).

The existing commercial ties, cooperative and integrated areas in East and Southeast Asia are currently characterized by informal organizational structures, and cooperative ventures therefore have a fundamentally different quality from those that existed in the early stages of the European Union. The unwillingness on the part of individual countries in Southeast, and also in Northeast Asia to cede their national rights as sovereign states to a supranational organization is the key reason for the low level of institutionalization in Asian economic relationships. One of the consequences of this is that decisions are frequently made on the basis of the smallest denominator, as all member states must agree. Fundamental structural reform and real turnarounds in economic, currency and security policy leading to closer cooperation and wider integration should not be expected in the near future.

Overview and regional specifics

One of the most important studies of Japanese–German third-country collaboration in the East and Southeast Asian region is the research report compiled by the ifo Institute for Economic Research from January 1995 to March 1997. The report is based mainly on research into the press and in databases and on consultations with managers working in Japanese–German third-country projects (Hilpert and Taube, 1997). Essentially, it represents a snapshot of March 1997.

To get a more precise picture, particularly for collaboration in China, the German Institute for Japanese Studies carried out a research project within the framework of its long-term programme 'Japan in Asia' with the title 'Focus on China – Collective Internationalization Strategies of German and Japanese Manufacturing and Technology Companies' (Haak, 2002b). This study examines primarily Japanese–German third-country collaboration in China. The research was based essentially on interviews with the management of Japanese–German cooperative ventures in China, Japan and Germany and on database research (newspapers, journals, the JETRO archive) and on evaluation and interpretation of other publications on this subject. Interviews were held with representatives from economic science, economic institutions and state-run institutions. First results from the research were discussed in depth with scientists from various disciplines and representatives from the business world and politics at a conference 'Japan and China – Economic Relation in Transition', organized jointly by the Fujitsu Research Institute and the German Institute for Japanese Studies and which took place in January 2001 in Tokyo.

In the study, each place of production shared by Japanese and German companies in a third country counts as a single case of collaboration. Individual Japanese–German projects in a third country, frequently defined to end at a certain point in time, count as independent cases. Empirical results clearly reveal that any successful Japanese–German third-country cooperative venture in an Asian country was preceded by successful involvement of a German company in Japan. A closer look at the distribution of Japanese–German third-county collaboration shows a clear concentration in East and Southeast Asia. Other regional markets, such as the USA, Western Europe, Central and Eastern Europe, Africa and Latin America are not considered here, although Japanese–German third-country cooperative ventures are also in operation there.

Of a total of 89 ventures, 52 are in the East and Southeast Asia. They are concentrated mainly in the People's Republic of China (19), followed by Indonesia (7) and South Korea (5). Less attractive countries for joint ventures are Vietnam, Malaysia and Taiwan, which each have only four instances of Japanese–German collaboration. In Thailand there are just three, and Hong Kong and Singapore each have two business partnerships. The focus of joint engagement in East and Southeast Asia is primarily on opening up and penetrating markets (for example the automobile industry, chemicals and pharmaceuticals, telecommunications) in the target countries. In large projects to build plant and create infrastructure (for example transport systems, chemical works, power stations, structural steel engineering and so on) the aim is to share risk and combine complementary strengths (Haak, 2002b; Hilpert and Taube, 1997).

Does it make sense for Japanese and German companies to collaborate in third-country markets? What are the lessons from China? The People's Republic of China is becoming increasingly significant as a market and as a production location for Japanese and German companies doing business on an international scale. At the same time, the Chinese government considers that these companies represent one of the most important mainstays for the economic and technological development of their country. From the point of view of strategic management of internationally active companies, current investment in the Chinese market is being swept along by globalization and sharper international competition (Konomoto, 1997, 1998; Li and Li, 1999; Taylor, 1996; Haak, 2003a).

One thing is certain: many high-tech companies are no longer tied to traditional locations. High-tech products such as cars, for example, can be manufactured all over the world in more or less the same quality. The particular features of the Chinese market and the specific benefits offered by its locations almost clamour for the commitment of internationally active companies. Intercompany ventures, joint development, production and sales, trade of components and technology are basic factors in the success of strategic management in the international organization of labour and decentralized production to secure a global presence. Only by being a leading technology producer based on faster and more target-oriented implementation of product and process innovation is it possible to gain long-term market leadership in China. Japanese and German companies are well-aware of this fact and try to use the requirements and challenges of China as a market and a production location to their strategic advantage (Konomoto, 2000; Kawashima and Konomoto, 1999; Köllner, 1997).

At the start of the new century, China is one of the most interesting but also one of the highest risk markets in Asia. Its economy is growing at a speed and on a scale that Germany and Japan only experienced during the years of their *Wirtschaftswunder*. China's business dynamic has been maintained in recent years with investment from abroad and the increase in exports that this has initiated. The Chinese government is promoting further development by more public investment to stimulate more growth. Joining the WTO is also fuelling development with its sustained impact on international companies.

China is not a homogeneous economic area. Commerce and buying power are concentrated mainly in the coastal areas, where most of the international companies have settled. In the north are the old heavy industry areas; in the east Shanghai is developing into a modern technology and services centre; and since the formation of the first special economic zone the economic dynamic in the southern regions is developing along the lines of Hong Kong, the former British Crown colony, now a Special Administrative Region (Ohmae, 2001).

The per capita income of the population is rising, particularly in the industrial centres, and new groups of consumers are ready to buy high-quality consumer goods, particularly modern products. German and Japanese companies active on a global basis can no longer omit China as a production base and as a market from their strategies. In fact no globally active company can seriously afford to ignore the Chinese market in the long term.

Market and technology leadership in China are considered to be key to the long-term successful penetration of other markets in Eastern and Southeastern Asia. To achieve such market and technology leadership, some companies see third-company collaboration as a promising organizational form. In 2002 there were 19 Japanese–German third-country collaborative ventures active in different sectors, including mechanical engineering, textiles, food, chemicals, cars, services and IT (Haak, 2003). From the point of view of Japanese and German management, what reasons are there to use a third-country collaborative strategy to become active in China?

Motives

Analysing the motivation for implementing a collective internationalization strategy in the form of a Japanese–German cooperative venture in a third country is a very complex undertaking. The basic motives for joint business engagement must be considered as much as the reasons why the German and Japanese managements chose a specific region or company.

The fundamental motives are shared costs and risk, access to external resources (management capacity, technology and so on) and new markets, synergy effects, influence on competition (power) and possibly also to safeguard the continuing existence of a company. What does the general motivation to share costs and risks really mean? In recent years, the proportion of costs for research and development and for carrying out marketing activities in more than one country in the course of internationalizing a business has increased considerably. Achieving the same performance and product quality worldwide requires more and more investment in production, in terms of capital and knowledge. From the point of view of profitability, too, companies are being forced to expand their international interests in order to maintain a presence in all the important markets in North America, West Europe and Japan. Furthermore, ever-shortening product life-cycles and the rising numbers of imitation strategies by competitors from Asia require that products are marketed as fast and as globally as possible. Progress in information and communication technology accelerates this process further (Deutsch–Japanischer Wirtschaftskreis, 1997; Haak, 2002b).

In the face of such developments and also taking into account the not inconsiderable political and economic risks in some countries in Asia, many Japanese and Germany companies are not able to maintain a presence and market on a global scale on their own. Under these conditions, a Japanese–German cooperative venture to open up a regional market seems a promising solution to drive on a company's internationalization and improve its position in global competition.

With large industrial or infrastructure projects in East and Southeast Asia, the financial risks often assume a magnitude that even big Japanese and German companies either cannot or do not want to bear on their own. Many managers also see the need for caution when deciding to enter into large industrial projects in a high-risk environment, and investing in the People's Republic of China is considered high-risk. Third-country collaboration between Japanese and German companies gives better protection from economic and political risk. There is also the option of export insurance to cover the risks taken by the partners (Hermes Insurance, METI) collaborating on projects in third countries (Deutsch–Japanischer Wirtschaftskreis, 1996).

A joint venture in the target country makes sense if the Japanese and German strengths complement each other. The partnership can provide access to the operational resources of the partner company – such as labour, manufacturing skills, management expertise, capital or even just to its image. Contact with customers and knowledge about the partner company's market and competition can also be acquired. Exchanging knowledge about the competition situation or finding missing pieces of information can also save time in such collaboration (Haak, 2001b, 2002b; Hilpert and Taube, 1997).

The question of whether combined and synergy effects can be achieved depends on the potential and circumstances of each partner. If two or more partners complement each other in a range of abilities, their capacity to compete is greatly improved. From the point of view of German management, working with a Japanese company in Asia offers unique advantages that would not be available with a company from another country. It is possible, for example, that business opportunities provided by the Japanese partner can only be accessed locally via Japanese personal and interfirm networks. Access to the Japanese general trading houses and banks are only one possible option here, and contacts to important and innovative suppliers can eventually benefit a Japanese–German venture long term. A German company can also share in the low-cost financing provided as development aid in Japan for the Asian economic region.

German and Japanese managements need to achieve further learning through collaboration (see also Chapter 6); if such reciprocal learning does not take place, continued collaboration in a third country may be threatened. Companies in the same sector which cooperate on production or marketing or in technological or manufacturing technology-related research and development will only improve their joint market position if they create added value as a result of the venture in the third country, provided they innovate to benefit the venture and therefore the parent company.

Another important driving factor for Japanese–German third-country collaboration from a general point of view is the pressure some companies are under to enter into a business collaboration in order to secure the future existence of the company. Small and medium-sized enterprises, frequently family-run, may avoid such collaboration as they fear losing freedom to make their own decisions (Deutsch–Japanischer Wirtschaftskreis, 1997, Haak, 2002b), but as difficulties in the Japanese economy have now continued for almost 12 years, many family enterprises are being forced to find a partner in order to stay in the East and Southeast Asian competitive arena. Safeguarding the existence of a company should not be underestimated as a motive for implementing a collective internationalization strategy, working together with a partner improves competitive advantage in technology, management expertise, regional presence, financial power and so on. The fundamental goal is to learn from the partner and to ensure the survival of the company by acquiring new knowledge and abilities (see also the earlier discussion of the learning organization). With this process, international management can hope to stand up to competing companies better (Haak, 2002a, p. 43; Hilpert and Taube, 1997, p. 91).

A closer look at what motivates Japanese companies shows that Japan-centred activity in Japanese general trading houses has become increasingly less significant in recent years. Company objectives are now to find new and profitable areas of business, through investing in production plant and involving themselves more and more in infra-structure projects abroad. Companies also undertaking consultancy, becoming active in IT and more active in logistics management. These activities are directed increasingly towards the Asian economic area. Business collaboration with Western industrial companies has become more important with the acceleration of internationalization in the Japanese economy and the long-term upwards revaluation of the yen. Forming consortia of purely Japanese companies to give quotations belongs to the past; today, European and American companies are also consulted with the objective of achieving competitive standards of quality and performance. The structural and economic crisis in the Japanese economy in the 1990s and at the beginning of the twenty-first century has led to a relaxation in the industrial supplier networks (vertical *keiretsu*) (see also the detailed description of the changes in the Japanese supplier networks in Chapter 6). Faced with the long-drawn-out stagnation of Japanese domestic production and the increasing tendency to move manufacturing to East and Southeast Asia, numerous small and medium-sized companies in Japan have had to regroup or actively aim to diversify in their customer relations. For many such enterprises, joining with a German company is a promising alternative to proceeding alone abroad, as costs and risk are shared (Haak, 2002b).

The Japanese economy has a higher share of the market in the Asian economic region than anywhere else in the world, and Japanese standards of quality in the processing and production areas are shining examples to many Asian companies. The great challenge to Japanese companies today is to hold onto the shares gained in Asian markets and to exploit new opportunities. There is growing resistance to 'Japanese dominance' of which they are often accused and Japanese companies are increasingly encountering problems in Asia. The economic policy of many developing and new industrialized countries in Asia is forcing a generally stronger involvement with European companies in order to combat the perceived threat of economic supremacy from Japanese and US companies (Hilpert and Taube, 1997).

The strong business involvement of Japanese companies in East and Southeast Asia, particularly in China but also in Indonesia, Thailand and Malaysia, has not resulted in the technology transfer the target countries had hoped for. They are now looking for this technology transfer from increased involvement with European companies, so investment particularly from Western Europe is now given a high priority. In South Korea, Taiwan and in China, there is open discrimination against Japanese imports and in the awarding of public contracts.

All these factors are making it more difficult for Japanese companies to work in the markets of the Asian economic region. Working with a German partner offers a way around the various problematic situations, making Japanese involvement more acceptable. As already noted, German companies which have a particularly positive image in the region are considered especially attractive as partners for Japanese companies in third-country collaboration (Haak, 2001b, 2002b; Hilpert and Taube, 1997; Deutsch–Japanischer Wirtschaftskreis, 1996, 1997).

What specifically motivates German management to enter into a third-country collaboration with a Japanese company? The answer lies in the experience and expertise that the Japanese management has in the region which is always highlighted as a strategic advantage (Haak, 2002b). Widespread protectionism in East and Southeast Asian markets means that penetrating a market frequently only promises success when investment is made directly in the target country, and therefore German management's search for a collaboration partner with whom to share costs and risks in the developing and newly industrialized countries is particularly compelling.

Particularly where a German company is inadequately prepared, the capabilities and knowledge of Japanese companies in Asian markets is not to be underestimated. East and Southeast Asia have always been the regional tied market for the Japanese economy; over decades, Japanese companies have become familiar with this region and Japanese managers are well-prepared for their work in the relevant target areas. This preparation goes beyond acquiring knowledge of the language of the target country. With the close ties of Japanese staff to the parent company in Japan, they represent a catalyst for change in both the parent company and in the Japanese subsidiary in Asia (Haak, 2002a). Mutual exchange of ability, skill and knowledge enable learning on both sides and improve competitiveness, not just in the parent company, but in the subsidiary at the same time.

The traditional Japanese trade brokers, the general trading houses (*sôgô shôshas*) mentioned previously, and the global Japanese banks play a key role in these knowledge and information networks of Japanese companies in East and Southeast Asia. They have a wealth of experience in local business and maintain close contact with the local economic and political decision-makers. As the Japanese companies are so well networked in each Asian target country, German management can gain access to these enmeshed networks of information and knowledge locally. Business opportunities can result that cannot be anticipated in advance when a collective internationalization strategy for Asia is planned (Haak, 2002b).

One of the key strengths of Japanese companies in the Asian economic region is the existence of extensive distribution channels, some of which were created by Japanese companies after the Second World War. In some countries, Japanese companies can also refer back to prewar traditions, allowing access to the market with no difficulty at all. A Germany company new to the Asian market need not build up its own sales and services networks (Deutsch–Japanischer Wirtschaftskreis, 1997), it can rely on the existing and functioning distribution structures put in place by the Japanese company locally. This saves the cost of preparing the market and lowers the risk of failure as the company starts to expand towards Asia (Haak, 2002b, p. 44; Hilpert and Taube, 1997, p. 94).

Another important factor is that Japanese technology and image lead the market in East and Southeast Asia, more so than in any other economic region in the world. This role-model function of Japanese products and Japanese technology in many Asian countries can be of use to the German company in that working together with the Japanese company will be visible proof of quality in the eyes of many Asians. This image transfer can have a positive effect on the market position of the German company (Deutsch–Japanischer Wirtschaftskreis, 1997; Haak, 2002b). Hilpert and Taube (1997) summarize the competitive advantage that Japanese companies in the region can offer German partner as:

- successful personnel management;
- a profound knowledge of Asian mentality and business style;
- careful protection of technology; and
- strategic planning and procedures.

8
Conflicts and Elements of Success

Japanese–German third-country cooperative ventures in China tend to enjoy the benefit of more flexibility compared to other forms of internationalization. However, this makes monitoring more difficult for the partners, as loose forms of collaboration do not allow fast and effective access particularly when changes to strategy are made in the parent companies. The advantage of flexibility is especially apparent when such ventures come to an end. Selling a foreign subsidiary is frequently very difficult and often incurs a loss, whereas a third-country cooperative venture can be brought to an end with comparatively little effort (Haak, 2001b, 2002b).

What are the criteria that determine the success of a Japanese–German cooperative venture in a third country? Compared to German or Japanese companies tackling the Chinese market on their own, a good partner is crucial for success. The venture has a good chance of success if the new markets to be opened up are in related areas. The success rates for Japanese–German collaboration are much higher here than where Japanese or German businesses already active in China are acquired whole or in part. Furthermore, both partners should come with the same assumptions and the venture should be equally important to both of them.

However, besides the benefits of improved competitiveness and greater profits, third-country collaboration is also often accompanied by friction and conflict resulting from different objectives, varying amounts of available resources, contrasting management styles and, as mentioned above, different corporate cultures with different traditions in decision-making and problem-solving (Hammes, 1993; Harzing, 1999).

Conflicts

What are the areas of conflict that must be overcome when Japanese and German companies enter into third-country collaboration, for example, in China? Assuming that the venture is put together from targets and with the means to achieve the goals set out by the company, it is possible to differentiate between target- and means-related conflicts (Haak, 2003; Hilpert and Taube, 1997).

Target-related conflicts in Japanese–German third-country collaboration are caused by the incompatibility of objectives for the partnership on the part of the German and Japanese parent companies. If one or even both of the partners pursue opportunistic goals, then the venture is very likely to fail in the short or mid-term. Conflicts around target agreement irrespective of whether they existed initially or became apparent in the course of the venture are one of the central threats to such projects in China, as they throw the basic consensus of the entire venture into doubt. A solid basic consensus on goals by the partners from the beginning is particularly crucial for success in the high-risk and dynamic Chinese markets. Ventures can only meet the challenges of the competitive Chinese environment if the targets are compatible (Haak, 2003).

The competitive environment in China is extraordinarily dynamic; in some markets, double-figure growth rates are targeted so that within short periods the position of market leaders and competition can change. Newcomers to the market are not a rarity under these dynamic conditions, all of which increases the pressure to get the collaboration on a sound footing from the start of the venture. If objectives which directly affect the whole joint venture are not aired or only communicated incompletely, misinterpretation may result leading to rapid destruction of the basis for further collaboration. Problems could arise, for example, if the German partner ties the success of the venture in China to a financial result, whilst the Japanese partner is pursuing a longer-term objective and accordingly values the knowledge that accrues from working together with the German partner more highly (Haak, 2002b, 2003).

Furthermore, apart from difficulties between the German and Japanese partners, targets set by the local company in China can also contribute to further conflict. In certain industries, including telecommunications, car manufacturing and the agroindustrial and chemical sectors, Chinese involvement is a legal requirement. Such three-sided collaboration increases further potential areas of target-related conflict, as under some circumstances political and social objectives on the part of the Chinese partner enter into strategic and operative decisions. Whilst German and Japanese companies are pursuing goals of opening up markets in China and using resources (labourforce, power and so on) to those ends, Chinese partners may be looking primarily for learning effects, in order to eventually become independent of the cooperative venture.

It is also possible that target-related conflicts will arise if objectives change during the course of the partnership. The reasons why a partner might shift its objectives are many and varied. For example, the significance of a partner might change over time; technological innovation in a parent company might mean that one side becomes financially more powerful and better placed globally, whilst the other company might suffer a collapse in profits, losing its financial clout and becoming overall less attractive as a partner. There is also the danger that learning effects within the Japanese–German venture are distributed unevenly, allowing one partner to benefit more from the collaboration than the other. Internal company changes such as new strategic alignments in association with newly appointed management or an increase in potential knowledge relevant to corporate policy might also remove the basis for working together in the third-country (Haak, 2003).

As well as these target-related areas of conflict, *means-related conflicts* might appear when the partners attempt to realize their joint targets. They take many forms and are a daily challenge to international management in Japanese–German third-country collaboration. Unlike target-related conflicts, however, most means-related conflicts do not represent a threat to the third-country venture in China, except as regards complementarity of resources; the venture's right to exist may be thrown into doubt if it transpires after the partners have started working together that they cannot contribute the amounts expected to the project or that these amounts are being knowingly withheld. Parallel to this is the much more frequently encountered situation where one of the partners develops capabilities or finds resources in the course of the partnership which fill gaps in its competence that existed before it entered into the partnership. If there are no other factors in favour of continuing the partnership, it is no longer meaningful for the newly strengthened partner to continue working with the other, as a weakened partner can become an encumbrance (Haak, 2002b, 2003).

The weight can also shift between partners when, whilst working together in China, one side is able to develop more competence in areas such as technology, expertise or customer contacts faster or to a greater extent than the other, again with the risk that the strengthened partner will end the cooperative venture as it will not be prepared to nurse the weaker partner along.

Conflicts can also arise if the two countries approach decision-making in different ways. Making decisions in a German company is usually a linear process; information is sorted by relevance to the company, different courses of action are identified and these are rejected one after the other according to criteria laid down previously. This process continues until a clear-cut decision can be made that is perceived to be the best one for the problem. Ideally, decisions are made by those highest in the company, then passed from senior management down the hierarchy. This is the classic 'top-down' approach. In contrast, decision-making in Japanese companies may be described as more circular. Before the decision is taken, management attempts to gain an integrated view of the situation with as little friction as possible, to find a natural solution which fits harmoniously with the environment. The consequence of this holistic view is that everyone affected by the decision is involved in one way or another in the decision-making process and can impact on it (Grawehl, 1996, p. 12).

The logic of the Japanese approach to decision-making means that senior management on the upper hierarchies takes on a guiding function, which moves through all the hierarchy levels. This Japanese way may even be called a 'bottom-up' process (Alston, 1986, p. 181). Kobayashi stresses, on the other hand, a more precise term which he calls 'top-directed bottom-up decision-making', primarily to make clear that in Japanese companies, too, senior management bears responsibility for the decision, even though the way in which the decision is reached is structured differently from the practice in German companies (Kobayashi, 1988, p. 33).

The different periods of time it takes in Japanese and German companies to make a decision and then to implement it can also result in conflict (Hilpert and Taube, 1997, p. 107). German managers find the long-winded process whereby a certain problem is discussed with different Japanese employees, each time starting from the beginning, irritating and time-consuming. However, the benefits of the Japanese procedure become apparent when the decision is implemented. Once the decision has been taken in a consensus, it is implemented much more quickly than by the German partner. On the German side, management might have to break down resistance from employees not involved in the decision-making process or find ways to avoid it, whilst on the Japanese side, all those affected have expressed their agreement and willingness to implement. The problems that German management may have in getting cooperation of their employees in implementing a decision they have imposed irritates the Japanese management, leading them to doubt the managerial ability of the Germans. Corporate culture expressed in these two different ways of arriving at a decision come face to face in Japanese–German third-country collaboration.

The organizational form of the cooperative venture also determines to a large degree whether there is potential for conflict. Many joint sales, research, development or production ventures are limited by different degrees of collaboration, and the greatest potential for conflict is in the equity joint venture in which many joint decisions have to be taken. In contrast, sales collaborations have relatively few complex structures for joint decision-making so their basic organizational design carries less potential for conflict.

Conflict can also arise in technology transfer and technology protection. Primarily, conflict occurs here when one partner does not consent to the use of certain technology in the collaboration, or one partner has different views on the speed and method of technology transfer into the third-country cooperative venture. According to Hilpert and Taube (1997, p. 108), the greatest potential for conflict is in the differences of opinion about the area of application for which the technology brought into the third-country collaboration is to be made available. These real problems in technology transfer are associated with the question of technology protection, essentially the question of protecting a company's technology from imitation by unauthorized third parties or by the unintentional and unplanned transfer of technology to the partner in the third-country collaboration.

Problems can even occur in negotiations before the companies engage jointly in the third country, if for example the two managements do not see eye to eye on the amount and quality of the technology which the partners are to bring to the cooperative venture. Conflicts in this early phase are still relatively harmless, as at this point there has not been a real transfer of technology or know-how. However, participants should be aware that strains at this early stage might mean that the collaboration in the third country might not happen. The Japanese and German managements must take this option on board and allow it to be a possible part of negotiations or even a way out of them (Haak, 2002b, 2003).

However, it is much more problematic if difficulties arise once a venture is underway, for example when the competition situation in the third country changes or if there are changes to the market structure in the target country and it becomes a matter of urgency to provide more technology or management expertise for the collaboration. Both partners will have already contributed a great deal to the third-country collaboration which would be irretrievably lost if it were to be cancelled. This kind of technology conflict can result in either the German or the Japanese parent company making concessions regarding the continuing transfer of technology or management expertise, which it would not be prepared to make under normal circumstances (Haak, 2002b).

The joint willingness to work effectively together can be considerably lessened by frustrations encountered in running the joint venture. Different documentation (languages, technical details and so on) or the limited ability of employees to work together on a cross-cultural basis can lead to delays in technology transfer or even to errors in using technology, in extreme cases endangering the continuing work of the Japanese–German third-country collaboration (*ibid.*). To avoid such conflict it is necessary to unambiguously establish the purpose of anything brought into the third-party collaboration to reduce the danger of the partner passing on technology or knowledge for use outside of the collaboration or to third parties (suppliers, companies in the same network, and so on). These safeguards are important to ensure that technology and management expertise does not drain away to external companies, but it can place a great strain on the trust between partners if one partner is accused of intentional misdemeanour (Hilpert and Taube, 1997).

Personnel conflicts also put a strain on collaboration. The worst staff-related problems are caused by lack of qualifications and loyalty of employees delegated by the parent company, and managers often complain that third-country collaboration is perceived as a siding for their careers. This aspect should not be underestimated as it can have considerable impact on the motivation of management (Haak, 2001b, 2002b). Lack of loyalty and willingness to perform can also result if the third-country collaboration is undervalued in the overall strategic concept of the parent company. Maintaining permanent managerial motivation is a basic condition for the success of such ventures.

Conflict due to personnel policies must be taken seriously by the parent companies; indeed it should not be allowed to arise at all. Permanent communication between managers involved in developing the third-party collaboration is important in ensuring timely notification of any potential danger at personnel level. The significance of the third-country collaboration in the overall strategic concept must be communicated to employees, and management in the joint venture must be shown that they have a career in the future in the parent company. If such cross-cultural engagement is seen to be particularly valuable for future careers in the parent companies or in 100 per cent subsidiaries it would not be a problem to find good staff (Haak, 2002b).

Another area of conflict not to be taken lightly concerns different rates of pay for Japanese and German managers in the collaboration. Different salary structures are especially problematic when the Japanese and German managers as delegates perceive a similar work structure in the collaboration, but receive different payment. Such difference in treatment might lead to conflict. However, Hilpert and Taube also note that in their empirical studies they found examples where there were no conflicts in some third-country collaborations where Japanese managers earned much less than their German colleagues (Hilpert and Taube, 1997, p. 110). Nevertheless, management must always keep in sight the danger that different salary structures for Japanese and German managers with comparable qualifications and duties can cause a strained working atmosphere resulting in serious tension between employees. This goes hand-in-hand with the problem of loss of motivation which can go as far as a refusal to work (Deutsch–Japanischer Wirtschaftskreis, 1997).

Another breeding ground for conflict in Japanese–German third-country collaboration is the form of selling, traditionally very different for each side. German companies are said to practice 'hard selling', which manifests itself in aggressive marketing and sales strategies, whereas the sales methods of Japanese companies are characterized as 'soft selling' with customer orientation at the centre. Japanese companies are not less aggressive towards their potential customers, but they proceed much more subtly than German companies in order to build up long-term customer loyalty (Hilpert and Taube, 1997, p. 111). Japanese companies try to create personal and above all trust-based relationships between the company and the potential customer (see also Bradach and Eccles, 1989). Only when this foundation has been laid will they make the customer aware of the superior benefits of the product they are trying to sell. Tailoring the product or the production process to the specific ideas and preferences of the customer is taken for granted as a service (Haak, 2001a,b, 2002b). For the German partner the sales process can't be fast enough, whilst the Japanese partner sees the German approach as too abrupt, risking the loss of the customer. Managements must be aware of these differences in the ways customers are approached and develop suitable strategies together to prevent conflict in this area.

Pricing policy might also generate conflict between the partners, as in Japan the prices for consumer and investment goods are not changed after they have been agreed with the negotiation partner for the whole package (Hilpert and Taube, 1997, p. 111). German companies find this procedure incomprehensible; in German pricing and product policy extras are added to bill separately.

Problems can also appear when one of the two partners seems to be investing a disproportionate amount of time in sales. Frequently in Asia, the Japanese side has better knowledge of the local markets and sales structures. Consequently, at first glance it seems sensible to the German management to use this Japanese strength in the third-country collaboration, but it must be aware that in the mid-term it can become very dependent on the Japanese side. If the collaborative venture is dissolved, the German partner will have none of its own customers and might possibly have done too little to become known, making it difficult to engage in the market alone.

Elements of success

As already seen, a Japanese–German third-country collaboration can only function successfully in the target country when the objectives of the parent companies for the joint venture are compatible. For both the Japanese and the German parent companies it is of utmost importance that the goals of the collaboration are clearly defined in their significance and order of importance. Insufficient precision in defining goals and their ranking can lead to conflict later (Haak, 2002b). Therefore, in the preparatory phase of the collaboration the managers responsible from each parent company should discuss the goals comprehensively; open communication is important for successful collaboration (*Asia Bridge*, 1996). Discussion of how goals are to be realized should also be as open as possible. The outcome of these discussions must clarify the shared or divergent positions, so that a decision about further joint involvement can be taken. After the cooperative venture has started up, the partners should continue their dialogue so that they can agree new objectives as they are modified over time.

A fundamental readiness on the part of Japanese and German management openly to discuss any imminent conflict regarding goals and to find a solution together represents an important factor for the success of the collaboration. However, real-life business shows that these discussions will never be completely candid; managers frequently pursue opportunistic goals, do not present all the facts and withhold information. Particularly in critical phases of the collaboration, this tendency increases which can then seriously endanger its success (Haak, 2002b).

Frank discussion on a personal level between German and Japanese management might well fail at exactly the point where it is urgently needed. There is no patent recipe for dealing with these problems, but it should be the job of both managements to observe their partner company and its environment carefully to gather information on whether decision parameters for the partner have changed. Observations must focus on the development of the partner's home market, but important decisions regarding personnel in the parent company must also be integrated permanently into the analysis. Market share, acquisitions, purchasing new technology, or a reorientation of the parent company's strategy are all important aspects to note when observing a partner (Deutsch–Japanischer Wirtschaftskreis, 1997).

Frequently, joint undertakings are founded without having carried out a detailed analysis of the partner company in advance. Lack of time, staff or finance are often given as reasons. However, even if there has been a business relationship with the potential partner for years, an exact analysis is indispensable. In the long term, the collaboration only makes sense when the resources each partner brings to the venture complement each other, enabling improved competitive positioning. Consequently, it should be ascertained that the companies' goals are compatible and there should be an investigation of the available resources and their complementarity. Hilpert and Taube suggest the following four-stage process:

1 Inventory of resources needed to achieve the goals of the collaborative venture;
2 Inventory of the resources available in own company;
3 List of resources required from partner(s) to fill the gap between inventory and requirement;
4 Gather information about resources held by potential collaboration partners and compare with requirement profile (Hilpert and Taube, 1997, p. 116).

The authors note that this process should not only take place at the planning stage of Japanese–German third-country collaborations, but also at regular intervals after it has started. With this procedure it is possible to establish whether costs were shared when the resources were deployed, and whether there is a need for German and Japanese management to act accordingly. They should examine, for example, whether there is a danger that the partner will break away or whether buying a company or including another partner in the collaboration will enable any resource deficits to be redressed in order to improve the competitive position of the cooperative venture. If an analysis of the resources used concludes that the partnership will not achieve its planned performance, then decisions must be made immediately in order not to jeopardize the venture's ability to survive. If the deficit in resources or skills is insignificant and can be met internally, or if the partner can be obliged through concessions or sanctions to provide the resources hitherto withheld, it might be possible to continue. If the deficits cannot be made up, then there is no basis for business between the Japanese and German partners (Haak, 2002b).

However, the analysis should not be directed exclusively at the partner company. The resources that a company is prepared to make available should also be reviewed at regular intervals to ensure the success of the venture. An analysis of the company's own strengths and weaknesses is imperative, and the only way to ensure that long-term commitment to the collaboration will be successful. It must also be made clear to the management that only the constant creation of knowledge, products and procedures will make the company more attractive and thus keep the partner motivated to continue.

Trust

What is the role of trust in handling conflict in Japanese–German third-country collaboration? Unlike conflict, trust is almost always associated with economically desirable consequences, which show up in more open communications, simpler coordination, lower transaction costs, additional opportunities to act, more effective learning processes and stable interpersonal and interorganizational relationships (see also Albach, 1980). Trust at organizational level can generate competitive advantage. For virtual organizations, trust is indispensable as a basis, although here it is particularly difficult to engender. It appears, overall, to be economically impossible to transact many payments or services without a minimum of trust. Trust is particularly relevant for complex deliverables which can only be produced with difficulty or perhaps not at all without complete cooperation of all those involved (customer, partner in the group of companies, or work partner).

Japanese–German joint ventures in Asia can only succeed if there is interplay between contracts and trust. This is not a static value, but a dynamic process under the influence of both the different histories and cultures of the partners and the changing conditions. Without a minimum of mutual trust, on an institutional or a personal basis, a Japanese–German joint venture in Asia will become dysfunctional very quickly.

On the other hand, Japanese and German collaboration also needs contractually fixed parameters to guide the venture to success through its different phases. These elements are intended to prevent opportunistic behaviour on the part of one or other partner. The rules, formulated jointly, set down the ways to solve differences of opinion (Beechler and Stucker, 1998; Beechler and Bird, 1999; Campell and Burton, 1994).

Contracts and trust can be seen as the central mainstay of a Japanese–German third-country collaboration. However, there is a difference, which should not be underestimated, in the ways that German and Japanese management weigh these two important aspects for the success of such a venture. German managers consider contracts more important than Japanese managers. From the German point of view, contracts should be as detailed and comprehensive as possible, and personal relationships based on trust are ranked as much less significant.

In contrast, personal relationships and the existence of mutual trust are of supreme importance for Japanese management. The contractual relationship is seen as the manifestation of trust between the German and Japanese partners and does not form the actual basis of the alliance. Japanese managers do not consider the contractual rendering of the relationship between the partners dogmatic. In their view, it is perfectly possible for them to renegotiate it in the course of the alliance and adapting the internal and external conditions as required presents no problems. These different points of view and patterns of behaviour present problems when the contracts governing the alliance are designed and drawn up. Different demands are made on the amount of detail in the contracts and there is also a discrepancy in the willingness to draw up flexible contracts (Haak, 2002b).

The distribution of the rights to take decisions and control over the companies involved is closely tied to the question of how much weight should be accorded to trust and to the wording of contracts. There is a risk that one of the partners will dominate the partnership and take decisions over the heads of the other. Whereas too great a concentration on the decision-making power can lead to a partner's rights being removed, there is also the danger that if control is too evenly distributed, work will be obstructed and possibly completely stifled (Haak, 2003; Hilpert and Taube, 1997).

Communication problems represent another level of means-related conflict. The organization and the structure of the communication process in Japanese–German third-country collaborations determines whether and how quickly the decision-makers can supply the employees carrying out the project with the relevant information. Breakdowns in communication can prove to be serious problems for third-country collaborations. Reasons for the breakdown might be that too little time was planned for dialogue with the partner, or even that the wrong group of people is taking part in the briefings.

The different languages and socio-cultural characters of the employees represent the central problem for Japanese–German third-country collaboration, and it is misleading to believe that the language barriers can be easily overcome with the use of English and the employment of interpreters. Japanese is a context-dependent language – meaning and sense can only be derived from the surrounding context. Even if both managements speak English, there is still a difference in communicative behaviour (Haak, 2002b, 2001b, 2003; Abegglen and Stalk, 1985). Japanese and German managers interpret the verbal messages of their partners according to the context of behaviour and values that they are familiar with. Under certain circumstances this can mean that verbal signals are misinterpreted and that non-verbal signals are not even noticed. This sociocultural conditionality of communication is a serious problem which can become even more critical when a three-sided alliance requires communication with a third-country management. Lack of knowledge of the partner's sociocultural background can lead to misunderstandings which delay or obstruct the daily routine of business in such collaborations. This can also delay the trust-building process, when for example traditional customs are not observed when invitations are issued or gifts exchanged (Hilpert and Taube, 1997).

In the past, trust has only been investigated on an interpersonal level, and has remained in the domain of psychoanalysis and social psychology. However, trust is conceptualized in many different ways. Sociologists such as Luhmann and Giddens try to associate the rational with the emotional, the cognitive with the affective, the descriptive with the normative in a systematic conception of trust. It is often assumed that a relationship based on trust can develop into a stronger personal emotional-normative secure relationship, but one should not lose sight of the fact that the person exhibiting the trust is always taking a certain risk. Trust always implies an advance payment with risk made in the expectation of later returns. Managements in Japanese–German third-country collaborations must be aware of this in order to establish a basis of trust in regular, mutual exchange of resources and information that is sufficiently resilient to take on the challenges of competition in the third country in Asia (Haak, 2003).

One of the crucial factors for the success of Japanese–German collaborations is the foundation of trust based on personal relationships between the key decision-makers in the cooperating companies. It is possible that a well-developed relationship based on trust could replace a contract completely, but even this should be backed up with a more or less detailed contract between Japanese and German management. In the early stages and again later on, contracts are particularly important, and in this context it is possible to distinguish between four key phases in the life-cycle development of a third-country collaboration: the early phase, the development phase, the mature phase and the decline.

During the early phase a clearly defined basis of trust has often not yet been established between the partners unless they are starting out with positive experience from collaborating on another project. Often the future partners do not yet know each other well, neither has any information about the other and about how they might react in conflict situations, for example. Knowing little about the partner and the imponderables of the economic success of the joint venture increase the uncertainty between partners in the early stages of the collaboration. A strong desire to secure the company's interests in a contract is felt under these circumstances, and, therefore in the early phase of the venture the contract is frequently accorded more weight than personal trust. However, particularly in these early stages, it is important to apply trust-building measures in order to get over the start phase of the collaboration as quickly as possible. These include, for example, arranging company events together, visiting parent companies, decision-makers attending company celebrations or the launching of new operations by the parent companies, and personal invitations at general manager and senior-management level to promote understanding in private conversation outside the work environment.

As collaboration progresses, personal trust between the decision-makers grows and the requirement for contractual regulation of business relations lessens considerably. Corporate relations have been established and are based essentially on trust between the collaboration partners. In this second phase, which I would like to refer to as the development phase, the partners are bound by the knowledge that the benefit in continuing the third-country collaboration exceeds the short-term gain that opportunistic violation of the trust would bring.

In the third phase, the mature phase of the third-country collaboration, there can be a growing interest in a contractual basis or in contractual safeguards if trust was breached during the months or years of the collaboration, for example by discontinuity at senior-management level in the parent companies. It can also happen that changed framework conditions in the target country, or in Japan or Germany, make the economic benefit of continuing the collaboration uncertain for one or more of the partners. In the fourth phase, contractual safeguards again carry more weight, as one or possibly both partners do not see the economic advantage of continuing to collaborate; the break-up of the collaboration might be imminent. The causes might lie in a loss of trust between the decision-makers of the joint project, but also in a strategic reorientation in the parent company, possibly in the course of modifications to national and international framework conditions.

Understanding the different weightings given to trust and contracts in the course of the collaboration allows both sides to meet the wishes of their partner. Conflicts can be avoided, or at least can be more easily dealt with. Cooperative relationships based on trust create space for the active use of management capacity to improve the competition and profit situation as the management is relieved of the need constantly to monitor the state of the venture (Haak, 2001b). Another point to note about the special role of trust between the partner managers is that it is a dynamic process. The constant process of evaluating internal and external data must not stop, as changes might occur. Phases 3 and 4 of the life-cycle, for example, might require stronger contractual cover. Finding the right balance between trust and contract requires trust-building measures that are specific to each situation, and a precise and detailed contract (Haak, 2002b).

How can trust be built up between the Japanese and the German managements? Is there an ideal way to plan strategically and implement in order to use trust to improve the competitive situation and increase profits? First of all, trust between Japanese and German management working in a third country does not appear *ad hoc*, it grows gradually over a period of time. It must be worked on again and again by both sides in the collaboration. Which measures promise most in building up a solid basis of trust in Japanese–German third-country collaborations? One of the most important starting points for establishing a solid basis of trust is the willingness of the partners to respond flexibly to the requirements and wishes of the other. Relaying a feeling of mutual personal appreciation is also a key component in building trust in the collaboration. For example, taking part in the religious ceremonies associated with the opening of new factories in Japan is a good opportunity to show how much a partner is esteemed. Ties can also be strengthened by inviting the partner to company events or celebrations. It should also be noted that there are very specific 'trust-building rituals' (Hilpert and Taube, 1997, p. 122) which can be deployed consciously as part of the mutual familiarization process to strengthen the basis of trust. Hilpert and Taube mention the raising of national and/or company flags for visits to the company, for example, but the basis of trust can also be reinforced by carrying out negotiations at locations with a very symbolic character or by visiting them together.

If the Japanese and German partners exchange gifts, it is important to note that estimation of the partner company by the Japanese side is reflected in the material value of the gift. Spending leisure time (for example golf, tennis, sailing and so on) or sightseeing together on visits to Japan, Germany or the third country also offer good opportunities to get to know the partner and their likes and dislikes better. Undertaking activities together before or after negotiations presents a good opportunity to convey one's own cultural background and the specific ways of thinking to one's partner. Whether, when the collaboration is more advanced and trust has been built up, integrating the partner into more out-of-work activities should be considered (invitations to a meal, visits together to a concert and so on) depends on the personalities of the management. Please note here, however, that out-of-work activities are not necessarily beneficial to the continued functioning of the collaboration as decisions taken by management at company level are deferred or not made at all due to personal relations and perceived moral obligations. This can, for example, play an important role when assessing managerial performance, the objectivity of which can be affected by personal preferences of the superior (Haak, 2002b, 2003).

The design of the contract is the second central mainstay of successful Japanese–German collaboration, and here it is important to maintain a balance between the needs of the partners. Whereas the German side requires more detailed formulation, the Japanese partner works more towards the creation of free space allowing the cooperative venture to be structured flexibly. Items included when a collaboration contract is drawn up are (Ernst *et al.*, 1992; Hilpert and Taube, 1997):

1. Specification of the cash, technology, equipment, real estate and so on that the partners are to contribute to the collaboration;
2. Appointments at managerial level of the collaboration;
3. Specification of the distribution of profits and loss in the collaboration;
4. Specification of the company language(s), working language and language used in the company documentation;
5. Leeway to act and limits to individual decision-making powers for management on both the Japanese and German sides and for both parent companies;
6. Technology protection clauses;

7. Specification of the duration of the collaboration;
8. Specification of the forms of conflict management in the collaboration;
9. Commitment to rights to give notice and notice periods;
10. Regulation of arrangements for the winding up of the collaboration;
11. Regulation of arrangements for transferring staff between the parent companies and the collaboration; and
12. Regulation of the organizational structure of collaboration and specification of the key features of personnel policy.

Human-resource management

Smooth communication between employees in the collaboration and also between the cooperative venture and the parent company is one of the factors contributing to the success of the venture. Breakdowns in communication have general causes and may also be due to specific socio-cultural factors. There are many reasons for problems in the flow of communication which cannot all be discussed in detail here.

German and Japanese management should concentrate on two options when they find that the communication process is not running satisfactorily. The origin of the problem might merely be that too little information is exchanged, and the reason for this might be that not enough time is allocated for dialogue with the partner (Ernst, 1999). It can also happen that the wrong group of people is taking part in certain discussions within the company and between the collaborating companies (Cascio and Serapio, 1991). However, it is also possible that one partner is intentionally withholding information so that the communication process becomes imprecise and inadequate. It is therefore imperative for successful communication that partners budget time for regular discussion and that the communication process takes place at the right company levels. Regular discussion costs time and money but this should not be accepted as the reason why these consultations do not take place; only continuous exchange of opinions at various company levels and between the collaborating companies will reveal problems and enable solutions to be agreed (Haak, 2002b).

Inefficient exchange of information can also be due to sociocultural misunderstandings between the German and Japanese managements, which might also be of a very basic linguistic nature. The communication paths may not function smoothly, and company-specific analysis must be used to deal with these problem areas, with the motivation to examine and improve the processes and structures of communication coming from senior management level.

Companies can use short or long-term strategies to deal with linguistic or socio-cultural misunderstandings. A simple, yet very effective response to this kind of problem which can be used in regular discussions and negotiations is the 'double-question' method. In order to be sure that the partner has understood the speaker's intention, the subject being dealt with should be introduced into the conversation twice. Using different formulations and questions, the subject is highlighted from different sides, allowing positions and opinions to be aired more clearly and to avoid misunderstandings at an early stage in the proceedings.

Improving language skills and step-by-step learning of the socio-cultural particularities of the collaboration partner should be long-term strategies for management in third-country collaborations. As one of the first steps, German management can make the partnership with the Japanese company the subject of a company meeting and inform employees of the third-country collaboration. Including the Japanese partner in the company brochure or on the company's home page would also be useful to circulate information about this form of collaboration more quickly. Employees should also be encouraged to show initiative particularly if they wish to learn the language. On a larger scale, it might be possible to outline the socio-cultural conditions in seminars (Hilpert and Taube, 1997).

In both business practice and in management theory there is frequently controversial discussion of an instrument to improve the communication process between Japanese and German partners in a collaboration: the 'cross-cultural seminar'. The idea behind this is that the personnel of a collaboration partner with whom a company works closely, regularly take part together in seminars about cross-cultural management. The intention is that the employees from the different corporate cultures and countries get to know each other better and, at the same time and under expert guidance, contribute to overcoming cultural barriers. However, it must be remembered that these seminars represent an additional load on the selected employees' time who have to continue to do their jobs in the parent company or the collaborative venture. There is also considerable danger that the 'expert guidance' which of necessity can be allowed only a short time, a few days at best, will offer more stereotypes about the country and style of management than is really the case.

There is another way which seems more promising: longer-term secondment of employees to take on duties in the partner company, improving communication and hence the exchange of information. The practice of secondment gives individual employees the opportunity to acquire a deeper understanding of the ways in which managers in the partner company think and behave. When such personnel return to their parent company, mutual understanding and experience of the decision-making process and cultural background in the partner company will enhance communication. However, Japanese and German companies have specific corporate cultures so that transferring experiences of work and ways of life in the secondment programme to other business collaborations might not necessarily provide the same benefit.

Improving the communication process is not the only factor that plays a crucial part in the success of Japanese–German third-country collaboration. Strategic personnel policy also has a positive long-term impact on the competitiveness of the company. Frequently, the reason for lack of loyalty and willingness on the part of staff working in such ventures is that senior management from the parent companies has not expressed its commitment to the project sufficiently strongly. It is the responsibility of management in the parent companies to make clear to employees that are going to work for the third-country collaboration that the project is very important. Delegation to the project should not be seen as banishment; employees should consider it a career opportunity and it should also be treated as such by the parent company. The delegated employees must not have the feeling that they have been forgotten or cut off from other career paths within the parent company (Haak, 2001b, 2002b).

Above-average pay and guarantees of relative autonomy represent effective motivation for working in collaborations in third countries. If the management in the parent company finds that employees are not showing commitment to joint projects, then it must find the reasons as quickly as possible. It might be due to inadequate communication between the employees in the collaboration and/or the management and the parent company. It might also be because the collaboration is not sufficiently highly valued. It must be established early on whether the collaboration partner can and is prepared to make qualified, motivated employees available to the joint venture. According to Hilpert and Taube (1997), in pursuing the goal of reinforcing a sense of communication and identification with the third-country joint venture, the collaboration partners should harmonize their personnel policies to avoid German and Japanese employees being paid differently for the same work in the collaboration.

Organizational structure

Different decision-making and organizational structures meet in Japanese–German third-country collaborations. Such differences in corporate culture may be beneficial in formulating joint responses to specific market challenges, but if the Japanese and German decision-making and organizational structures obstruct each other the result may be a loss of competitive position. This means that for such collaborations, a decision-making and organizational structure must be created that does justice to the demands of the market and the competition (Deutsch– Japanischer Wirtschaftskreis, 1997; Hilpert and Taube, 1997). Ways must be found that allow the partner companies to cooperate efficiently, with the extent to which decision-making and organizational structures should be harmonized being decided for each venture separately. It might not be worth the effort of introducing new forms of decision-making and a new structure specially for the third-country collaboration. It could make sense to transfer the German model, or to use the Japanese decision-making and organizational structures. The efficiency of the organizational structure will become apparent as the business develops in the third-country, and adaptation and modification may then be appropriate if they improve the competitive position of the venture.

The way in which the sales strategy is organized in the target country is one of the success-critical factors in Japanese–German involvement in a third country. It is fundamental that the sales strategy and the price and product policy are tailored to the target customer base, the target group in the third country. If Japanese-oriented customers dominate in a third country, then soft selling should be preferred to hard selling. Pricing should also follow the existing patterns so as not to irritate the target group. However, if the customers are Western or Western-oriented, then the marketing strategies used in the same sector in Germany can be used, modified as appropriate for the specific target group.

The organizational form of the marketing structures must be realized on the borderline between two important aspects. On the one hand, it is important to adapt sales and marketing procedures to the situation in the third country or to the markets that are supplied from the third country. The result of this is that responsibility for sales is then in the hands of the partner who is most familiar with those markets and who might well have many years of experience in them. Over the years, this partner will have trained staff who are now also available for the new work. The partner's investment in the human-resource factor would then be profitable for the other partner. On the other hand, it must be avoided that one of the two partners dominates in sales so that a position of power is built up in the collaboration which forces the other, less-strong partner to become dependent in issues of local target-oriented sales.

How should this dilemma be dealt with? Although the responsibility for sales is clearly with the collaborative venture, depending on conditions in the target market it could be arranged that both companies meet the customer together. If there are third-country collaborative ventures in several countries, it might be preferable to split the responsibility for sales, depending on the markets. This would allow each of the partners to dominate in a regional market, avoiding one-sided dependency relationships. Senior management in the Japanese and German parent companies might decide that sales are no longer a matter for collaboration, and that the joint activities will be limited to production and product development.

One factor that affects success is the legal form of the collaboration partners. Family-run enterprises are much more flexible in the organizational form of their relations to collaboration partners than joint-stock companies, for example, which are subject to many regulations to protect their shareholders. The greater room for manoeuvre enjoyed by management of family companies allows them to shake off contract restraints and enter into trust-based, flexible and pragmatic relationships with business partners. Small and medium-sized enterprises which are frequently run as family companies have in this case a better starting position than joint-stock companies.

Technology protection

Areas of conflict between partners in technology transfer and technology protection place a serious strain on a partnership in a third country. Overcoming these conflicts must start with a survey of the home company in order to find where its core competence lies. Management must establish at which stage or stages of the value-adding process in the company important knowledge that particularly needs protecting is located. After this analysis has been carried out, management must establish which technological know-how and which knowledge must be specifically protected when brought into the third-country collaboration (Haak, 2002b, 2003).

Management must think carefully about how far it wants to go and define clear boundaries which determine when it would be preferable to break off the collaboration rather than lose core competence. Losing sensitive knowledge can place a strain on the competitive position of the parent company in the mid or long term, and even taking into account the costs of breaking off the collaboration this must be the way forward if it becomes clear that the third-country collaboration will cause important technological core competence to be lost.

When technology transfer is negotiated it is important to be as open as possible about which technological components will be contributed to the collaboration and which will not be available. It should also be established as early as possible how much new technology will be made available to the collaboration and what is to happen with technological improvements or innovations acquired during the collaboration. In any case, the technology should be protected with appropriate contractual arrangements in the early phase of the venture.

What applies to other business collaborations is also valid for Japanese–German cooperative ventures in a third country: finding the exact balance between contractual regulation of technology transfer, technology protection and a collaboration based on trust is one of the most difficult tasks facing international management. If both partners place excessive value on safeguarding their technological potential, the learning effects and the complementary interaction of operational strengths that are hoped for from a collaboration might remain elusive. There is then doubt whether there is any point in a joint venture in the third country. The key task of strategic international senior management in the Japanese and German parent companies is to recognize whether and when technological collaboration can be intensified to the benefit of both sides and to provide additional technological investment (Hilpert and Taube, 1997, p. 129).

Conflicts that can arise in technology transfer are usually due to inadequate communication between the Japanese and German partners. Technical manuals about products and processing technology are mostly only available in one language. Translations take time, which is frequently not available, so a lack of language skills on both sides can cause problems when new products or processes are transferred and implemented. Improving communication represents a solution which should be embedded in conveying all the necessary socio-cultural aspects to make technology transfer a success. When the staff responsible for technology transfer and for overseeing the implementation of new technology for the cooperative venture is selected, managers should look for social and cross-cultural skills as well as technical expertise.

In the organization of technology transfer, there is a differentiation between embedded and mobile knowledge (Granrath, 1994), and depending on the level on which the transferring knowledge is located, quite specific protection mechanisms can be developed by the company. For more information about technology protection in German–Japanese collaboration in Japan and in Asia see Ernst *et al.* (1992) and Hilpert *et al.* (1997).

9
Conclusion

Many cases of Japanese–German third-country collaboration have proved successful. By combining complementary strengths, and not least due to cost and risk-sharing, competitiveness on foreign markets can be improved. This organizational form of collective internationalization does indeed make economic sense. Faster access to the difficult markets in East and Southeast Asia is one of the most important benefits of joint international ventures. New market shares can be gained and the competitive position of the third-country collaboration and also that of the parent companies can be much improved.

These positive aspects, which can be seen as opportunities, are countered by the not inconsiderable risks of joint ventures in third countries. For example, if the objectives of the Japanese and the German managements are incompatible, then the collaboration is doomed to failure. Furthermore, conflicts can emerge at different levels of the cooperative venture which affect its competitiveness or cause it to fail completely. Conflicts in operation can result from differences in the corporate cultures, different concepts of marketing strategies, or in technology transfer and protection. Conflicts amongst personnel or conflicts due to inadequate communication can place a great strain on the ability of the whole joint venture to function. Personnel-related conflict in particular should be taken very seriously by managements in the Japanese and German parent companies, as the motivation of management seconded abroad is one of the crucial factors for the success of third-country cooperative ventures. Such management should be chosen very carefully on both the Japanese and the German sides.

As joint ventures in third countries can fail, it is advisable that both the Japanese and German sides scrutinize a potential collaboration carefully. Basic scepticism about joint Japanese–German projects in third countries is, however, not appropriate as this form of collective internationalization can make economic sense.

Third-country collaborative ventures in those sectors on which globalization has had a particularly noticeable effect are a promising way to realize collective internationalization strategies in East and Southeast Asia. In the automobile manufacturing and supply sectors, in pharmaceuticals and chemistry, electrotechnology and electronics, telecommunications and environmental technology the proportion of total costs spent on research and development and marketing have increased continuously. Companies are directing their efforts towards building up their core competences and are trying to cover other, in their view less important, areas of value-added with partnerships. Japanese and German companies affected by globalization must therefore look for business solutions which optimize their international activities with their own limited operational resources in the course of concentrating their activities on their core competences. The collective internationalization strategy, whether in the form of a strategic alliance, a strategic interfirm network or as documented here in the form of a Japanese–German third-country collaboration offers a meaningful form for internationalization and for achieving comprehensive advances in learning.

The trend towards collective internationalization strategies has also grown in recent years in the infrastructure sector. Japanese and German companies in energy technology, telecommunications, logistics and construction are looking for global partners to combine business strengths and also to share the costs and risks of international involvement. In the search for an appropriate partner company, the determining criteria are primarily technological expertise, financial power, project and country-related experience and marketing skills. Irrespective of whether the object of the joint venture is a large project or to open up a market in third country, in both cases the target is to work in a regional market where both business partners complement each other and where, ideally, no conflicts occur. If conflicts do arise, appropriate conflict management on both the Japanese and German sides must harness the positive effects to benefit the further development of the collective strategy.

Adept and experienced Japanese and German management is able to work successfully in foreign markets at reduced costs and risk with the organizational form of third-country collaborations as part of implementing their collective internationalization strategies. Third-country collaboration can be positively evaluated from both the German and the Japanese points of view. To make such a venture successful requires consideration of a series of crucial aspects. Frank and open consultation on targets between the managers responsible on both sides is extremely important, and the management of the collaboration makes many demands of managerial capabilities, skills and knowledge. Social and intercultural skills are required in local management to guide third-country collaborations in East and Southeast Asian target markets to success. Knowledge alone is not sufficient to operate the company in the third country. Companies who are successful in finding managers with these skills and who bring great commitment to the leadership of the third-country collaboration to meet the many challenges can achieve an important headstart in international competition.

In principle, then, it is to be expected that the collective internationalization strategy will become more important for German and Japanese companies working in foreign markets. What are the consequences, in concrete terms? It is certain that it will become increasingly important for German and Japanese management to build up their own collaboration expertise and to present themselves to the outside world as solid and reliable partners in whom one can invest a great deal of trust. Collaboration expertise increases as a company concentrates more on its core competence and therefore relies on partner companies to provide the necessary value-added processes both in national and international environments. It is crucial, then, that new collective internationalization strategies are only agreed with companies that enjoy good reputations. Companies that acquire a reputation of pursuing largely exploitative or opportunistic goals will be avoided in collective internationalization strategies.

In view of these developments it can be assumed that in the course of advancing internationalization of both the Japanese and German economies, third-country collaboration will continue to expand in the future. Many managers are already complaining about the high degree of complexity of their business relations, which with increasing international presence will continue to grow. As the number of collaboration partners grows, together with the number of ways in which collective internationalization strategies are implemented, managing these co-operative relationships requires more and more company resources. Third-country collaboration offers the opportunity of reducing complexity for international management and strengthening internationalization of a company. The crucial advantage of Japanese–German third-country collaboration is the chance to enter into a joint venture with just one partner but in many different countries. Third-country collaboration can thus reduce complexity for collaboration management by limiting the internationalization of the business activity and contribute to reducing the load on international management.

Reducing the consumption of resources for cooperating management creates new potential for the international management of German and Japanese companies which can be used to improve their competitive positions. Under the conditions of globalization, third-country collaboration as a form of implementing a collective internationalization strategy presents a promising way to improve a company's position in international competition. Of all the regions in the world, the potential for a combination of Japanese and German strengths in a third-country collaboration is greatest in East and Southeast Asia, especially in mainland China. Accordingly, this economic region will remain in the future the focus of such collaborations. It is incumbent on international management of German and Japanese companies to tap the full potential of this approach purposefully with creative solutions for internationalization to improve the companies' competitive positions. Third-country collaboration offers this opportunity in an organizational form that should not be underestimated.

Bibliography

Abegglen, J. C. and G. Stalk (1985) *Kaisha: The Japanese Corporation*. New York: Basic Books.

Abo, T. (1989) 'The Emergence of Japanese Multinational Enterprise and the Theory of Foreign Direct Investment', in K. Shibagaki, M. Trevor and T. Abo (eds), *Japanese and European Management*. Tokyo: University of Tokyo Press, pp. 3–17.

Abrahamson, E. (1996) 'Management Fashion', *Academy of Management Review* 21, pp. 254–85.

Adler, N. J. and F. Ghadar (1990) 'Strategic Human Resource Management: A Global Perspective', in R. Pieper (ed.), *Human Resource Management: An International Comparison*. Berlin and New York: de Gruyter, pp. 235–60.

Adler, P. S. (1988) 'Managing Flexible Automation', *California Management Review* 30 (3), pp. 34–56.

Albach, H. (1980) 'Vertrauen in der ökonomischen Theorie', *Zeitschrift für die gesamte Staatswissenschaft* 136 (1), pp. 2–11.

Albach, H. (1981) 'Die internationale Unternehmung als Gegenstand betriebswirtschaftlicher Forschung', *Zeitschrift für Betriebswirtschaft* 51, Ergänzungsheft nr. 1, pp. 13–24.

Albach, H. (1992) 'Strategische Allianzen, strategische Gruppen und strategische Familien', *Zeitschrift für Betriebswirtschaft* 62 (6), pp. 663–70.

Albrecht, F. (1993) *Strategisches Management der Unternehmensressource Wissen*. Frankfurt am Main: Lang.

Alchian, A. A. and S. Woodward (1988) 'The Firm is Dead, Long Live the Firm: A Review of Oliver E. Williamson's "The Economic Institutions of Capitalism"', *Journal of Economic Literature* (March), pp. 65–79.

Aldrich, H. E. (1979) *Organizations and Environments*. Englewood Cliffs, New Jersey: Prentice-Hall.

Aldrich, H. E. and D. A. Whetten (1981) 'Organization-sets, Action-sets and Networks: Making the Most of Simplicity', in P. C. Nystrom and W. H. Starbuck (eds), *Handbook of Organizational Design*, vol. 1. Oxford: Oxford University Press, pp. 385–408.

Allaire, Y. and M. E. Firsirotu (1984) 'Theories of Organizational Culture', *Organization Studies*, pp. 193–226.

Alston, J. P. (1986) *The American Samurai*. Berlin and New York: de Gruyter.

Altmann, N. and D. Sauer (eds) (1989) *Systemische Rationalisierung und Zulieferindustrie*. Frankfurt and New York: Campus-Verlag.

Anderson, J. C. and J. A. Narus (1990) 'A Model of Distributor Firm and Manufacturer Firm Working Partnerships', *Journal of Marketing* (January), pp. 42–58.

Anderson, J. C. and J. A. Narus (1991) 'Partnering as a Focused Market Strategy', *California Management Review* (Spring), pp. 95–113.

Anderson, O. (1993) 'On the Internationalization Process of Firms: A Critical Analysis', *Journal of International Business Studies* 24 (2), pp. 209–31.

Anderson, O. (1997) 'Internationalization and Market Entry Mode: A Review of Theories and Conceptual Frameworks', *Management International Review Studies* 37 (special issue 2), pp. 27–42.

Andrews, K. R. (1980) *The Concept of Corporate Strategy*. Homewood, Illinois: R. D. Irwin.

Argyris, C. (1980) *The Inner Contradictions of Rigorous Research*. New York: Academic Press.

Argyris, C. (1982) *Reasoning, Learning and Action. Individual and Organizational*. San Francisco: Jossey-Bass.

Argyris, C. (1990) *Overcoming Organizational Defenses. Facilitating organizational learning*. Boston, London and Sydney: Allyn & Bacon.

Argyris, C. and D. A. Schön (1978) *Organizational Learning. A Theory of Action Perspective*. Reading, Massachusetts: Addison-Wesley.

Argyris, C. and D. A. Schön (1999) *Die lernende Organisation*. Stuttgart: Klett-Cotta.

Arndt, H. and S. Pflüger (1995) 'Das Grünbuch der Kommission. Ein Meilenstein auf dem Weg zur europäischen Währungsunion?' *Wirtschaftsdienst* 95 (7), pp. 371–5.

Asanuma, B. (1989) 'Manufacturer–supplier relationships in Japan and the concept of relation-specific skills', *Journal of the Japanese and International Economies* (3), pp. 1–30.

Ashby, W. R. (1968) 'Principles of the self organizing system', in W. Buckley (ed.), *Modern Systems Research for the Behavioral Scientist*. Chicago: Aldine Publishing Co.

Asia Bridge (ed.) (1996) 'Japan, Deutschland. Nippons Deutschland Initiative. Was bringen strategische Allianzen mit japanischen Partnern in Asien?' *Asia Bridge*, 10 July, pp. 14–15.

Astley, W. G. (1984) 'Toward an appreciation of collective strategy', *Academy of Management Review* 9 (3), pp. 526–35.

Auster, E. R. (1987) 'International corporate linkages: Dynamic forms in changing environments', *Columbia Journal of World Business* (Summer), pp. 3–6.

Axelrod, R. (1991) *Die Evolution der Kooperation*. Munich: Oldenbourg.

Bach, N. and C. Homp (1998) 'Objekte und Instrumente des Wissensmanagements', *Zeitschrift für Organisation und Führung* 67 (3), pp. 139–46.

Bach, V., H. Österle and P. Vogler (2000) *Business Knowledge Management in der Praxis. Prozessorientierte Lösungen zwischen Knowledge Portal und Kompetenz management*. Berlin and Heidelberg: Springer.

Backhaus, K. and M. Meyer (1993) 'Strategische Allianzen und strategische Netzwerke', *Wirtschaftswissenschaftliches Studium* (7), pp. 330–4.

Backhaus, K. and R. Piltz (1990) 'Strategische Allianzen – eine neue Form kooperativen Wettbewerbs', *Zeitschrift für betriebswirtschaftliche Forschung*, special issue, pp. 1–10.

Balling, R. (1998) *Kooperation. Strategische Allianzen, Netzwerke, Joint Ventures und andere Organisationsformen zwischenbetrieblicher Zusammenarbeit in Theorie und Praxis*. Frankfurt am Main: Lang.

Bandura, A. (1969) *Principles of Behavior Modification*. New York: Holt, Rinehart & Winston.

Bandura, A. (1977) *Social Learning Theory*. Englewood Cliffs, New Jersey: Prentice-Hall.

Bandura, A. (1986) *Social Foundations of Thought and Action. A Social Cognitive Theory*. Englewood Cliffs, New Jersey: Prentice-Hall.

Bandura, A. (1990) 'Reflection on nonability determinants of competence', in R. J. Sternberg and J. Kolligian (eds), *Competence Considered: Perceptions of Competence and Incompetence across the Lifespan*. New Haven, Connecticut: Yale University Press, pp. 315–62.

Bandyk, C. (1988) *Vertikale Integration als wettbewerbspolitisches Problem*. Dissertation Nr. 1066 der Hochschule St. Gallen, Zürich.

Barney, J. B. and W. G. Ouchi (1986) *Organizational Economics*. San Francisco: Jossey-Bass.

Barney, J. B. (1991) 'Firm resources and sustained competitive advantage', *Journal of Management Studies* 17 (1), pp. 99–120.

Bartlett, C. A. (1982) 'How multinational organizations evolve', *Journal of Business Strategy* 3 (1), pp. 20–32.

Bartlett, C. A. (1986) 'Building and managing the transnational: The new organizational challenge', in M. E. Porter (ed.), *Competition in Global Industries*. Boston: Harvard Business School Press, pp. 367–401.

Bartlett, C. A. (1989) 'Aufbau und Management der transnationalen Unternehmung: Eine organisatorische Herausforderung', in M. E. Porter (ed.), *Globaler Wettbewerb*. Wiesbaden: Gabler, pp. 425–64.

Bartlett, C. A. and S. Ghoshal (1985) *Transnational Mangement*, second edition. Chicago: Irwin.

Bartlett, C. A. and S. Ghoshal (1989) *Managing Across Borders. The Transnational Solution*. Boston: Harvard Business School Press.

Bartlett, C. A. and S. Ghoshal (1990a) *Internationale Unternehmensführung*. Frankfurt and New York: Campus-Verlag.

Bartlett, C. A. and S. Ghoshal (1990b) 'Matrix management: Not a structure, a frame of mind', *Harvard Business Review* 68 (July–August), pp. 138–45.

Bartlett, C. A. and S. Ghoshal (1992) 'What is a global manager?', *Harvard Business Review* 70 (September–October), pp. 124–32.

Bartlett, C. A. and S. Ghoshal (1997) *The Individualized Corporation. A Fundamentally New Approach to Management*. New York: Harper Business.

Bartlett, C. A. and S. Ghoshal (2000) 'Going global: Lessons from late movers', *Harvard Business Review* 78 (March–April), pp. 132–42.

Bateson, G. (1985) *Ökologie des Geistes*. Frankfurt am Main: Suhrkamp.

Baur, C. (1990) *Make-or-Buy-Entscheidungen in einem Unternehmen der Automobilindustrie: Empirische Analyse und Gestaltung der Fertiggungstiefe aus transaktionskostentheoretischer Sicht*. Munich: VVF.

Bayerisches Staatsministerium für Wirtschaft und Verkehr (ed.) (1992) *Kooperation und Wettbewerb. Ein Ratgeber für kleine und mittlere Unternehmen*. Munich: Bayerisches Staatsministerium für Wirtschaft und Verkehr.

Bea, F. X. (2000) 'Wissensmanagement', *Wirtschaftswissenschaftliches Studium* 29 (7), pp. 362–67.

Bea, F. X. and J. Haas (2001) *Strategisches Management*. Stuttgart: Lucius & Lucius.

Beamish, P. W. (1988) *Multinational Joint Ventures in Developing Countries*. London: Routledge.

Beamish, P. W. (ed.) (1998) *Strategic Alliances*. Cheltenham, Northampton: Edward Elgar.

Beamish, P. W. and J. C. Banks (1987) 'Equity joint venture and the theory of multinational enterprise', *Journal of International Business Studies* 18 (2), pp. 1–16.

Beamish, P. W. and A. C. Inkpen (1995) 'Keeping international joint ventures stable and profitable', *Long Range Planning* 28 (3), pp. 26–36.

Beason, R. and D. E. Weinstein (1994) 'Growth, economies of scale, and industrial targeting in Japan (1955–1990)', Harvard Institute of Economic Research Discussion Paper 1644. Boston, 10 June.

Bechert, H. and R. Gombrich (eds) (1995) *Der Buddhismus. Geschichte und Gegenwart.* Munich: Beck.

Bechtle, G. (1980) *Betrieb als Strategie.* Frankfurt am Main: Campus.

Beechler, S. L. and A. Bird (eds) (1999) *Japanese Multinationals Abroad. Individual and Organizational Learning.* New York and Oxford: Oxford University Press.

Beechler, S. L. and K. Stucker (1998) *Japanese Business.* London and New York: Routledge.

Behrendt, W. K. (1982) 'Die frühen Jahre der NC-Technologie: 1954 bis 1963', *Technische Rundschau* (19), pp. 19–21.

Benson, J. K. (1975) 'The interorganizational network as a political economy', *Administrative Science Quarterly* (June), pp. 229–49.

Berg, C. C. (1981) *Beschaffungsmarketing.* Würzburg: Physica-Verlag.

Berger, M. and L. Uhlmann (1985) *Auslandsinvestitionen kleiner und mittlerer Unternehmen.* Berlin: Duncker & Humblot.

Bergius, R. (1972) *Psychologie des Lernens.* Stuttgart: Kohlhammer.

Bergsten, C. F. (2000) 'East Asian regionalism, towards a tripartite world', *The Economist*, 15 July, pp. 19–21.

Bidlingmaier, J. (1967) 'Begriff und Formen der Kooperation im Handel', in J. Bidlingmaier, J. Jacobi and E. W. Uherek (eds), *Absatzpolitik und Distribution.* Wiesbaden: Gabler, pp. 353–95.

Binderhofer, E., I. Getreuer-Kargl and H. Lukas (eds) (1996) *Das pazifische Jahrhundert?* Vienna: Brandes & Apsel.

Blair, R. D. and D. L. Kaserman (1983) *Law and Economics of Vertical Integration and Control.* New York: Academic Press.

Blau, P. (1964) *Exchange and Power in Social Life.* New York: Wiley.

Bleackley M. and G. Devlin (1988) 'Strategic Alliances – Guidelines for Success', *Long Range Planning* (5), pp. 18–23.

Bleeke, J. and D. Ernst (1991) 'The way to win cross-border alliances', *Harvard Business Review* 69 (November–December), pp. 127–35.

Bleeke, J. and D. Ernst (eds) (1994) *Rivalen als Partner. Strategische Allianzen und Akquisitionen im globalen Markt.* Frankfurt am Main and New York: Campus-Verlag.

Bleicher, K. (1991) *Organisation. Strategien – Strukturen – Kulturen.* Wiesbaden: Gabler.

Bleicher, K. (1992) 'Organisation der Corporation', in E. Frese (ed.), *Handwörterbuch der Organisation.* Stuttgart: Poeschel, col. 441–54.

Blohm, H. (1969) 'Kooperation', E. Grochla (ed.), *Handwörterbuch der Organisation.* Stuttgart: Poeschel, col. 890–93.

Boddewyn, J. J. (1988) 'Political aspects of MNE theory', *Journal of International Business Studies* 19 (3), pp. 341–63.

Boesenberg, D. and H. Metzen (eds) (1993) *Lean Management. Vorsprung durch schlanke Konzepte.* Landsberg/Lech: Verlag Moderne Industrie.

Böhn, D. (1992) *Der asiatisch-pazifische Raum.* Berlin: Cornelsen.

Borrmann, A., M. Holthus, K.-W. Menck and B. Schnatz (1996) *Kleine und mittlere deutsche Unternehmen in Asien. Investitionschancen und Erfahrungen.* Baden-Baden: Nomos.

Borys, B. and D. B. Jemison (1989) 'Hybrid arrangements as strategic alliances: Theoretical issues in organizational combinations', *The Academy of Management Review* (2), pp. 234–48.

Bosse, F. (1996) 'Das japanische Management in der Krise – nach der Rezession bleiben die strukturellen Probleme', in Institut für Asienkunde (ed.), *Japan. Wirtschaft, Politik, Gesellschaft* 4 (5), pp. 535–42.

Bosse, F. (2000) 'Keiretsu vor dem Aus?' *Japan aktuell, Wirtschaft, Politik, Gesellschaft*, (April), pp. 139–46.

Böttcher, E. (1974) *Kooperation und Demokratie in der Wirtschaft. Schriften zur Kooperationsforschung.* Tübingen: Mohr.

Böttcher, R. (1996) *Global Network Management. Context – Decision Making – Cooordination.* Wiesbaden: Gabler.

Bradach, J. and R. G. Eccles (1989) 'Price, authority and trust: from ideal types to plural forms', *Annual Review of Sociology* 15, pp. 97–118.

Brandstätter, H., H. Schuler and G. Stocker-Kreichgauer (1978) *Psychologie der Person.* Stuttgart: Kohlhammer.

Bresser, R. K. F. (1989) 'Kollektive Unternehmensstrategien', *Zeitschrift für Betriebswirtschaft* 59 (5), p. 545–64.

Bresser, R. K. F. (1998) *Strategische Managementtheorie.* Berlin and New York: de Gruyter.

Brockhaus (2002) http://brockhaus.xipolis.net/suche/suche_treffer_detail.php-lemma=Lernen&werk_id=3&artikel_id=30077800&PHPSESSID=fc0f1ab1cca945b58db3942869a772ca (found 21 July 2002).

Brödner, P. (1991) 'Maschinenbau in Japan. Nippons Erfolgskonzept: so einfach wie möglich', *Technische Rundschau* (37), pp. 54–62.

Bromann, S. (2001) 'Japans kleine und mittelständische Zulieferer vor neuen Herausforderungen', *Japan Markt* (May), pp. 15–6.

Bromiley, P. and L. L. Cummings (1995) 'Transaction costs in organisations with trust', *Research on Negotiation in Organisations* (5), pp. 219–47.

Bronder, C. (1992) *Unternehmensdynamisierung durch strategische Allianzen*, Dissertation. St Gallen.

Bronder, C. (1993) 'Was einer Kooperation den Erfolg sichert', *Harvard Business Manager* 15 (1), pp. 20–8.

Bronder, C. and R. Pritzl (1991) 'Strategische Allianzen zur Steigerung der Wettbewerbsfähigkeit', *io Management Zeitschrift* 60 (5), pp. 27–30.

Bronder, C. and R. Pritzl (1992) 'Ein konzeptioneller Ansatz zur Gestaltung und Entwicklung Strategischer Allianzen', in C. Bronder and R. Pritzl (eds), *Wegweiser für strategische Allianzen.* Wiesbaden: Gabler, pp. 17–44.

Brown, D. L. (1980) 'Planned change in underorganized systems', in T. G. Cummings (ed.), *Systems Theory for Organization Development.* Chichester: Wiley, pp. 181–203.

Brucker, A. (ed.) (1990) *Japan – China – Korea. Der asiatisch-pazifische Raum.* Munich: Oldenbourg.

Bruhn, M., H. Meffert and F. Wehrle (eds) (1994) *Marktorientierte Unternehmensführung im Umbruch. Effizienz und Flexibilität als Herausforderungen des Marketings.* Stuttgart: Schäffer-Poeschel.

Buckley, P. J. (1993) 'The role of management in internationalisation theory', *Management International Review* 33 (3), pp. 193–207.

Buckley, P. J. (ed.) (1994) *Cooperative Forms of Transnational Corporation Activity.* London and New York: Routledge.

Buckley, P. J. and M. Casson (1976) *The Future of the Multinational Enterprise.* London: Macmillan – now Palgrave Macmillan.

Buckley, P. J. and M. Casson (1988) 'A theory of cooperation in international business', in F. J. Contractor and P. Lorange (eds), *Cooperative Strategies in International Business*. Lexington, Massachusetts, and Toronto: Lexington Books, pp. 31–53.

Buckley, P. J. and M. Z. Brooke (1992) *International Business Studies*. Oxford: Blackwell.

Bucklin, L. P. and S. Sengupta (1993) 'Organizing successful co-marketing alliances', *Journal of Marketing* (April), pp. 32–46.

Bühner, R. (1989) 'Strategie und Organisation. Neuere Entwicklungen', *Zeitschrift Führung+Organisation* 58 (4), pp. 223–32.

Bühner, R. (1991) *Grenzüberschreitende Zusammenschlüsse deutscher Unternehmen*. Stuttgart: Poeschel.

Bullinger, H. J. (1994) *Einführung in das Technologiemanagement*. Stuttgart: B. G. Teubner.

Bullinger, H.-J., I. Haus and P. Ohlhausen (1998) 'Produktionsfaktor Wissen', *Personalwirtschaft* 25 (5), pp. 22–6.

Bundesministerium für Wirtschaft (ed.) (1963) *Zwischenbetriebliche Zusammenarbeit im Rahmen des Gesetzes gegen Wettbewerbsbeschränkungen*. Bergisch Gladbach: Heider.

Bürklin, W. (1993) *Die vier kleinen Tiger. Die pazifische Herausforderung*. Munich: Langen Müller.

Burton, F. and F. Saelens (1994) 'International alliances as a strategic tool of Japanese electronic companies', in N. Campbell and F. Burton (eds), *Japanese Multinationals*. London: Routledge, pp. 58–70.

Busch, S., K.-H. Fink and R. Mikton, (1982) *Ost-West-Zusammenarbeit in dritten Ländern. Unternehmenserfahrungen bei Drittlandskooperationen, dargestellt an 20 Beispielen*, BDI-Drucksache 156. Cologne: Verlag Industrieförderung.

Buzan, B. and G. Segal (1994) 'Rethinking East Asian security', in *Survival* 36 (2), pp. 3–21.

Calori, R., G. Johnson and P. Sarnin (1992) 'French and British top managers' understanding of the structure and the dynamics of their industries: a cognitive analysis and comparison', *British Management Journal* 3 (2), pp. 61–78.

Campbell, N. and F. Burton (eds) (1994) *Japanese Multinationals. Strategies and Management in the Global Kaisha*. London and New York: Routledge.

Caruth, D. L. and S. A. Stovall, (1994) *NTC's American Business Terms Dictionary*. Lincolnwood, Illinois: National Textbook Co.

Cascio, W. F. and M. G. Serapio (1991) 'Human resources systems in an international alliance: The undoing of a done deal', *Organizational Dynamics* (Winter), pp. 63–74.

Cassell, C. and G. Symon (eds) (1994) *Qualitative Methods in Organizational Research*. Thousand Oaks. California: Sage.

Casson, M. (1990) *Enterprise and Competitiveness: A Systems View of International Business*. Oxford, England: Clarendon Press and New York: Oxford University Press.

Caves, R. E. (1982) *Multinational Enterprise and Economic Analysis*. Cambridge: Cambridge University Press.

Chalmers, J. (1982) *MITI and the Japanese Miracle. The Growth of the Industrial Policy, 1925–1975*. Stanford: Stanford University Press.

Champy, J. and M. Hammer (1994) *Business Reengineering – Die Radikalkur für das Unternehmen*. Frankfurt and New York: Campus.

Chandler, A. D. (1962) *Strategy and Structure*. Cambridge, Massachusetts: MIT Press.

Chandler, A. D. (1977) *The Visible Hand*. Cambridge, Massachusetts: Harvard University Press.

Chen, M. (1995) *Asian Management Systems. Chinese, Japanese and Korean Styles of Business*. London: International Thomson Business.

Child, J. (1998) 'Trust and international strategic alliances: The case of Sino-foreign joint ventures', in C. Lane and R. Bachmann (eds), *Trust within and between Organizations. Conceptual Issues and Empirical Applications*. Oxford: Oxford University Press, pp. 241–72.

Child, J. (2000)'Management and organizations in China: Key trends and issues', in J. T. Li, A. Tsui and E. Weldon (eds), *Management and Organizations in the Chinese Context*. Basingstoke: Macmillan – now Palgrave Macmillan, pp. 33–62.

Child, J. and D. Faulkner (1998) *Strategies of Cooperation. Managing Alliance, Networks, and Joint Ventures*. Oxford: Oxford University Press.

Chokki, T. (1986) 'A history of the machine tool industry in Japan', in M. Fransman (ed.), *Machinery and Economic Development*. New York: St Martin's Press, pp. 124–52.

Chowdhury, J. (1992) 'Performance of international joint ventures and wholly owned foreign subsidiaries: A comparative perspective', *Management International Review* 32 (2), pp. 115–33.

Christelow, D. B. (1987) 'International joint ventures: How important are they?', *Columbia Journal of World Business* (Summer), pp. 7–14.

Cichon, W. and H. H. Hinterhuber (1989) 'Globalisierung und Kooperation im Wettbewerb', *Journal für Betriebswirtschaft* 39 (3), pp. 139–54.

Clark, K. B., T. Fujimoto and E. C. Stotko, (eds/trans.) (1992) *Automobilentwicklung mit System. Strategie, Organisation und Management in Europa, Japan und USA*. Frankfurt am Main: Campus-Verlag.

Classen, M. and R. Becker (1999) 'Wissensmanagement in der Praxis. Vom Geben und Nehmen', *Organisationsentwicklung* 18 (4), pp. 24–35.

Clegg, S. R. (1990) *Modern Organizations: Organization Studies in the Postmodern World*. London: Sage.

Clegg, S. R. and C Hardy (1996) 'Organizations, organization and organizing', in S. R. Clegg, C. Hardy and W. R. Nord (eds), *Handbook of Organization Studies*. London: Sage, pp. 1–28.

Coase, R. (1937) 'The Nature of the firm', *Economica* 4 (16), pp. 386–405.

Collis, D. J. (1988) 'The machine tool industry and industrial policy 1955–1988', in M. E. Spence and H. A. Hazard (eds), *International Competitiveness*. Cambridge, Massachusetts: Ballinger, pp. 75–114.

Collis, D. J. (1991) 'A resource-based analysis of global competition: The case of the bearings industry', *Strategic Management Journal* 12 (special issue), pp. 49–68.

Contractor, F. J. (1990) 'Contractual and co-operative forms of international business: Towards a unified theory of modal choice', *Management International Review* 30 (1), pp. 31–54.

Contractor, F. J. and P. Lorange (eds) (1988) *Cooperative Strategies in International Business*. Lexington, Massachusetts: Lexington Books.

Contractor, F. J. and P. Lorange (1998) 'Competition vs. co-operation: A benefit/cost framework for choosing between fully-owned investments and co-operative relationships', *Management International Review* 28 (special issue), pp. 5–18.

Cook, K. S. (1977) 'Exchange and power in networks of interorganizational relationships', *The Sociological Quarterly* (Winter), pp. 62–82.

Coser, L. (1956) *The Function of Social Conflicts*. New York.

Currall, S. C. and T. A. Judge (1995) 'Measuring trust between organisational boundary role persons', *Organisational Behavior and Human Decision Processes* 64 (2), pp. 151–70.

Cyert, R. M. and J. G. March (1963) *A Behavioral Theory of the Firm*. Englewood Cliffs, New Jersey: Prentice-Hall.

Daft, R. L. and K. E. Weick (1984) 'Toward a model of organizations as interpretation systems', *Academy of Management Review* 9 (2), pp. 284–95.

Dams, T. and M. Mizuno (eds) (1985) *Entscheidungsprozesse auf mikro- und makroökonomischer Ebene dargestellt an ausgewählten Beispielen in Japan und in der Bundesrepublik Deutschland*. Berlin: Duncker & Humblot.

Dahrendorf, R. (1959) *Sozialstruktur des Betriebes – Betriebssoziologie*. Wiesbaden: Gabler.

Dahrendorf, R. (1972) *Konflikt und Freiheit*. Munich: Piper.

Dathe, J. (1998) *Kooperationen. Leitfaden für Unternehmen*. Munich and Vienna: Hanser.

Davenport, T. H. (1996) 'Some principles of knowledge management', *Strategy and Business* 1 (2), pp. 34–40.

Deiter, R. (1991) 'Cooperatives', in F. N. Magill (ed.), *Survey of Social Science. Economic Series*. Pasadena and Englewood Cliffs, New Jersey: Salem Press, pp. 409–13.

Dessler, G. (1976) *Organization and Management: A Contingency Approach*. Englewood Cliffs, New Jersey: Prentice-Hall.

Deutsch-Japanischer Wirtschaftskreis (ed.) (1996) *Der Nutzen von Handels- und Investitionsversicherungen für deutsch-japanische Kooperationen in Drittländern*. Düsseldorf: Deutsch-Japanischer Wirtschaftskreis.

Deutsch-Japanischer Wirtschaftskreis (ed.) (1997) *Gemeinsam in Zukunftsmärkte? Möglichkeiten deutsch-japanischer Kooperation in dritten Ländern*. Düsseldorf: Deutsch-Japanischer Wirtschaftskreis.

Devlin, G. and M. Bleackley (1988) 'Strategic alliances: Guidelines for success', *Long Range Planning* (5), pp. 18–23.

Dill, P. (1986) *Unternehmenskultur. Grundlagen und Anknüpfungspunkte für ein Kulturmanagement*. Bonn: BDW Service- und Verlagsgesellschaft Kommunikation.

DiMaggio, P. J. and W. W. Powell (1983) 'The iron cage revisited: Institutional isomorphism and collective rationality in organizational fields', *American Sociological Review* 48, pp. 147–60.

Dirks, D. (1995) *Japanisches Management in internationalen Unternehmen. Methodik interkultureller Organisation*. Wiesbaden: Deutscher Universitäts-Verlag; Wiesbaden: Gabler.

Dirks, D. (1999) 'Konzentration auf das Wesentliche durch Outsourcing', in J. Legewie and H. Meyer-Ohle (eds), *Japans Wirtschaft im Umbruch*. Munich: Iudicium, pp. 65–8.

Dirks, D., J. F. Huchet and T. Ribault (eds) (1999) *Japanese Management in the Low Growth Era. Between External Shocks and Internal Evolution*. Berlin, Heidelberg and New York: Springer.

Dolezalek, C. M. (1956) 'Grundlagen und Grenzen der Automatisierung', *VDI-Z* 98 (12), pp. 564–9.

Dolezalek, C. M. (1960) 'Einfluß der Automatisierung auf die Entwicklung der Werkzeugmaschinenindustrie', *Verein Deutscher Ingenieure-Nachrichten* 14 (24), pp. 1–4.

Dorow, W. (1978) *Unternehmungskonflikte als Gegenstand unternehmungspolitischer Forschung*. Berlin: Duncker & Humblot.

Dorow, W. (1982) *Unternehmungspolitik*. Stuttgart: Kohlhammer.

Doz, Y. and G. Hamel (1998) *Alliance Advantage. The Art of Creating Value through Partnering*. Boston: Harvard Business School Press.

Doz, Y. L. and C. K. Prahalad (1991) 'Managing DMNCs: A search for a new paradigm', *Strategic Management Journal* 12 (special issue), pp. 145–64.

Doz, Y., C. K. Prahalad and G. Hamel (1990) 'Control, change, and flexibility: The dilemma of transnational collaboration', in C. A. Bartlett, Y. Doz and G. Hedlund (eds), *Managing the Global Firm*. London and New York: Routledge, pp. 117–43.

DuBrin, A. J. (1974) *Fundamentals of Organizational Behavior – An Applied Perspective*. New York: Pergamon Press.

Dülfer, E. (ed.) (1982) *Projektmanagement – International*. Stuttgart: Poeschel.

Dülfer, E. (1985) 'Die Auswirkungen der Internationalisierung auf Führung und Organisationsstruktur mittelständischer Unternehmen', *Betriebswirtschaftliche Forschung und Praxis* 37 (6), pp. 493–514.

Dülfer, E. (1991) *Internationales Management*. Munich: Oldenbourg.

Dülfer, E. (1997) *Internationales Management in unterschiedlichen Kulturbereichen*. Munich and Vienna: Oldenbourg.

Duncan, R. B. and A. Weiss (1979) 'Organizational learning: Implications for organizational design', in B. W. Staw (ed.), *Research in Organizational Behavior*, vol. 1, pp. 75–123.

Duncan, W. J. (1975) *Essentials of Management*. Hinsdale, Illinois: Dryden Press.

Dunning, J. H. (1980) 'Towards an eclectic theory of international production', *Journal of International Business Studies* 11, pp. 9–31.

Dunning, J. H. (1988) 'The eclectic paradigm of international production: A restatement and some possible extensions', *Journal of International Business Studies* 19, pp. 1–31.

Dunning, J. H. (1993) *Multinational Enterprises and the Global Economy*. Wokingham, UK: Addison-Wesley.

Dürr, H. and R. Hanisch (1986) *Südostasien. Tradition und Gegenwart*. Braunschweig: Westermann.

Ebers, M. (ed.) (1997) *The Formation of Inter-organizational Networks*. Oxford: Oxford University Press.

Eccles, R. G. (1981) 'The quasifirm in the construction industry', *Journal of Economic Behavior and Organization* (December), pp. 335–57.

Edsman, C.-M. (1976) *Die Hauptreligionen des heutigen Asiens*. Tübingen: Mohr.

Effenberger, J. and H. Goecke (1994) *Das Management strategischer Allianzen*. Arbeitspapier der Technischen Universität Braunschweig, AP-Nr. 94/7, TU Braunschweig.

Eisele, J. (1995) *Erfolgsfaktoren des Joint-Venture-Management*. Wiesbaden: Gabler.

Endress, R. (1991) *Strategie und Taktik der Kooperation. Grundlagen der zwischen- und innerbetrieblichen Zusammenarbeit*. Berlin: Erich Schmidt.

Engelhard, J. and E. J. Sinz (1999) *Kooperation im Wettbewerb. Neue Formen und Gestaltungskonzepte im Zeichen der Globalisierung und Informationstechnologie*. Wiesbaden: Gabler.

Erdmann, C. and W. Kreisel (1994) 'Die pazifische Herausforderung. Globale Konkurrenz, regionale Zusammenarbeit', *Geographische Rundschau* 46 (11), pp. 610–5.

Ernst, A. (1999) 'Personnel management of Japanese firms and information flows', in H. Albach , U. Görtzen and R. Zobel (eds), *Information Processing as a Competitive Advantage of Japanese Firms*. Berlin: Edition Sigma, pp. 239–53.

Ernst, A., R. Hild, H. G. Hilpert and S. Martsch (1992) 'Technologieschutz in Japan: Strategien für Unternehmenskooperationen', *ifo Studien zur Japanforschung* (9). Munich: Ifo-Institut für Wirtschaftsforschung.

Eschenburg, R. (1971) *Ökonomische Theorie der genossenschaftlichen Zusammenarbeit. Schriften zur Kooperationsforschung*. Tübingen: Mohr.

Fama, E. (1980) 'Agency problems and the theory of the firm', *Journal of Political Economy* 88, pp. 288–307.

Fama, E. F. and M. C. Jensen (1980) 'Agency problems and residual claims', *Journal of Labor Economics* 26, pp. 327–49.

Feske, S. (1991) *ASEAN: Ein Modell für regionale Sicherheit: Ursprung, Entwicklung und Bilanz sicherheitspolitischer Zusammenarbeit in Südostasien*. Baden-Baden: Nomos.

Fieten, R., F. Werner and B. Lageman (1997) *Globalisierung der Märkte. Herausforderungen und Optionen für kleine und mittlere Unternehmen, insbesondere für Zulieferer*. Stuttgart: Schäffer-Poeschel.

Filley, A. C. (1975) *Interpersonal Conflict Resolution*. Glenview, Illinois: Scott, Foresman.

Fiol, C. M. and M. A. Lyles (1985) 'Organizational learning', *Academy of Management Review* 4, pp. 803–13.

Fischer, M. (1993) 'Distributionsentscheidungen aus transaktionskostentheoretischer Sicht', *Marketing – Zeitschrift für Forschung und Praxis* (4), pp. 249–58.

Fischer, W. (1979) *Die Weltwirtschaft im 20. Jahrhundert*. Göttingen: Vandenhoeck & Ruprecht.

Flecker, J. and G. Schienstock (1991) 'Betriebsübernahmen und Konzernstrukturen', in J. Flecker and G. Schienstock (eds), *Flexibilisierung, Deregulierung und Globalisierung*. Munich and Mering: Hampp, pp. 225–41.

Forrest, J. E. (1990) 'Strategic alliances and the small technology based firm', *Journal of Small Business Management* (July), pp. 37–45.

Forsgren, M. (1989) *Managing the Internationalization Process*. London: Routledge.

Forsgren, M. and J. Johanson (eds) (1992) *Managing Networks in International Business*. Philadelphia: Gordon & Breach.

Frazier, G. L. (1983) 'Interorganizational exchange behavior in marketing channels: A broadened perspective', *Journal of Marketing* (Fall), pp. 68–78.

Freiwald, E. (1996) *Asiens Osten. Wirtschaftsraum der Zukunft?* Hamburg: Toro-Verlag.

Friedman, D. (1988) *The Misunderstood Miracle. Industrial Development and Political Change in Japan*. Ithaca, London: Cornell University Press.

Fritz, W. (1988) 'Der kartellrechtliche Kooperationsspielraum mittelständischer Unternehmen', *Wirtschaftswissenschaftliches Studium* (2), pp. 58–64.

Fuchs, J. (2001) 'Wissens-Management: Perversitäten und Perspektiven eines Modeworts', *Personal* 53 (5), p. 240.

Fundenberg, D. and J. Tirole (1991) *Game Theory*. Cambridge, Massachusetts: MIT Press.

Fürstenberg, F. (1972) *Japanische Unternehmensführung: Management-Strukturen in der japanischen Industrie*. Zürich: Verlag Moderne Industrie.

Gaffga, P. (1996) 'Südostasien – Heimat der kleinen Tiger und Drachen', *Praxis Geographie* 26 (9), pp. 40–3.

Gahl, A. (1991) *Die Konzeption strategischer Allianzen*. Berlin: Duncker & Humblot.

Galbraith, J. K. (1954) 'Countervailing power', *American Economic Review* 44 (2), pp. 1–6.

Garcia-Canal, E. (1996) 'Contractual form in domestic and international strategic alliances', *Organization Studies* 17, pp. 773–94.

Garratt, B. (1990) *Creating a Learning Organisation. A Guide to Leadership, Learning and Development*. Cambridge: Director Books.

Gatignon, H. and E. Anderson (1988) 'The multinational corporation's degree of control over foreign subsidiaries: An empirical test of a transaction cost explanation', *Journal of Labour Economics* 4, pp. 305–36.

Geißler, H. (1996) 'Vom Lernen in der Organisation zum Lernen der Organisation', in Sattelberger, T. (ed.), *Die lernende Organisation: Konzepte für eine neue Qualität der Unternehmensentwicklung*. Wiesbaden: Gabler, pp. 79–95.

Geringer, M. J. and L. Hebert (1991) 'Measuring performance of international joint ventures', *Journal of International Business Studies* 22 (Summer), pp. 249–63.

Gerth, E. (1971) *Zwischenbetriebliche Kooperation*. Stuttgart: Poeschel.

Ghoshal, S. (1987) 'Global strategy: An organizing framework', *Strategic Management Journal* 8 (5), pp. 425–40.

Ghoshal, S. and C. A. Bartlett (1990) 'The multinational corporation as an international network', *Academy of Management Review* 15 (4), pp. 603–25.

Giddens, A. (1976) *New Rules of Sociological Method: A Positive Critique of Interpretative Sociologies*. London: Hutchinson.

Giddens, A. (1979) *Central Problems in Social Theory*. London: Macmillan– now Palgrave Macmillan.

Giddens, A. (1988) *Die Konstitution der Gesellschaft*. Frankfurt and New York: Campus-Verlag.

Gist, M. E. and T. R. Mitchell (1992) 'Self-efficacy: A theoretical analysis of its determinants and malleability', *Academy of Management Review* 17 (2), pp. 183–211.

Glasl, F. (1980) *Konfliktmanagement – Diagnose und Behandlung von Konflikten in Organisationen*. Berne and Stuttgart: Haupt.

Gomes-Casseres, B. (1987) 'Joint venture instability: Is it a problem?', *Columbia Journal of World Business* (Summer), pp. 97–102.

Gomes-Casseres, B. (1989) 'Ownership structures of foreign subsidiaries', *Journal of Economic Behavior and Organization* 12, pp. 1–25.

Görgens, J. (1994) *Just in time Fertigung. Konzept und modellgestützte Analyse*. Stuttgart: Schäffer-Poeschel.

Graham, E. M. (1994) 'Joint venture', in D. Greenwald (ed.), *The McGraw-Hill Encyclopedia of Economics*. New York: McGraw-Hill, pp. 591–3.

Granovetter, M. (1985) 'Economic action and social structure: The problem of social embeddedness', *American Journal of Sociology* 91, pp. 481–510.

Granrath, L. (1994) *Technologieaustausch versus Technologieprotektion Anforderungen an ein Kooperationskonzept für eine Zusammenarbeit zwischen westlichen und japanischen Unternehmen in Japan*. Hochschule St Gallen, Dissertation 1994, Hallstadt.

Grant, R. (1998) *Contemporary Strategy Analysis*. Cambridge, Massachusetts: Cambridge University Press.

Grawehl, A. (1996) 'Entscheiden auf Japanisch', *Personalwirtschaft* (23) 7, pp. 10–5.

Griese, J. (1992) 'Auswirkungen globaler Informations- und Kommunikationssysteme auf die Organisation weltweit tätiger Unternehmen', *Managementforschung* 2, pp. 164–79.

Griffin, G. C. (1955) 'Maschinensteuerung – die Grundlage der Automatisierung', *Machine Shop Management* 16, pp. 46–50.

Grossekettler, H. (1978) 'Die volkswirtschaftliche Problematik von Vertriebskooperationen', *Zeitschrift für das gesamte Genossenschaftswesen* 28, pp. 325–74.

Grossmann, S. J. and O. D. Hart (1986) 'The costs and benefits of ownership: A theory of vertical and lateral integration', *Journal of Political Economy* 94, pp. 691–719.

Grün, O. (1989) 'Projektmanagement, internationales', in K. Macharzina and M. K. Welge (eds), *Handwörterbuch Export und Internationale Unternehmung*. Stuttgart: Poeschel, col. 1736–46.

Grunwald, W. and H.-G. Lilge (1982) *Kooperation und Konkurrenz in Organisationen*. Berne and Stuttgart: Haupt.

Gulati, R. (1995) 'Social structure and alliance formation patterns: A longitudinal analysis', *Administrative Science Quarterly* 40, pp. 619–52.

Gümbel, R. (1992) 'Marketing-Ökonomie', in H. Diller (ed.), *Vahlens großes Marketinglexikon*. Munich: Vahlen, pp. 686–91.

Haak, R. (1997) *Die Entwicklung des deutschen Werkzeugmaschinenbaus in der Zeit von 1930 bis 1960*. Berlin: Institut für Produktionsanlagen und Konstruktionstechnik Berlin.

Haak, R. (2000a) 'Lernen als Erfolgsfaktor – Internationale Unternehmenskooperationen als Managementaufgabe', *Japan Markt* (January), pp. 13–4.

Haak, R. (2000b) 'Kollektive Internationalisierungsstrategien der japanischen Industrie – Ein Beitrag zum Management internationaler Unternehmungskooperationen', *Zeitschrift für wirtschaftlichen Fabrikbetrieb (ZWF)* 95 (3), pp. 113–6.

Haak, R. (2000c) 'Zwischen Internationalisierung und Restrukturierung – Kooperationsmanagement der japanischen Industrie in fortschrittlichen Technologiefeldern', *Industrie-Management* 16 (6), pp. 64–8.

Haak, R. (2001a) 'Japanese–German interfirm networks in China', in Fujitsu Research Institute (ed.), *Conference Papers, Japan and China. Economic Relations in Transition*, Paper 18. Tokyo: Fujitsu Research Institute.

Haak, R. (2001b) 'Strategisches Management in dynamischer Umwelt – Markt- und Technologieführerschaft in der chinesischen Automobilindustrie', *Zeitschrift für wirtschaftlichen Fabrikbetrieb (ZWF)* 96 (1/2), pp. 46–51.

Haak, R. (2002a) 'Japanese business strategies towards China: A theoretical approach', in H. G. Hilpert and R. Haak (eds), *Japan and China. Cooperation, Competition and Conflict*. Basingstoke: Palgrave, pp. 158–73.

Haak, R. (2002b) Research Project at the German Institute for Japanese Studies. Interviews with German and Japanese Management in China, Germany and Japan. Documentation at the German Institute for Japanese Studies.

Haak, R (2003) 'Strategy and organization of international enterprises – Japanese-German business cooperation in third markets: The case of China', in R. Haak and H. G. Hilpert (eds) (2003), *Focus China – The New Challenge for Japanese Management*. Munich: Iudicium.

Haak, R. and H. G. Hilpert (eds) (2003) *Focus China. The New Challenge for Japanese Management*. Munich: Iudicium.

Haigh, R. W. (1992) 'Building a strategic alliance: The Hermosillo experience as a Ford-Mazda proving ground', *Columbia Journal of World Business* (Spring), pp. 60–73.

Hakansson, H. (ed.) (1982) *International Marketing and Purchasing of Industrial Goods – An Interaction Approach*. Chichester: Wiley.

Hakansson, H. (ed.) (1987) *Industrial Technological Development: A Network Approach*. London, Sydney and Dover, New Hampshire: Croom Helm.

Hakansson, H. and J. Johanson (1988) 'Formal and informal cooperation strategies in international industrial networks', in F. J. Contractor and P. Lorange (eds), *Cooperative Strategies in International Business*. Lexington, Massachusetts: Lexington Books, pp. 369–79.

Hakansson, H. (1989) *Corporate Technological Behaviour: Co-operation and Networks*. London and New York: Routledge.

Hakansson, H., H. Kjellberg and A. Lundgren (1993) 'Strategic alliances in global biotechnology: A network approach', *International Business Review*, (1), pp. 65–82.

Hakansson, H. and I. Snehota (1989) 'No business is an island: The network concept of business strategy', *Scandinavian Journal of Managemnt* 5 (3), pp. 187–200.

Halberstam, D. (1991) *Das 21. Jahrhundert. Japan und Europa. Die neuen Zentren der Macht*. Munich: Droemer-Knaur.

Haller, M. (ed.) (1993) *Globalisierung der Wirtschaft – Einwirkungen auf die Betriebswirtschaftslehre*. Berne and Stuttgart: Haupt.

Hamel, G. (1991) 'Competition for competence and interpartner learning within international strategic alliances', *Strategic Management Journal* (12), pp. 83–103.

Hamel, G., Y. L. Doz and C. K. Prahalad (1989) 'Collaborate with your competitors – and win', *Harvard Business Review* 67 (January–February), pp. 133–39.

Hammes, W. (1993) *Strategische Allianzen als Instrument der strategischen Unternehmensführung*. Wiesbaden: Gabler.

Hanft, A. (1996) 'Organisationales Lernen und Macht – Über den Zusammenhang von Wissen, Lernen, Macht und Struktur', in G. Schreyögg and P. Conrad (eds), *Wissensmanagement*. Berlin and New York: de Gruyter, pp. 133–62.

Hansen, M. T., N. Nohria and T. Tierney (1999) 'Wie managen Sie das Wissen in Ihrem Unternehmen?', *Harvard Business Manager* 21 (5), pp. 85–96.

Hansen, U., H. Raffee, M. Riemer and K. Segler (1983) *Kooperation zwischen deutschen und japanischen Unternehmen*. Arbeitspapiere Nr. 23. Mannheim: Universität Mannheim.

Harnisch, S. and H. W. Maull (2000) *Kernwaffen in Nordkorea, Regionales Krisenmanagement und Stabilität durch das Genfer Rahmenabkommen*. Bonn: Europa Union.

Harrigan, K. R. (1985) *Strategies for Joint Ventures*. Lexington, Massachusetts: Lexington Books.

Harrigan, K. R. (1986) *Managing for Joint Venture Success*. Lexington, Massachusetts: Lexington Books.

Harrigan, K. R. (1987) 'Strategic alliances: Their new role in global competition', *Columbia Journal of World Business* (Summer), pp. 67–9.

Harrigan, K. R. (1988) 'Strategic alliances and partner asymmetries', *Management International Review*, Special Issue: Cooperative Strategy in International Business, pp. 53–72.

Harzing, A. W. (1999) *Managing the Multinationals. An International Study of Control Mechanisms*. Cheltenham: Edward Elgar.

Haury, S. (1989) *Grundzüge einer ökonomischen Theorie lateraler Kooperation.* Dissertation Nr. 1126 der Hochschule St Gallen, Grüsch, Switzerland: Hochschule St. Gallen.

Hauschildt, J. (1977) *Entscheidungsziele.* Tübingen: Mohr.

Hayashi, S. (1991) *Culture and Management in Japan.* Tokyo: University of Tokyo Press.

Hedlund, G. (1986) 'The hypermodern MNC – a heterarchy?', *Human Resource Management* 25 (1), pp. 9–36.

Hedlund, G. and D. Rolander (1990) 'Action in heterarchies: New approaches to managing MNC', in C. A. Bartlett, Y. Doz and G. Hedlund (eds): *Managing the Global Firm.* London and New York: Routledge, pp. 15–46.

Heidenreich, M. and G. Schmidt (eds) (1991) *International vergleichende Organisationsforschung.* Opladen: Westdeutscher Verlag.

Heimerl-Wagner, P. (1992) *Strategische Organisationsentwicklung: inhaltliche und methodische Konzepte zum Lernen in und von Organisationen.* Heidelberg: Physica-Verlag.

Heinen, E. (1987): *Unternehmenskultur.* Munich and Vienna: Hanser.

Heitger, B. (1996) 'Chaotische Organisationen – organisiertes Chaos? Der Beitrag des Managements zur lernenden Organisation', T. Sattelberger (ed.): *Die lernende Organisation: Konzepte für eine neue Qualität der Unternehmensentwicklung.* Wiesbaden: Gabler, pp. 111–23.

Hellriegel, D. and J. W. Slocum (1976) *Organizational Behavior.* St Paul: West Publishing Co.

Hellriegel, D. and J. W. Slocum (1986) *Management.* Reading, Massachusetts: Addison-Wesley.

Hemm, H. and P. Diestsch (1992) 'Internationale Kooperationen und strategische Allianzen. Ziele, Probleme und praktische Gestaltung unternehmerischer Partnerschaft', in B. N. Kumar and H. Hausmann (eds): *Handbuch der internationalen Unternehmenstätigkeit,* pp. 531–47.

Hemmert, M. (1993) *Vertikale Kooperation zwischen japanischen Industrieunternehmen.* Wiesbaden: Deutscher Universitäts-Verlag.

Hemmert, M. (1995) 'Technologieführer Japan? Die Umstrukturierung der japanischen Forschungslandschaft', in *Japanstudien. Jahrbuch des deutschen Instituts für Japanstudien der Philipp-Franz-von-Siebold-Stiftung* 7, pp. 239–78.

Hemmert, M. (1997) 'Innovationsstrategien und Technologiepolitik in Japan: Ein Aufholersystem im Umbruch', in K. Lichtblau and F. Waldenberger (eds): *Planung, Wettbewerb und wirtschaftlicher Wandel. Ein japanisch-deutscher Vergleich.* Cologne: Deutscher Instituts-Verlag, pp. 84–106.

Hemmert, M. (1999) 'Die Reorganisation industrieller Keiretsu', in J. Legewie and H. Meyer-Ohle (eds), *Japans Wirtschaft im Umbruch.* Munich: Iudicium, pp. 55–8.

Hemmert, M. and R. Lützeler (1994) 'Einleitung: Landeskunde und wirtschaftliche Entwicklung seit 1945', in Deutsches Institut für Japanstudien (ed.), *Die japanische Wirtschaft heute.* Munich: Iudicium, pp. 23–44.

Hemmert, M. and C. Oberländer (eds) (1998) *Technology and Innovation in Japan. Policy and Management for the Twenty-First Century.* Routledge Studies in the Growth Economies in Asia. London: Routledge.

Hennart, J.-F. (1991a) 'The transaction costs theory of joint ventures: An empirical study of Japanese subsidiaries in the United States', *Management Science* 37, pp. 483–97.

Hennart, J.-F. (1991b) 'The transaction cost theory of the multinational enterprise', in C. N. Pitelis and R. Sugden (eds), *The Nature of the Transnational Firm*. London: Routledge, pp. 81–116.

Hennart, J.-F. (1993) 'Explaining the swollen middle: Why most transactions are a mix of market and hierarchy', *Organization Science* 4, pp. 529–47

Hennart, J.-F. (1998) 'Upstream vertical integration in the aluminium and tin industries', *Journal of Economic Behavior and Organization* 9, pp. 281–99.

Herzig, N., C. Watrin, C. and H. Ruppert (1997) 'Unternehmenskontrolle in internationalen Joint Ventures – Eine agencytheoretische Betrachtung', *Die Betriebswirtschaft* 57 (6), pp. 764–76.

Hildebrandt, L. and C. A. Weiss (1997) 'Internationale Markteintrittsstrategien und der Transfer von Marketing-Know-How', *Zeitschrift für betriebwirtschaftliche Forschung* 49, pp. 3–25.

Hilpert, H. G. (1992a) 'APEC – Das Entstehen eines pazifischen Pendants zur EG?', *Ifo Schnelldienst* 14, pp. 14–29.

Hilpert, H. G. (1992b) 'Marktstrategien deutscher und japanischer Unternehmen in der asiatisch-pazifischen Region', *Ifo Studien zur Japanforschung* 6. Munich: Ifo-Institut für Wirtschaftsforschung.

Hilpert, H. G. (1993) 'Die wirtschaftliche Verflechtung Japans mit der asiatisch-pazifischen Region', *Ifo Schnelldienst* 3, pp. 14–31.

Hilpert, H. G. and R. Haak (eds) (2002) *Japan and China. Cooperation, Competition and Conflict*. Basingstoke: Palgrave.

Hilpert, H. G. and M. Taube (1997) *Deutsch-Japanische Unternehmenskooperationen in Drittmärkten*. Munich: ifo Institut für Wirtschaftsforschung e.V. München.

Hilpert, H. G., S. Martsch, and C. Heath (1997) *Technologieschutz für deutsche Investitionen in Asien. Die Situation in China, Indien, Indonesien, Korea und Vietnam.* Ifo Studien zur Entwicklungsforschung 30. Munich: Weltforum-Verlag.

Hinck, M. (1997) *Deutsch-japanische Unternehmenskooperationen. Studie im Auftrag der DIHKJ*. Tokyo: Deutsche Industrie- und Handelskammer.

Hinings, C. R. and R. Greenwood (1988) *The Dynamics of Strategic Change*. Oxford: Blackwell.

Hirschman, A. O. (1974): *Abwanderung und Widerspruch*. Tübingen: Mohr.

Hirsch-Kreinsen, H. (1989) 'Entwicklung einer Basistechnik. NC-Steuerung von Werkzeugmaschinen in den USA und der BRD', in K. Düll and B. Lutz (eds), *Technikentwicklung und Arbeitsteilung im internationalen Vergleich*. Frankfurt am Main and New York: Campus.

Hirsch-Kreinsen, H. (1993) *NC-Entwicklung als gesellschaftlicher Prozeß. Amerikanische und deutsche Innovationsmuster der Fertigungstechnik*. Frankfurt am Main and New York: Campus.

Hirschmann, A. O. (1991) 'Exit and voice', in J. Eatwell, M. Millgate and P. Newman (eds), *The New Palgrave. A Dictionary of Economics* 2, reprinted with corrections. London: Macmillan – now Palgrave Macmillan, pp. 219–24.

Hakansson, H. and I. Snehota (1989) 'No business is an island: The network concept of business strategy', *Scandinavian Journal of Management* 5 (3), pp. 187–200.

Hitachi Seiki Kabushiki Kaisha (1991) *Hito ni yasashii gijutsu: Chie to sôi no 55 nen: Sôritsu 55 shûnen* [Hitachi Seiki Co., People-friendly technology: Fifty-five years of experience and creativity: Celebrating the fifty-fifth anniversary of the foundation of the company]. Tokyo: Hitachi Seiki.

Hobday, M. (1995) *Innovation in East Asia. The Challenge to Japan*. Aldershot: E. Elgar.

Hofstede, G. (1980) *Culture's Consequences*. London: Sage.

Hoßfeld, D. (1991) *Joint Ventures als Markteintrittsstrategie japanischer Unternehmen für Osteuropa*. diploma thesis, Universität Gesamthochschule Essen, Essen.

Hulbert, J. M. and K. Brandt (1980) *Managing the Multinational Subsidiary*. New York: Holt, Rinehart & Winston.

Huntington, S. P. (1994) 'The clash of civilizations?', in A. Clesse, R. Cooper and Y. Sakamoto (eds), *The International System after the Collapse of the East-West Order*. Dordrecht: M. Nijhoff, pp. 7–27.

Hyodo, T. (1987) 'Participatory management and Japanese workers consciousness', in J. Bergmann and S. Tokunaga (eds), *Economic and Social Aspects of Industrial Relations. A Comparison of the German and the Japanese Systems*. Frankfurt am Main and New York: Campus, pp. 261–70.

Imai, M. (1993) *Kaizen*. Frankfurt am Main: Ullstein.

Inkpen, A. (1995) *The Management of International Joint Ventures. An Organizational Learning Perspective*. London and New York: Routledge.

Inkpen, A.C. and P. W. Beamish (1997) 'Knowledge, bargaining power, and the instability of international joint venture', *Academy of Management Review* 22 (1), pp. 177–202.

Inoue, R. (1995) 'Stable strategic alliance between Mitsubishi and Benz', *International Business Alliances* 1 (1), p. 2.

Inoue, R. (1996) 'Alliances: Western style and Asian style', *International Business Alliances* 2 (4), p. 1.

Irrgang, W. (1989) *Strategien im vertikalen Marketing: handelsorientierte Konzeptionen der Industrie*. Munich: Vahlen.

Irrgang, W. (ed.) (1993) *Vertikales Marketing im Wandel: aktuelle Strategien und Operationalisierungen zwischen Hersteller und Handel*. Munich: Vahlen.

Itaki, M. (1991) 'A critical assessment of the eclectic theory of the multinational enterprise', *Journal of International Business Studies* 22 (3), pp. 445–60.

Itô, T. (1992) *The Japanese Economy*. Cambridge Massachusetts and London: MIT Press, pp. 181–9.

James, B. G. (1984) *Business Wargames*. Tunbridge Wells: Abacus.

James, B. G. (1985) 'Alliance: The new strategic focus', *Long Range Planning* (6), pp. 76–81.

Jarillo, J. C. (1988) 'On strategic networks', *Strategic Management Journal* 9 (1), pp. 31–41.

JETRO (ed.) (1999) *International Business Alliances* 6 (1).

JETRO (ed.) (1995a) 'Japan Vilene and Carl Freudenberg to produce non-woven fabric in China', *International Business Alliances* 1 (3), p. 4.

JETRO (ed.) (1995b) 'Meg-Maruka and Hennecke unite to produce PUR processing equipment in Asia', *International Business Alliances* 1 (3), p. 4.

JETRO (ed.) (1995c) 'Sumitomo Metal Mining teams up with a German firm to produce lead frames in Asia', *International Business Alliances* 1 (3), p. 2.

JETRO (ed.) (1995d) 'What it takes to make an international corporate alliance to succeed', *International Business Alliances* 3 (1), pp. 2–5.

JETRO (ed.) (1996) 'Third-country corporate alliances', *International Business Alliances* 3 (2), pp. 2–9.

JETRO (ed.) (1997) 'The current state of corporate alliances', *International Business Alliances* 3 (3) pp. 2–5.

Johanson, J. and L. G. Mattsson (1988) 'Internationalisation in industrial systems: A network approach', in N. Hood and J.-E. Vahlne (eds), *Strategies in Global Competition*. London: Croom Helm, pp. 287–314.

Johnson, G. and K. Scholes (1997) *Exploring Corporate Strategy*. London: Prentice-Hall.

Johnston, R. and P. R. Lawrence (1988) 'Beyond vertical integration: The rise of the value-adding partnership', *Harvard Business Review* 66 (July–August), pp. 94–101.

Jürgens, U., T. Malsch and K. Dohse, (1989) *Moderne Zeiten in der Automobilfabrik. Strategie der Produktmodernisierung im Länder- und Konzernvergleich*. Berlin, Heidelberg and New York: Springer.

Kaas, K. P. (1992) 'Kontraktgütermarketing als Kooperation zwischen Prinzipalen und Agenten', *Zeitschrift für betriebswirtschaftliche Forschung* (10), pp. 884–901.

Kanter, R. M. (1994) 'Collaborative advantage', *Harvard Business Review* 72 (July–August), pp. 96–108.

Kantzenbach, E. (1967) *Die Funktionsfähigkeit des Wettbewerbs*. Göttingen: Vandenhoeck & Ruprecht.

Kappich, L. (1989) *Theorie der internationalen Unternehmungstätigkeit*. Munich: VVF.

Karmann, A. (1992) 'Principal-Agent-Modelle und Risikoallokation. Einige Grundprinzipien', *Wirtschaftswissenschaftliches Studium* (11), pp. 557–62.

Kast, F. E. and J. E. Rosenzweig (1985) *Organization and Management, a Systems and Contingency Approach*. New York and Tokyo: McGraw-Hill.

Kato, T. (1996) 'Reinventing the business: Japan's trading companies on the move', *Nomura Research Institute Quarterly* 5 (2), pp. 36–59.

Katz, D. and R. L. Kahn (1966) *The Social Psychology of Organizations*. New York and London: Wiley.

Kawashima, I. and S. Konomoto (1999) 'Time for more autonomy: Problems of Japanese companies in East and Southeast Asia', *Nomura Research Institute Quarterly* 8 (3), pp. 18–31.

Keesing, R. (1974) 'Theories of culture', *Annual Review of Anthropology* 3, pp. 73–93.

Keizai Kikakuchô (1994) *Kokumin keizai keisan nenpô* (Annual report on National Accounts). Tokyo: Keizai Kikakuchô Keizai Kenkyûjo, pp. 46–7.

Kelly, J. (1970) 'Make conflict work for you', *Harvard Business Review*, pp. 103–13.

Kelting-Büttner, F. (1991) *Ergebnisse der RKW-Kooperationsumfrage*. Eschborn.

Kennedy, P. (1954) 'Automatic controls takes over in automotive manufacturing', *Automotive Industry* 111, pp. 62–7 and 138–44.

Kern, H. and M. Schumann (1986) *Das Ende der Arbeitsteilung?*. Munich: Beck.

Kief, H. B. (1991) 'Von der NC zur CNC: Die Entwicklung der numerischen Steuerungen', *Werkstatt und Betrieb* 124 (5), pp. 385–91.

Kieser, A. (1989) 'Organisationsstruktur, empirische Befunde', in K. Macharzina and M. K. Welge (eds), *Handwörterbuch Export und Internationale Unternehmung*. Stuttgart: Poeschel, col. 1574–90.

Kieser, A., U. Koch and M. Woywode (1999) 'Wie man Bürokratien das Lernen beibringt', *Zeitschrift für Organisation und Führung* 68 (3), pp. 128–33.

Kilduff, M. (1992) 'Performance and interaction routines in multinational corporations', *Journal of International Business Studies* 23 (1), pp. 133–45.

Killing, J. P. (1983) *Strategies for Joint Venture Success*. London: Croom Helm.

Klein, S. (1989) 'A transaction cost explanation of vertical control in international markets', *Journal of the Academy of Marketing Science* (Summer), pp. 253–60.

Knyphausen-Aufseß, D. zu (1995) *Theorie der strategischen Unternehmensführung. State of the Art und neue Perspektiven*. Wiesbaden. Gabler.

Kobayashi, N. (1988) 'Strategic alliances with Japanese firms', *Long Range Planning* 21 (2), pp. 29–34.

Kogut, B. (1988) 'A study of the life cycle of joint ventures', in F. J. Contractor and P. Lorange (eds), *Cooperative Strategy in International Business*. Lexington: Lexington Books, 1988, pp. 169–85.

Kogut, B. (1988a) 'Joint venture: theoretical and empirical perspectives', *Strategic Management Journal* 9, pp. 319–32

Kogut, B. (1988b) 'A study in the life cycle of joint ventures', *Management International Review* 28, Special Issue, pp. 39–51.

Kogut, B. (1989) 'The stability of joint ventures: Reciprocity and competitive rivalry', *Journal of Industrial Economics* (December), pp. 183–98.

Kohn, A. (1989) *Mit vereinten Kräften. Warum Kooperation der Konkurrenz überlegen ist*. Weinheim and Basel: Beltz.

Köllner, P. (1997) 'Japans Rolle in der industriellen Arbeitsteilung in Ostasien: Theorie und Praxis', *Japan aktuell Wirtschaft Politik Gesellschaft* 5 (4), pp. 171–7.

Konomoto, S. (1997) 'Japanese manufacturing in Asia: Time for a reassessment', *Nomura Research Institute Quarterly* 6 (3), pp. 70–83.

Konomoto, S. (1998) 'Industrial policy in China and the strategies of Japanese transplants', *Nomura Research Institute Quarterly* 7 (3), pp. 36–47.

Konomoto, S. (2000) *Problems of Japanese Companies in East and Southeast Asia*. Nomura Research Institute Papers, no. 18. Tokyo: Nomura Research Institute.

Koontz, H. (1961) 'The management theory jungle', *Academy of Management Journal* 4 (3), pp. 174–88.

Koontz. H., C. O'Donnell and H. Weihrich (1984) *Management*. New York: McGraw-Hill.

Korhonen, P. (1998) *Japan and Asia-Pacific Integration. Pacific Romances 1968–1996*. London and New York: Routledge.

Kreikebaum, H. (1998) *Organisationsmanagement internationaler Unternehmen. Grundlagen und neue Strukturen*. Wiesbaden: Gabler.

Kreps, D. M. (1990) *A Course in Microeconomic Theory*. Princeton, New Jersey: Princeton University Press.

Kroeber, A. L. and C. Kluckhohn (1952) *Culture: A Critical Review of Concepts and Definitions*. Cambridge, Massachusetts: Peabody Museum.

Krüger, W. (1972) *Grundlagen, Probleme und Instrumente der Konflikthandhabung in der Unternehmung*. Berlin: Duncker & Humblot.

Kumar, B. (1989) 'Internationale(n) Unternehmenstätigkeit, Formen der', in K. Macharzina and M. K. Welge (eds), *Handwörterbuch Export und internationale Unternehmung*. Stuttgart: Poeschel, col. 914–26.

Kumar, B. N. (1975) 'Joint ventures', *Wirtschaftswissenschaftliches Studium* 4 (6), pp. 257–63.

Kunz, G. C. (1999) 'Führung und Kooperation in der lernenden Organisation', *Personalführung* (2), pp. 44–50.

Kutschker, M. (1989) 'Akquisition, internationale', in K. Marcharzina and M. K. Welge (eds), *Handwörterbuch Export und Internationale Unternehmung*. Stuttgart: Schäffer-Poeschel, col. 1–2.

Kutschker, M. (1994a) 'Strategische Kooperationen als Mittel der Internationalisierung', in L. Schuster (ed.), *Die Unternehmung im internationalen Wettbewerb*. Berlin: Erich Schmid Verlag, pp. 121–57.

Kutschker, M. (1994b) 'Dynamische Internationalisierungsstrategie', in J. Engehard and H. Rehkugler (eds), *Strategien für nationale und internationale Märkte. Konzepte und praktische Gestaltung*. Wiesbaden: Gabler, pp. 221–48.

Kutschker, M. (1995) 'Konzepte und Strategien der Internationalisierung', in H. Corsten and M. Reißer (eds), *Handbuch Unternehmensführung*. Wiesbaden: Gabler, pp. 647–60.

Kutschker, M. (1996) 'Evolution, Episoden und Epochen: Die Führung von Internationalisierungsprozessen', in J. Engelhard (ed.), *Strategische Führung internationaler Unternehmen. Paradoxien, Strategien, Erfahrungen*. Wiesbaden: Gabler, pp. 1–37.

Kutschker, M. (ed.) (1998) *Integration der internationalen Unternehmung*. Wiesbaden: Gabler.

Kutschker, M. and I. Bäurle (1997) 'Three+one: Multidimensional Strategy of internationalization', *Management International Review* 37 (2), pp. 103–25.

Kutschker, M. and S. Schmid (1999) 'Organisationsstrukturen internationaler Unternehmen', in M. Kutschker (ed.), *Perspektiven der internationalen Wirtschaft*. Wiesbaden: Gabler, pp. 361–411.

Kutschker, M. and S. Schmid (2002) *Internationales Management*. Munich and Vienna: Oldenbourg.

Lane, C. (1998) 'Theories and issues in the study of trust', in C. Lane and R. Bachmann (eds), *Trust within and between Organizations. Conceptual Issues and Empirical Applications*. Oxford: Oxford University Press, pp. 1–30.

Lane, C. and R. Bachmann, (1996) 'The social constitution of trust: Supplier relations in Britain and Germany', *Organisational Studies* 17, (3), pp. 365–95.

Larsson, A. (1985) *Structure and Change: Power in Transnational Enterprise*. Uppsala: Uppsala University.

Latham, G. P. and L. M. Saari (1979) 'Application of social learning theory to training supervisors through behavioural modelling', *Journal of Applied Psychology* 3, pp. 239–46.

Laux, H. (1990) *Risiko, Anreiz und Kontrolle: Principal-Agent-Theorie; Einführung und Verbindung mit dem Delegationswert-Konzept*. Heidelberg: Springer.

Levin, S. and P. E. White (1961) 'Exchange as a conceptual framework for the study of interorganizational relationships', *Administrative Science Quarterly* (March), pp. 583–601.

Levitt, T. (1965) 'Exploit the product life cycle', *Harvard Business Review* 43 (November–December), pp. 81–94.

Lewicki, R. J. and B. B. Bunker (1996) 'Developing and maintaining trust in work relationships', in R. M. Kramer and T. R. Tyler (eds), *Trust in Organizations. Frontiers of Theory and Research*. Thousand Oaks: Sage, pp. 114–39.

Li, F. and J. Li (1999) *Foreign Investment in China*. Basingstoke: Macmillan – now Palgrave Macmillan.

Link, A. N. and L. L. Bauer (1989) *Cooperative Research in U.S. Manufacturing: Assessing Policy Initiatives and Corporate Strategies*. Lexington, Massachusetts: Lexington Books.

Lorange, P. and G. J. B. Probst (1987) 'Joint ventures as self-organizing systems: A key to successful joint venture design and implementation', *Columbia Journal of World Business* (Summer), pp. 71–7.

Lorange. P., J. Roos, and P. S. Bronn (1992) 'Building successful strategic alliances', *Long Range Planning* (6), pp. 10–7.

Lubman, S. (1995) 'The future of Chinese law', *China Quarterly* 141, Special Issue, pp. 1–21.

Lück, W. and M. Trommsdorf (1982) *Internationalisierung der Unternehmung als Problem der Betriebswirtschaftslehre*. Berlin: E. Schmidt.

Luhmann, N. (1973) *Vertrauen. Ein Mechanismus der Reduktion sozialer Komplexität.* Stuttgart: Ferdinand Enke.

Luhmann, N. (1987) *Soziale Systeme. Grundriß einer allgemeinen Theorie.* Frankfurt: Suhrkamp.

Luhmann, N. (1988) 'Familiarity, confidence, trust: problems and alternatives', in D. Gambetta (ed.), *Trust: Making and Breaking Co-operative Relations.* Oxford: Basil Blackwell, pp. 94–107.

Lullies, V., H. Bollinger and F. Weltz (1993) *Wissenslogistik.* Frankfurt: Suhrkamp.

Luthans, F. (1985) *Organizational Behavior.* New York and Tokyo: McGraw-Hill.

Luthans, F. and R. Kreitner (1985) *Organizational Behavior Modification and Beyond: An Operant and Social Learning Approach.* Glenview and London: Scott, Foresman.

Lyles, M. A. (1987) 'Common mistakes of joint venture experienced firms', *Columbia Journal of World Business* (Summer), pp. 79–85.

Macharzina, K. (1992) 'Internationalisierung und Organisation', *Zeitschrift Führung und Organisation* 61 (1), pp. 4–11.

Macharzina, K. (1999) *Unternehmensführung – Das internationale Managementwissen. Konzepte. Methoden. Praxis.* Wiesbaden: Gabler.

Macharzina, K. and J. Engelhard (1987) 'Internationales Management', *Die Betriebswirtschaft* 47 (3), pp. 319–44.

Macharzina, K. and M. K. Welge (eds) (1989) *Handwörterbuch Export und internationale Unternehmung.* Stuttgart: Poeschel.

MacNeil, I. R. (1974) 'The many futures of contracts', *Southern California Law Review* 47, pp. 691–816.

MacNeil, I. R. (1978) 'Contracts: Adjustments of long-term economic relations under classical, neoclassical and relational contact law', *Northwestern University Law Review* 72, pp. 854–905.

Mahoney, J. T. and D. A. Crank (1993) *Vertical Coordination: The Choice of Organizational Form.* Faculty Working Paper 93-0169, College of Commerce and Business Administration: University of Illinois at Urbana-Champaign.

Mannesmann Demag A. G. (ed.) (1995) *Mannesmann Demag und Komatsu Unterzeichnen Joint Venture,* information for the press, 8 November. Duisburg: Mannesmann Demag AG.

Markides, C. C. (1992) 'The economic characteristics of de-diversifying', *British Journal of Management* 3 (2), pp. 91–100.

Martinez. J. I. and J. C. Jarillo (1991) 'Coordination demands of international strategies', *Journal of International Business Studies* 22 (3), pp. 429–443.

Masten, S. E. (1984) 'Organization of production: Evidence from the aerospace industry', *Journal of Labor Economics* 27, pp. 403–18.

Masten, S. E. (1993) 'Transaction costs, mistakes, and performance: Assessing the importance of governance', *Managerical and Decision Economics* (14), pp. 119–29.

Masten, S. E. (1996) 'Empirical research in transaction cost economics: Challenges, progress and direction', in J. Groenewegen (ed.), *Transaction Cost Economics and Beyond.* Boston and London: Kluwer Academic Publishers, pp. 43–64.

Masten, S. E. and K. J. Crocker (1985) 'Efficient adaptation in long-term contracts: Take-or-pay provisions for natural gas', *American Economic Review* 75, pp. 1083–93.

Masten, S. E., J. W. Meehan and E. A. Snyder (1989) 'Vertical integration in the U.S. auto industry', *Journal of Economic Behavior and Organization* 12, pp. 265–73.

Mattsson, L.-G. (1987) 'Management of strategic change in a "markets-as-networks" perspective', in A. M. Pettigrew (ed.), *The Management of Strategic Change*. Oxford: Basil Blackwell, pp. 234–56.

Maull, H. W. and D. Nabers (2001) 'Einleitung', in H. W. Maull and D. Nabers (eds), *Multilateralismus in Ostasien-Pazifik. Probleme und Perspektiven im neuen Jahrhundert*. Hamburg: Deutsches Übersee Institut, pp. 11–20.

Mayntz, R. (1963) *Soziologie der Organisation*. Reinbek bei Hamburg: Rowohlt.

Mayring, P. (1990) *Einführung in die qualitative Sozialforschung. Eine Anleitung zum qualitativem Denken*. Munich: Psychologie Verlags Union.

Meckl, R. (1993) *Unternehmenskooperationen im EG-Binnenmarkt*. Wiesbaden: Deutscher Universitäts-Verlag.

Meffert, H. (1986) 'Marketing im Spannungsfeld von weltweitem Wettbewerb und nationalen Bedürfnissen', *Zeitschrift für Betriebswirtschaft* 56, pp. 689–712.

Meffert, H. (1994) *Marketing-Management: Analyse, Strategie, Implementierung*. Wiesbaden: Gabler.

Mertens, P. (1994) 'Virtuelle Unternehmen', *Wirtschaftsinformatik* 36 (2), pp. 169–72.

Miles, R. E. and Ch. C. Snow (1986) *Unternehmensstrategien*. Hamburg: McGraw-Hill.

Miller, D. (1984) 'Quantum structural change in organizations', in D. Miller, P. H. Friesen and H. Mintzberg (eds), *Organizations: A Quantum View*. Englewood Cliffs, New Jersey: Prentice-Hall, pp. 207–19.

Mintzberg, H. (1991) *Mintzberg über Management*. Wiesbaden: Gabler.

Mommertz, K. H. (1981) *Bohren, Drehen und Fräsen. Geschichte der Werkzeugmaschinen*. Reinbek bei Hamburg: Rowohlt.

Monteverde, K. and D. J. Teece (1982) 'Supplier switching costs and vertical integration in the automobile industry', *British Journal of Economics* 13, pp. 206–13.

Moore, J. F. (1993) 'Predators and prey: A new ecology of competition', 71 *Harvard Business Review* (May–June), pp. 75–86.

Morris, D. and M. Hergert (1987) 'Trends in international collaborative agreements', *Columbia Journal of World Business* (Summer), pp. 15–21.

Mosakowski, E. (1991) 'Organizational boundaries and economic performance: An empirical study of entrepreneurial computer firms', *Strategic Management Journal* 12, pp. 115–33.

Moss Kanter, R. (1994) 'Collaborative advantage', *Harvard Business Review* (July–August), pp. 96–108.

Müller, K. and E. Goldberger (1986) *Unternehmens-Kooperation bringt Wettbewerbsvorteile. Notwendigkeit und Praxis zwischenbetrieblicher Zusammenarbeit in der Schweiz*. Zürich: Verlag Industrielle Organisation.

Müller, S. (1991) *Die Psyche des Managers als Determinante des Exporterfolges*. Stuttgart: M & P Verlag für Wissenschaft und Forschung.

Murphy, W. J. (1988) 'Interfirm cooperation in a competitive economic system', *American Business Law Journal*, pp. 29–45.

Naujoks, W. and R. Pausch (1977) *Die Bedeutung der zwischenbetrieblichen Kooperation in der betrieblichen Praxis. Hauptergebnisse einer empirischen Untersuchung*. Bonn: Institut für Mittelstandsforschung, Forschungsgruppe Bonn.

Neuberger, O. (1997) 'Individualisierung und Organisierung. Die wechselseitige Erzeugung von Individuum und Organisation durch Verfahren', in G. Ortmann, J. Sydow and K. Türk (eds), *Theorien der Organisation. Die Rückkehr der Gesellschaft*. Opladen: Westdeutscher Verlag, pp. 487–522.

Neumann, J. von and O. Morgenstern (1944) *Theory of Games and Economic Behaviour*. Princeton: Princeton University Press.

Niehans, J. (1991) 'Transaction costs', in J. Eatwell, M. Millgate and P. Newman (eds), *The New Palgrave. A Dictionary of Economics*. London: Macmillan–Palgrave, pp. 676–80.

Nihon Kôsaku Kikai Kôgyôkai (1982) *Haha-naru kikai: 30 nen no ayumi* [Japan Machine Tool Builders Association, The Mother of Machines: Thirty Years of History], Tokyo: Nihon Kôsaku Kikai Kôgyôkai, pp. 81–3.

Nohria, N. and R. G. Eccles (eds) (1992) *Networks and Organizations: Structure, Form, and Action*. Boston: Harvard Business School Press.

Nonaka, I. (1990) 'Redundant, overlapping organization: A Japanese approach to managing the innovation process', *California Management Review* 32 (3), pp. 27–38.

Nonaka, I. and H. Takeuchi (1997) *Die Organisation des Wissens. Wie japanische Unternehmen eine brachliegende Ressource nutzbar machen*. Frankfurt am Main, New York: Campus-Verlag.

Nystrom, P. C. and W. H. Starbuck (1984) 'To avoid organizational crisis, unlearn', *Organizational Dynamics* (Spring), pp. 53–65.

Oberender, P. and A. Väth (1989) 'Von der Industrieökonomie zur Marktökonomie', in P. Oberender (ed.), *Marktökonomie. Marktstruktur und Wettbewerb in ausgewählten Branchen der Bundesrepublik Deutschland*. Munich: Vahlen.

Ohmae, K. (1985) *Macht der Triade*. Wiesbaden: Gabler.

Ohmae, K. (1986) *Japanische Strategien*. Hamburg: McGraw-Hill.

Ohmae, K. (1989) 'The global logic of strategic alliances', *Harvard Business Review* 67 (March–April), pp. 143–54.

Ohmae, K. (1990) 'Strategic alliances in the borderless world', *Zeitschrift für betriebswirtschaftliche Forschung*, special issue 27, pp. 11–20.

Ohmae, K. (2001) 'Asia's next crisis: Made in China. Rapid evolution of Chinese economy threatens regional status quo', *The Japan Times*, Tokyo, 30 July.

Okumura, H. (1998) *Japan und seine Unternehmen*. Munich and Vienna: Oldenbourg.

Oliver, C. (1991) 'Strategic responses to institutional processes', *Academy of Management Review* 16 (1), pp. 145–79.

Ortmann, G., A. Windeier, A. Becker and H.-J. Schulz (1990) *Computer und Macht*. Opladen: Westdeutscher Verlag.

Osborn, R. N. and C. C. Baughn (1990) 'Forms of interorganizational governance for multinational alliances', *Academy of Management Journal* 33, pp. 503–19.

Papmehl, A. and R. Siewers (eds) (1999) *Wissen im Wandel. Die lernende Organisation im 21. Jahrhundert*. Vienna: Wirtschaftsverlag Ueberreuter.

Park, S.-J. (1975) 'Die Wirtschaft seit 1868', in H. Hammitzsch (ed.), *Japan*. Nürnberg: Glock und Lutz, pp. 123–44.

Park, S.-J. (ed.) (1985) *Japanisches Management in der Praxis: Flexibilität oder Kontrolle im Prozess der Internationalisierung und Mikroelektronisierung*. Berlin: Express-Edition.

Parkhe, A. (1993) 'Strategic alliance structuring: A game theoretic and transaction cost examination of interfirm cooperation', in *Academy of Management Journal* 36, pp. 794–829.

Pausenberger, E. (ed.) (1981) *Internationales Management*. Stuttgart: Poeschel.

Pausenberger, E. and R. Nöcker (2000) Kooperative Formen der Auslandsmarktbearbeitung', *Zeitschrift für betriebswirtschaftliche Forschung* 63 (6), pp. 393–412.

Pautzke, G. (1989) *Die Evolution der organisatorischen Wissensbasis*. Herrsching: Kirsch.

Pearce, J. and R. Robinson (1997) *Strategic Management*. Chicago and London: Irwin.

Pena, N. A. and J. C. Fernández de Arroyabe (2002) *Business Cooperation. From Theory to Practice*. Basingstoke: Palgrave.

Pennings, J. M. (1981) 'Strategically interdependent organizations', in P. C. Nystrom and W. H. Starbuck (eds), *Handbook of Organizational Design*. Oxford: Oxford University Press, pp. 433–55.

Perlitz, M. (1994): 'Internationales Management', in W. Wittmann *et al.* (eds), *Handwörterbuch der Betriebswirtschaft*. Stuttgart: Schäffer-Poeschel, col. 1855–71.

Perlitz, M. (1997a) *Internationales Management*. Stuttgart: Lucius & Lucius.

Perlitz, M. (1997b) 'Spektrum kooperativer Internationalisierungsformen', in K. Marcharzina and M.-J. Oesterle (eds), *Handbuch Internationales Management*. Wiesbaden, Gabler, pp. 441–57.

Perlitz, M. (1999) 'Neue Märkte', in M. Perlitz and M. Rheinhardt (eds), *Neue Märkte. Strategien für das 21. Jahrhundert*. Munich and Vienna: Hanser, pp. 3–17.

Perlitz, M. and F. Seger (2000) 'Konzepte internationaler Markteintrittsstrategien', in D. von der Oelsnitz (ed.), *Markteintrittsmanagement. Probleme, Strategien, Erfahrungen*. Stuttgart: Schäffer-Poeschel, pp. 89–110.

Perlmutter, H. V. (1969) 'The tortuous evolution of the multinational corporation', *Columbia Journal of World Business* 4, pp. 9–18.

Perlmutter, H. V. and D. A. Heenan (1986) 'Cooperate to compete globally', *Harvard Business Review* 64 (March–April), pp. 136–52.

Perridon, L. and M. Rössler (1980) 'Die internationale Unternehmung: Entwicklung und Wesen', *Wirtschaftswissenschaftliches Studium* 9 (5), pp. 211–17.

Perrow, Ch. (1970) *Organizational Analysis: A Sociological View*. London: Tavistock.

Pfeffer, J. and P. Nowak (1976) 'Joint venture and interorganizational dependence', *Administrative Science Quarterly* (September), pp. 398–418.

Pfeffer, J. and G. Salancik (1978) *The External Control of Organizations: A Resource Dependence Perspective*. New York: Harper & Row.

Piaget, J. (1985) *Meine Theorie der geistigen Entwicklung*. Frankfurt am Main: Fischer Taschenbuch Verlag.

Picot, A. (1990) 'Vorwort zur deutschen Ausgabe', in O. E Williamson, *Die ökonomischen Institutionen des Kapitalismus. Unternehmen, Märkte, Kooperationen. Die Einheit der Gesellschaftswissenschaften*. Tübingen: Mohr.

Picot, A. (1991) 'Ein neuer Ansatz zur Gestaltung der Leistungstiefe', *Zeitschrift für betriebswirtschaftliche Forschung* (4), pp. 336–57.

Picot, A. and E. Franck (1993) 'Vertikale Integration', in J. Hauschildt and O. Grün (eds), *Ergebnisse empirischer betriebswirtschaftlicher Forschung: Zu einer Realtheorie der Unternehmung*. Stuttgart: Schäffer-Poeschel, pp. 179–219.

Picot, A. and H. Ronald (1992) 'Coase – Nobelpreisträger 1991. Transaktionskosten: Ein zentraler Beitrag zur wirtschaftswissenschaftlichen Analyse', *Wirtschaftswissenschaftliches Studium* (2), pp. 79–83.

Picot, A., D. Schneider and U. Laub (1989) 'Transaktionskosten und innovative Unternehmensgründung', *Zeitschrift für betriebswirtschaftliche Forschung* (5), pp. 358–87.

Picot, A. and E. Wenger (1988) 'The employment relation from the transaction cost perspective', in G. Dlugos, W. Dorow and K. Weiermair (eds): *Management under Differing Labour Market and Employment Systems*. Berlin: de Gruyter, pp. 29–43.

Piore, M. J. and C. F. Sabel (1984) *The Second Industrial Divide*. New York: Basic Books.

Platz, R. and G. Rieger (eds) (1996) *Südostasien im Wandel*. Stuttgart: Schmetterling-Verlag.

Pohl, M. (1994) 'Japans Rolle in Ostasien: Großmacht wider Willen?', *Aus Politik und Zeitgeschichte* B 50, pp. 27–38.

Pohl, M. and O. Weggel (1994) 'Südostasien – Japan', *Informationen zur politischen Bildung* (147/148).

Poppal, R. (1995) 'Virtuelle Leistungsorganisation. Die neue Qualität strategischer Allianzen', *Absatzwirtschaft* (5), pp. 66–7.

Popper, K. (1989) *Logik der Forschung. Die Einheit der Gesellschaftswissenschaften*. Tübingen: Mohr.

Porter, M. E. (1980) *Competitive Strategy: Techniques for Analyzing Industries and Competitors*. New York: Free Press.

Porter, M. E. (1985) *Competitive Advantage: Creating and Sustaining Superior Performance*. New York: Free Press.

Porter, M. E. (ed.) (1986) *Competition in Global Industries*. Boston: Harvard Business School Press.

Porter, M. E. (ed.) (1989) *Globaler Wettbewerb*. Wiesbaden: Gabler.

Porter, M. E. (1990a) *The Competitive Advantage of Nations*. New York: Free Press.

Porter, M. E. (1990b) 'The competitive advantage of nations', *Harvard Business Review* (3–4), pp. 73–93.

Porter, M. E. (1990c) *Wettbewerbsstrategie: Methoden zur Analyse von Branchen und Konkurrenten*. Frankfurt and New York: Campus-Verlag.

Porter, M. E. (1999) *Nationale Wettbewerbsvorteile*. Vienna and Frankfurt am Main: Wirtschaftsverlag Carl Ueberreuter.

Porter, M. E. and M. Fuller (1986) 'Coalitions and global strategy', in M. E. Porter (ed.) *Competition in Global Industries*. Boston: Harvard Business School Press, pp. 315–44.

Porter, M. E., E.E. Lawler III and J. R. Hackman (1975) *Behavior in Organizations*. New York.

Porter, M. E., H. Takeuchi and M. Sakakibara (2000) *Can Japan Compete?* Basingstoke: Macmillan–Palgrave.

Prahalad, C. K. and G. Hamel (1990) 'The core competence of the corporation', *Harvard Business Review* 68 (May–June), pp. 79–91.

Pratt, J. W. and R. J. Zweckhauser (1985) 'Principals and agents: An overview', in J. W. Pratt and R. J. Zweckhauser (eds), *Principals and Agents: The Structure of Business*. Boston: Harvard Business School Press, pp. 1–35.

Rath, H. (1990) *Neue Formen der internationalen Unternehmenskooperation*. Hamburg: S + W Steuer- und Wirtschaftsverlag.

Reber, G. (1992) 'Lernen, Organisationales', in E. Frese (ed.), *Handwörterbuch der Organisation*. Stuttgart: Poeschel, col. 1240–55.

Reed, M. (1992) *The Sociology of Organizations*. New York and London: Harvester Wheatsheaf.

Reed, M. I. (1984) 'Management as social practice', *Journal of Management* 21 (3), pp. 273–85.

Reich, R. B. (1994) *Die neue Weltwirtschaft*. Frankfurt am Main: Büchergilde Gutenberg.

Reiß, M., L. von Rosenstiel and A. Lanz (eds) (1997) *Change Management: Programme, Projekte und Prozesse*. Stuttgart: Schäffer-Poeschel.

Renkel, H.-P. (1985) *Technologietransfer-Management in Japan. Gründung, Innovation und Beratung*. Bergisch Gladbach, Cologne: Eul.

Reynolds, J. I. (1984) 'The pinched shoe effect of international joint ventures', *Columbia Journal of World Business* 19 (Summer), pp. 23–9.

Ring, P. S. and A. H. van de Ven (1994) 'Developmental process of co-operative interorganisational relationships', *Academy of Management Review* 19, pp. 90–118.

Rinsche, G. (1996) 'Die asiatische Herausforderung. Zum Verhältnis zwischen Europa und Asien', *Konrad-Adenauer-Stiftung, Auslands-Informationen* (12), pp. 3–23.

Robert, M. (1992) 'The dos and don'ts of strategic alliances', *The Journal of Business Strategy* (March–April), pp. 50–3.

Robbins, St. P. (1974) *Managing Organizational Conflict: A Nontraditional Approach*. Englewood Cliffs, New Jersey: Prentice-Hall.

Rominski, D. (1995) 'Gemeinschaftsmarketing. Mit Konkurrenten gewinnen', *Absatzwirtschaft* (5), pp. 40–6.

Ruekert, R. W. and O. C. Walker, Jr. (1987) 'Marketing's interaction with other functional units: A conceptual framework and empirical evidence', *Journal of Marketing* (January), pp. 1–19.

Rüland, J. (1995) 'Die Gemeinschaft Südostasiatischer Staaten (ASEAN): Vom Anti-kommunismus zum regionalen Ordnungsfaktor', *Aus Politik und Zeitgeschichte* (B 13–14), pp. 3–12.

Ruppert, W. (1992) 'Unternehmensstrategien und Marktposition deutscher Unternehmen in der asiatisch-pazifischen Region', *ifo Studien zur Japanforschung* (6), pp. 47–173.

Rust, W. L. (1985) *ASEAN – Regionale Zusammenarbeit im Schatten der Großmächte*. Frankfurt am Main: Lang.

Rüttinger, B. (1977) *Konflikt und Konfliktlösen*. Munich: Goldmann.

Sako, M. (1992) *Prices, Quality and Trust: Inter-firm Relations in Britain and Japan*. Cambridge: Cambridge University Press.

Samuelson, P. A. (1975) *Volkswirtschaftslehre*. Cologne: Bund-Verlag.

Sasaki, T. (1993) 'What the Japanese have learned from strategic alliances', *Long Range Planning* 26 (6), pp. 41–53.

Schacher, D. (1998) 'Vernetzte Zusammenarbeit – Neue Formen der Organisation in globalen Produktionsunternehmen', in L. Krause and E. Uhlmann (eds), *Innovative Produktionstechnik*. Munich and Vienna: Hanser.

Schaude, G. (1991) *Kooperation, Joint Venture, Strategische Allianzen. Wie finde ich meinen Kooperationspartner*. Informationsheft des Rationalisierungs-Kuratoriums der Deutschen Wirtschaft. Eschborn: RKW.

Scheel, H. D. (1986) 'Die Charakteristika der japanischen Wirtschaft', in M. Pohl (ed.), *Japan*. Stuttgart: Thienemann, pp. 282–310.

Schein, E. H. (1980) *Organisationspsychologie*. Wiesbaben: Gabler.

Scherm, M. and P. R. Bischoff (1994) 'Lean Management – stereotype Sichtweisen japanischer Unternehmensphänomene', in M. Esser and K. Kobayashi (eds), *Kaishain. Personalmanagement in Japan. Sinn und Werte statt Systeme, Psychologie für das Personalmanagement*. Göttingen: Verlag für Angewandte Psychologie, pp. 100–7.

Scheurer, S. and M. Zahn (1998) 'Organisationales Lernen – Von den theoretischen Grundlagen zur praktischen Umsetzung', *Zeitschrift für Organisation und Führung* 67 (3), pp. 174–89.

Schienstock, G. (1991) 'Managementsoziologie – ein Desiderat der Industriesoziologie?' *Soziale Welt* 42 (3), pp. 349–70.

Schmitt, W. W. (1998) *Management japanischer Niederlassungen. Strukturen und Strategien.* Bonn: Institut für Wissenschaftliche Publikationen.

Scholz, C. (1994) *Die virtuelle Organisation als Strukturkonzept der Zukunft?* Arbeitspapier Nr. 30 des Lehrstuhls für Betriebswirtschaftslehre, insbesondere Organisation-, Personal- und Informationsmanagement der Universität des Saarlandes. Saarbrücken: Universität Saarbrücken.

Schrader, S. (1993) 'Kooperation', in J. Hauschildt and O. Grün (eds), *Ergebnisse empirischer betriebswirtschaftlicher Forschung: Zu einer Realtheorie der Unternehmung.* Stuttgart: Schäffer-Poeschel, pp. 221–54.

Schreyögg, G. (1987) 'Verschlüsselte Botschaften – Neue Perspektiven einer strategischen Personalführung', *Zeitschrift Führung und Organisation* 56 (3), pp. 151–58.

Schreyögg, G. (1991) 'Der Managementprozeß – neu gesehen', *Managementforschung* 1, pp. 255–89.

Schreyögg, G. (1998) *Organisation: Grundlagen moderner Organisationsgestaltung.* Wiesbaden: Gabler.

Schröder, S. (1995) *Innovation in der Produktion.* Munich and Vienna: Hanser.

Schubert, W. and K. Küting (1981) *Unternehmungszusammenschlüsse.* Munich: Vahlen.

Schüppel, J. (1996) *Wissensmanagement: organisatorisches Lernen im Spannungsfeld von Wissens- und Lernbarrieren.* Wiesbaden: Gabler.

Schütte, H. and P. Lasserre (1996) *Management-Strategien für Asien-Pazifik.* Stuttgart: Schäffer-Poeschel.

Schwarz, R. and S. Martsch (1995) 'Das Japan-Engagement der bayerischen Wirtschaft – Ergebnisse einer Unternehmensbefragung', *Japan-Analysen Prognosen* no. 113, pp. 1–47.

Scott, W. R. (1987) *Organizations: Rational, Natural and Open Systems.* Englewood Cliffs, New Jersey: Prentice-Hall.

Sebestyén, O. G. (1994) *Management-Geheimnis Kaizen. Der japanische Weg zur Innovation.* Vienna: Wirtschaftsverlag Ueberreuter.

Senge, P. M. (1999) *Die fünfte Disziplin. Kunst und Praxis der lernenden Organisation.* Stuttgart: Klett-Cotta.

Shan, W. (1990) 'An empirical analysis of organizational strategies by entrepreneurial hightechnology firms', *Strategic Management Journal* (2), pp. 129–39.

Sheppard, B. H. and M. Tuchinsky (1996) 'Micro-OB and the network organization', in R. M. Kramer and T. R. Tyler (eds.) *Trust in Organizations. Frontiers of Theory and Research.* Thousand Oaks: Sage, pp. 140–65.

Shibagaki, K., M. Trevor and T. Abo (eds) (1989) *Japanese and European Management. Their International Adaptability.* Tokyo: University of Tokyo Press.

Shimizu, T. (1988) 'Japanisches Management', in W. Busse von Colbe, K. Chmielewicz, E. Gaugler and G. Laßmann (eds), *Betriebswirtschaftslehre in Japan und Deutschland. Unternehmensführung, Rechnungswesen und Finanzierung.* Stuttgart: Poeschel, pp. 173–91.

Shrivastava, P. (1983) 'A typology of organizational learning systems', *Journal of Management Studies* 1 (1983), pp. 7–28.

Sieber, P. (1998) *Virtuelle Unternehmen in der IT-Branche*. Berne: Haupt.

Siebert, H. (1991) 'Ökonomische Analyse von Unternehmensnetzwerken', *Managementforschung* 1, pp. 291–311.

Simon, W. (1957) 'Steuerungsprinzipien an Werkzeugmaschinen', *Werkstatt und Betrieb* 90 (11), pp. 791–8.

Simon, W. (1969) *Produktivitätsverbesserungen mit NC-Maschinen und Computern*. Munich: Hanser.

Skinner, J. S., J. B. Gassenheimer and S. W. Kelley (1992) 'Cooperation in supplier-dealer relations', *Journal of Retailing* (2), pp. 174–93.

Smith, K. G., S. J. Carroll and S. J. Ashford (1995) 'Intra- and interorganisational co-operation', *Academy of Management Journal* 38, pp. 7–23.

Spur, G. (1979) *Produktionstechnik im Wandel*. Munich and Vienna: Hanser.

Spur, G. (1991a) *Vom Wandel der industriellen Welt durch Werkzeugmaschinen*. Munich and Vienna: Hanser.

Spur, G. (1991b) 'Intensive Zusammenarbeit: Werkzeugmaschinenbau und Produktionswissenschaft', *Industrie-Anzeiger* 113 (14), pp. 16–8.

Spur, G. (1998a) *Technologie und Management. Zum Selbstverständnis der Technikwissenschaften*. Munich and Vienna: Hanser.

Spur, G. (1998b) *Fabrikbetrieb*. Munich and Vienna: Hanser.

Spur, G. and J. Ebert (1993) *Automatisierung und Wandel der betrieblichen Arbeitswelt*. Berlin, New York: de Gruyter.

Spur, G. and D. Specht (1990) *Die Numerische Steuerung – Fallstudie einer erfolgreichen Innovation aus dem Bereich des Maschinenbaus. Forschungsbericht*. Berlin: Akademie der Wissenschaften zu Berlin.

Staehle, W. (1989) 'Human Resource Management und Unternehmungsstrategie', *Mitteilungen aus der Arbeitsmarkt- und Berufsforschung* 22 (3), pp. 388–96.

Staehle, W. (1991) 'Redundanz, Slack und lose Kopplung in Organisationen – Eine Verschwendung von Ressourcen?', *Managementforschung* 1, pp. 313–45.

Staehle, W. (1999) *Management*. Munich: Vahlen.

Staehle, W. and J. Sydow (1992) 'Managementphilosophie', in E. Frese (ed.), *Handwörterbuch der Organisation*. Stuttgart: Poeschel, col. 1286–302.

Stahl, B. (1998) *Warum gibt es die EU und die ASEAN? Institutionalisierungsfaktoren in vergleichender Analyse*. Baden-Baden: Nomos.

Stahl, B. (2001) 'Die Gemeinschaft südostasiatischer Staaten (ASEAN)', in H. W. Maull and D. Nabers (eds), *Multilateralismus in Ostasien-Pazifik. Probleme und Perspektiven im neuen Jahrhundert*. Hamburg. Deutsches Übersee Institut, pp. 23–67.

Stahl, G. K. (1997) *Internationaler Einsatz von Führungskräften*. Munich and Vienna: Oldenbourg.

Steers, R. M. (1975) 'Problems in the measurement of organizational effectiveness', *Administrative Science Quarterly* (December), pp. 546–58.

Steffenhagen, H. (1975) *Konflikt und Kooperation in Absatzkanälen. Ein Beitrag zur verhaltensorientierten Marketingtheorie*. Wiesbaden: Gabler.

Steinmann, H. (1989) 'Mittelständische(n) Unternehmungen, Internationalisierung der', in K. Macharzina and M. K. Welge (eds): *Handwörterbuch Export und Internationale Unternehmung*. Stuttgart: Poeschel, col. 1508–19.

Steinmann, H. and G. Schreyögg (1997) *Management*. Wiesbaden: Gabler.

Stinchcombe, A. (1985) 'Contracts as hierarchical documents', in A. Stinchcombe and C. Heimer (eds), *Organization Theory and Management*. Oslo: Norwegian University Press, pp. 121–71.

Stopford, J. M. and L. T. Wells (1972) *Managing the Multinational Enterprise.* New York: Basic Books.

Stuckey, J. (1983) *Vertical Integration and Joint Ventures in the Aluminium Industry.* Cambridge, Mass: Harvard University Press.

Sydow, J. (1985) *Organisationsspielraum und Büroautomation.* Berlin and New York: de Gruyter.

Sydow, J. (1992) *Strategische Netzwerke – Evolution und Organisation.* Wiesbaden: Gabler.

Sydow, J. (1993) 'Strategie und Organisation international tätiger Unternehmen – Managementprozesse in Netzwerkstrukturen', in H.-D Ganter and G. Schienstock (eds), *Management aus soziologischer Sicht.* Wiesbaden: Gabler, pp. 47–82.

Sydow, J. (1995) 'Netzwerkbildung und Kooptation als Führungsaufgabe', in A. Kieser, G. Reber and R. Wunderer (eds), *Handwörterbuch der Führung.* Stuttgart: Schäffer-Poeschel, pp. 1622–35.

Sydow, J. (1998a) *Postmoderne Konzerne? Zum Verhältnis von Konzern und Netzwerk.* Berlin: Freie Universität Berlin.

Sydow, J. (1998b) 'Understanding the constitution of interorganizational trust', in C. Lane and R. Bachmann (eds), *Trust within and between Organizations. Conceptual Issues and Empirical Applications.* Oxford: Oxford University Press, pp. 31–63.

Sydow, J. (ed.) (1999) *Management von Netzwerkorganisationen.* Wiesbaden: Gabler.

Sydow, J. and B. van Well (1996) 'Wissenintensiv durch Netzwerkorganisation – Strukturationstheoretische Analyse eines wissenintensiven Netzwerkes', *Managementforschung* 6, pp. 191–234.

Sydow, J. and A. Windeler (1998) 'Organizing and evaluating interfirm networks: A structurationist perspective on network processes and effectiveness', *Organization Science* 9 (3), pp. 265–84.

Sydow, J., A. Windeler, M. Krebs and A. Loose van Well (1995) *Organisation von Netzwerken-Strukturationstheoretische Analysen der Vermittlungspraxis in Versicherungsnetzwerken.* Opladen: Westdeutscher Verlag.

Takahashi, Y., M. Murata and K. M. Rahman (eds) (1998) *Management Strategies of Multinational Corporations in Asian Markets.* Tokyo: Chuo University Press.

Takayama, K. (1997) 'Machine tool industry', in ifo Institute for Economic Research and Sakura Institute of Research (ed.), *A Comparative Analysis of Japanese and German Economic Success.* Tokyo and New York: Springer, pp. 427–40.

Taubman, J. (1956) 'What constitutes a joint venture', *Cornell Law Quarterly* (Summer), pp. 640–55.

Taylor, R. (1996) *Greater China and Japan. Prospects for an Economic Partnership in East Asia.* London and New York: Routledge.

Teramoto, Y., F. J. Richter, N. Iwasaki, T. Takai and Y. Wakuta (1994) 'Global strategy in the Japanese semiconductor industry: Knowledge creation through strategic alliances', in: N. Campbell (1994) *Japanese Multinationals.* London: Routledge, pp. 71–84.

Teubner, G. (1992) 'Die vielköpfige Hydra: Netzwerke als kollektive Akteure höherer Ordnung', in W. Krohn and G. Küppers (eds), *Emergenz: Die Entstehung von Ordnung, Organisation und Bedeutung.* Frankfurt: Suhrkamp, pp. 189–216.

Thimm, H.-U. and M. Besch (1971) *Die Nahrungswirtschaft. Zunehmende Verflechtung der Landwirtschaft mit vor- und nachgelagerten Wirtschaftsbereichen.* Hamburg and Berlin: Parey.

Thompson, J. D. (1967) *Organizations in Action: Social Science Bases of Administrative Theory*. New York: McGraw-Hill.

Tichy, N. A. (1980) 'Social network model for organization development', in T. G. Cummings (ed.), *Systems Theory for Organization Development*. Chichester: Wiley, pp. 115–62.

Toyne, B. (1989) 'International exchange: A foundation for theory building in international business', *Journal of International Business Studies* 20 (1), p. 117.

Tôyô Keizai (2000) *Kaigai shinshutsu kigyô sôran, kigyôbetsu-hen* [General Survey of Japanese Companies Abroad, Volume by firms]. Tokyo: Tôyô Keizai Shinpôsha.

Tröndle, D. (1987) *Kooperationsmanagement: Steuerung interaktioneller Prozesse*. Bergisch Gladbach and Cologne: Eul.

Tsuchiya, M. and Y. Konomi (1997) *Shaping the Future of Japanese Management: New Leadership to Overcome the Impending Crisis*. Tokyo: LTCB International Library Foundation.

Tsuruta, T. (1988) 'The rapid growth era', in R. Komiya, M. Okuno and K. Suzumura (eds), *Industrial Policy in Japan*. Tokyo; New York: Academic Press, pp. 49–87.

Turpin, D. (1993) 'Strategic alliances with Japanese firms: Myths and realities', *Long Range Planning* 26 (5), pp. 11–6.

Uhlig, H. (1992) 'Südostasien vor dem Jahr 2000. Die industrielle und agrarische Entwicklung der ASEAN-Länder', *Geographische Rundschau* 44 (1), pp. 10–7.

Ulrich, H. (1984) *Management*. Berne: Haupt.

Ulset, S. (1996) 'R&D outsourcing and contractual governance: An empirical study of commercial R&D projects', *Journal of Economic Behavior and Organization* 30, pp. 63–82.

Useem, M. (1996) 'Corporate education and training', in C. v. Kaysen (ed.), *The American Corporation Today. Examining the Questions of Power and Efficiency at the Century's End*. New York, Oxford: Oxford University Press, pp. 292–326.

Van de Ven, A. H. (1976) 'On the nature, formation, and maintenance of relations among organizations', *Academy of Management Review* (October), pp. 24–36.

Van de Ven, A. H. and D. L. Ferry (1980) *Measuring and Assessing Organizations*. New York: Wiley.

Van Gils, M. R. (1984) 'Interorganizational relations and networks', in P. J. Drenth (eds), *Handbook of Work and Organizational Psychology*. Chichester: Wiley, pp. 1073–100.

Varadarajan, P. R. and I. Rajaratnam (1986) 'Symbiotic marketing revisited', *Journal of Marketing* (January), pp. 7–17.

Vestal, J. E. (1993) *Planning for Change. Industrial Policy and Japanese Economic Development 1945–1990*. Oxford: Oxford University Press.

Vettel, K. and M. Krischek (1994) *Deutsch–Japanische Kooperationen. Option für den Mittelstand*. Mainz-Saarbrücken and Tokyo: Deutsche Industrie- und Handelskammer.

Voigt, S. (1993) 'Strategische Allianzen – Modisches Schlagwort oder Antwort auf globale Herausforderungen?', *Wirtschaftswissenschaftliches Studium* (5), pp. 246–49.

Vranic, J. (1995) 'Ausbau der regionalen Wirtschaftsbeziehungen in Ostasien', *Aus Politik und Zeitgeschichte* B 13–14, pp. 20–4.

Waldenberger, F. (1994) 'Grundzüge der Wirtschaftspolitik', in Deutsches Institut für Japanstudien (ed.), *Die japanische Wirtschaft heute*. Munich: Iudicium, pp. 23–44.

Waldenberger, F. (1996) 'Die Montageindustrien als Träger des japanischen Wirtschaftswunders. Die Rolle der Industriepolitik', in W. Schaumann (ed.), *Gewollt oder geworden? Planung, Zufall, natürliche Entwicklung in Japan.* Munich: Iudicium, pp. 259–71.

Waldenberger, F. (1998) 'Wirtschaftspolitik', in Deutsches Institut für Japanstudien (ed.): *Die Wirtschaft Japans. Strukturen zwischen Kontinuität und Wandel.* Berlin: Springer, pp. 19–54.

Walker, G. and D. Weber (1984) 'A transaction cost approach to make-or-buy decisions', *Administrative Science Quarterly* 29, pp. 373–91.

Wallraff, W. (1996) 'Wirtschaftliche Integration im asiatisch-pazifischen Raum', *Asien* 59 (April), pp. 7–33.

Walton, R. E. (1987) *Managing Conflict.* Reading, Massachusetts: Addison-Wesley.

Webster, F. E. (1992) 'The changing role of marketing in the cooperation', *Journal of Marketing* (October), pp. 1–17.

Weggel, O. (1989) *Die Asiaten.* Munich: C.H. Beck.

Weindl, J. (1994) *Europäische Gemeinschaft.* Munich: Oldenbourg.

Weiss, S. E. (1987) 'Creating the GM-Toyota joint ventures: A case in complex negotiation', *Columbia Journal of World Business* (Summer), pp. 23–7.

Welge, M. (1990) 'Globales Management', in M. Welge (ed.), *Globales Management. Erfolgreiche Strategien für den Weltmarkt.* Stuttgart: Poeschel, pp. 1–16.

Welge, M. K. and R. Böttcher (1991) 'Globale Strategien und Probleme ihrer Implementierung', *Die Betriebswirtschaft* 51 (4), pp. 435–54.

Wernerfeldt, B. (1984) 'A resource-based view of the firm', *Strategic Management Journal* 5 (2), pp. 171–80.

Westphal, J. (1991) *Vertikale Wettbewerbsstrategien in der Konsumgüterindustrie.* Wiesbaden: Gabler.

Wheelen, T. and Hunger, D. (1995) *Strategic Management and Business Policy.* Reading: Addison-Wesley.

Whetten, D. A. (1987) 'Interorganizational relations', in J. W. Lorsch (ed.), *Handbook of Organizational Behavior.* Englewood Cliffs, New Jersey: Prentice-Hall, pp. 238–53.

Wiegand, M. (1996) *Prozesse organisationalen Lernens.* Wiesbaden: Gabler.

Wiesenthal, H. (1995) 'Konventionelles und unkonventionelles Organisationslernen: Literaturreport und Ergänzungsvorschlag', *Zeitschrift für Soziologie* 24 (2), pp. 137–55.

Willamson, O. E. (1975) *Markets and Hierarchies.* New York: The Free Press.

Williamson, O. E. (1985) *The Economic Institutions of Capitalism.* New York: Free Press.

Williamson, O. E. (1988) 'The logic of economic organization', *Journal of Law, Economics and Organization* 4, pp. 65–93.

Williamson, O. E. (1990) *Die ökonomischen Institutionen des Kapitalismus: Unternehmen, Märkte, Kooperationen,* Die Einheit der Gesellschaftswissenschaften 64. Tübingen: Mohr.

Williamson, O. E. (1991a) 'Comparative economic organization: The analysis of discrete structural alternatives', *Adminstrative Science Quarterly* 36, pp. 269–96.

Williamson, O. E. (1991b) 'Vergleichende ökonomische Organisationstheorie: Die Analyse diskreter Strukturalternativen', in D. R. Ordelheide and E. Büsselmann (eds), *Betriebswirtschaftslehre und ökonomische Theorie.* Stuttgart: Poeschel, pp. 13–49.

Williamson, O. E. (1993) 'Calculativeness, trust, and economic organization', *Journal of Law and Economics* 36, pp. 453–86.

Williamson, O. E. (1996) 'Economic organization: The case for candor', *Academy of Management Review* 21, pp. 48–57.

Williamson, O. E. (ed.) (1990) *Organization Theory. From Chester Barnard to the Present and Beyond.* New York: Oxford University Press.

Williamson, O. E. and M. L. Wachter and J. E. Harris (1975) 'Understanding the employment relation: The analysis of idiosyncratic exchange', *British Journal of Economics* 6, pp. 250–78.

Williamson, O. E. and S. G. Winter (eds) (1991) *The Nature of the Firm.* New York: Oxford University Press.

Willke, H. (1987) 'Kontextsteuerung durch Recht? Zur Steuerungsfunktion des Rechts in polyzentrischer Gesellschaft', in M. Glagow, and H. Willke (eds), *Dezentrale Gesellschaftssteuerung.* Pfaffenweiler: Centaurus-Verlagsgesellschaft, pp. 3–26.

Wollnik, M. (1991) 'Das Verhältnis von Organisationsstruktur und Organisationskultur', in E. Dülfer (ed.), *Organisationskultur.* Stuttgart: Poeschel, pp. 65–92.

Womack, J., D. Jones and D. Ross (1990) *The Machine that Changed the World: The Story of Lean Production.* New York: Harper Perennial.

Woronoff, J. (1983) *Japan's Wasted Workers.* Totowa, New Jersey: Allanheld, Osmun.

Yamagishi, T. and M. Yamagishi (1994) 'Trust and commitment in the United States and Japan', *Motivation and Emotion* 18 (12), pp. 129–66.

Yamashiro, A. (1997) *Japanische Managementlehre. Keieigaku.* Munich: Oldenbourg.

Yoshihara, K. (1978) *Japanese Investment in Southeast Asia.* Honolulu: The University Press of Hawaii.

Yui, T. (1999) 'Japanese management practices in historical perspective', in D. Dirks, J. F. Huchet and T. Ribault (eds), *Japanese Management in the Low Growth Era. Between External Shocks and Internal Evolution.* Berlin, Heidelberg and New York: Springer, pp. 13–8.

Zaheer, A., B. McEvily and V. Perrone (1998) 'Does trust matter? Exploring the effects for interorganisational trust and interpersonal trust on performance', in *Organisation Science* 9 (2), pp. 141–59.

Zahn, E. (ed.) (1995) *Handbuch Technologiemanagement.* Stuttgart: Schäffer-Poeschel.

Zielke, A. E. (1992) *Erfolgsfaktoren internationaler Joint Ventures. Eine empirische Untersuchung der Erfahrungen deutscher und amerikanischer Industrieunternehmen in den USA.* Frankfurt am Main: Lang.

Zinkhau, G. M. and A. Pereira (1994) 'An overview of marketing strategy and planning', *International Journal of Research in Marketing* (3), pp. 185–218.

Index

Key: f=figure; n=note; **bold**=extended discussion or heading exphasized in main text.